WITHDRAWN BY THE
UNIVERSITY OF MICHIGAN

Albert Kahn
ARCHITECT OF FORD

Federico Bucci
Introduction by Giancarlo Consonni

Princeton Architectural Press

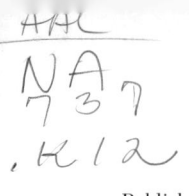

Published by
Princeton Architectural Press
37 East 7th Street
New York, New York 10003
(212) 995-9620

English translation © 1993 by
Princeton Architectural Press, Inc.
All rights reserved
97 96 95 94 93   5 4 3 2 1

No part of this book may be used or
reproduced in any manner without
written permission from the publisher
except in the context of reviews.

Original texts and photographic materials
© 1991 CittàStudi, Milan
Authorized translation from the Italian language edition
published by CittàStudi.

Printed and bound in Canada by Friesen Printers

Editing and production
Allison Saltzman

Translation from the Italian
Carmen DiCinque

Library of Congress Cataloguing-in-Publication Data
Bucci, Federico, 1959–
    [Architetto di Ford. English]
    Albert Kahn : architect of Ford / Federico Bucci.
       p. cm.
    Includes bibliographical references.
    ISBN 1–878271–84–9 : $24.95
    1. Kahn, Albert, 1869–1942--Criticism and interpretation.
  2. Industrial buildings--United States--History--20th century.
  I. Title.
NA737.K28B8313   1993
720'.92--dc20   93–36693
                                             CIP

Albert Kahn

CONTENTS

7 Introduction: Order without a City *Giancarlo Consonni*
23 Author's Preface

FROM SELF-EDUCATION TO PIONEER WORK WITH FORD
29 From Rhaunen to Detroit: The Birth of a Self-Made Man
31 Reinforced Concrete and Typological Invention
39 Highland Park: A Space Made to Order for the Assembly Line
50 River Rouge: The Second Fordist Revolution
60 Manufacturing Decentralization: The Third Fordist Revolution

PRODUCER OF PRODUCTION LINES 1929–1942
73 Theory and Practice of Industrial Architecture
90 The Soviet Adventure
97 Chicago 1934, New York 1939: Architecture for the Expositions
105 Plans for the Arsenal of Democracy

TEMPOS AND METHODS OF THE CREATIVE PROCESS
125 Scientific Management of Design Work
132 Fordism and Architecture Firms

ECLECTICISM FOR MOTOR CITY
143 Detroit: Architecture and a City Between Modernity and Tradition
166 Fordist Architecture: A Model for Europe
173 American Style versus International Style

186 Illustration Sources

✗ ORDER WITHOUT A CITY

Modernity perceives time and space as obstacles. Everything in opposition to movement (movement of goods, primarily, and of the matter that makes goods as they revert to a state of formless matter) and its acceleration is eliminated. Postmodernity, in turn, must be understood in relation to the increasing weight of intangible matter (technical/scientific knowledge, concepts, information, images, etc.) in the production and the accumulation of economic wealth.

The modern utopic vision is found within the metaphor of the machine, whose motor is the aspiration to mechanical order. What motivates postmodernity is the model of the automaton: the aspiration to imbue material reality with a "nervous system" that would render it "intelligent." While the first vision left a "monstrous harvest of goods"[1] (and refuse) on the field, the second vision adds immaterial goods (and refuse), as well as the bombardment of messages and virtual images that now invade the human psyche and the soul of the world.

The advent of a new condition does not eliminate the preceding one: rather, the former condition is instead subsumed into the new. The growing weight of the commodity of "information" and its easy transmission seem to fulfill the aspiration to annul spatial/temporal resistance and open new horizons. But its translation into economic value still requires the production and consumption of physical commodities, whose flow on the world scene encounters yet further incentives. Thus, in the advancement of the artificialization of landscapes and in the manipulation of living matter itself, the process of dematerialization thought to be the neotechnical frontier has its own counter-tendency: the conditions and obsessions of postmodernity.

Symptomatic of this is the fact that while Taylorism and Fordism have been surpassed in the most advanced industrial areas, some of their founding principles remain as reference models beyond the labor sphere.

The influence that the methods of labor management exercised over society did not escape the observant eyes of Taylor's and Ford's contemporaries, even among those furthest from their way of thinking and outside their professions. The director of public relations of the Ford Motor Company, W.J. Cameron, stated in 1937: "While we are producing useful products, we are also shaping human life, and the conditions of social life."[2] Cameron could not have conceived of according with a leader of a workers' movement who, in the fascist prison of Turi three years later, wrote in one of his notebooks: "The new methods of labor are indissoluble from the determined way of living, thinking and experiencing life…"[3]

Neither Cameron nor Gramsci could have foreseen how widespread and penetrating Fordism would be on cultural mentalities and ways of living. The tendency to specialize and fragment the pace of daily life, the race to economize time and space, the increasing subjection of space to motion, the imposition of ever accelerating social rhythms, and finally, the search for synchronicity between production and consumption (with the consequent propensity to attribute to objects an ever-decreasing duration): these inclinations and ways of living are greatly imbued with the principles that Henry Ford eventually clarified and established as he experimented in his production empire.

While there is no question that the world of production was a fundamental laboratory of modern temporality and spatiality, it also bore consequences for architects and urban planners: those who concerned themselves with ways of organizing, living and experiencing modern space. For this kind of study, the exploration of factory development from the industrial revolution on is obligatory, but it is necessary to examine more of history to shed light on the complexity of the processes that promoted the change in the perception of time and space.

Significantly, works like those of Wolfgang Schivelbusch and Stephen Kern[4] confirm the interpretative categories which took shape in that era. From these categories emerges the social rhythm and social relativity of time enunciated by Emile Durkheim at the beginning of the twentieth century. Time can also be considered as active tension, in which time of the individual combines with time of the community, a theory which was elaborated a few years after Durkheim by Henri Hubert and Marcel Mauss, based on the philosophy of Henry Bergson. Production discoveries and breakthroughs in the field of natural science—it is enough to cite the names Mach, Poincaré and Einstein—testified to epistemological revolutions that were simultaneously an active part and consequence of the general change, as well as essential references for its comprehension.

It should be noted, on the other hand, particularly with regard to Kern's study, that the revolutions which appeared in the most varied fields—from the exact sciences to the human sciences, from art to literature to music, and from economics to politics, down to ways of relating and rhythms of life—did not present the vectorial convergence that he tends to confirm. His argument is convincing when, operating in a zone of specialized knowledge and artistic creation, it sheds light on the importance of the relativist and subjectivist swing. However, what remains unexplained are the tangible ways of experiencing time and space, particularly the penetrating, conservative—if not exactly counter-revolutionary—action exercised on society by means of the organization of the industrial production sphere. Here the rise of scientific management (the scientific management of labor inaugurated by Frederick W. Taylor) in fact established a hegemony of new objectivism.

This new objectivism was not, however, a victory won from a free confrontation of ideas, for on the contrary, deterministic mechanism and positivism seem to be decisively in retreat. This objectivism was a supreme tax which the economic power exercised, taking advantage of the pervasive influence that organizational models of production have on society. In singling out work as a scientific object, controllable and modifiable from without, Taylor allowed eighteenth-century paradigms to continue to translate themselves into social rules, applying the same kind of action previously taken in medicine to an industrial setting.

While Bentham's *Panopticon* (1790) anticipated the new power of observation—"observation that keeps watch and that everyone, feeling its weight upon himself, internalizes so as to observe himself,"[5] its combination with the chronometer made the eye a mechanical instrument from which the observation of labor derived its status as scientific method. Authorized by the "objectivity" of measurement, this branch of science ultimately broke down the laborer's gestures into elementary movements, evaluated their efficacy and then prescribed the optimal recomposition of space and time.

For more than twenty years, Lilian and Frank B. Gilbreth, brilliant students of Taylor's, examined and synthesized the principles of scientific management that their teacher had studied at the beginning of the twentieth century.[6] In reducing the laborers' gestures to trajectories, the Gilbreths' work revealed how the space and time to which Taylorism referred were those of a mechanical rationale; likewise, it demonstrated that Taylor's main objective was the victory over spatial and temporal resistances which obstruct the optimal and regular operation of the production process.

After the substantial results obtained with Taylor's methods, there were developments in the production line which signaled further victories. A new phase began with the introduction of the assembly line in Ford's Highland Park plant (1913), followed by the River Rouge plant, which linked the assembly lines of the various departments, thus connecting all production units—even those far away—along the entire labor cycle. Later, the same relationship was effected between production, distribution and consumption. This experience reached mature development in a little more than ten years and was destined to become successful well beyond the automobile manufacturing sphere, to the point that Fordism speaks of an entire epoch whose influence reaches through the 1950s.

Although Ford followed Taylorist principles quite closely, he also introduced important innovations. The control of the individual worker assigned to monitoring work tempo was replaced by control disseminated within the organization of the production flow itself. Eventual inadequacies of a single worker or of a single department were revealed by irregularities in the rhythm of the labor cycle. Surveillance became even more objective and authoritative as it became inseparable from the total mechanism.

The imposing power of such a system was an appealing model for a society in which cities were merely groups of buildings held together by transportation and communications. Although not quite as thoroughly implemented as in Socgorad, the utopian city that Miljutin designed in 1931 as an immense assembly line, many aspects of the functioning and organization of many metropolitan areas carry the Fordist stamp.

Within this scenario, modern art emerged in its full revolutionary importance. Fully concerned with the perception of time and space as obstacles, and only incidentally concerned with power, the art of the eighteenth and nineteenth centuries assumed the role of interpreter and promoter of forces toward liberation and valorization of subjectivity, in open conflict with the new constrictions that assailed daily life.

Thus, while the organizational sciences sought to bring order to the chaos (understood as all that opposed the regular and increasingly rapid flow of production and accumulation), the intellectual vanguards, particularly the artistic vanguard, not only measured themselves against the chaos induced by the industrial revolution but went still further. They ventured into the depths of the psyche, yearning to bring to the surface a new order and to reveal it in the forms of the world. While the methods of the scientific management of production are motivated by the "desire to transform the divinity into a pure machine,"[7] the artistic avant-garde seem to voluntarily contract the virus of dehumanization generated by the "substitution of the mechanical principle for the organic,"[8] so as to acquire the antibodies with which to establish a new phase of radical humanization of the artificial order. These two opposing aspirations were both totalitarian and inevitable, although in a less tragic measure than the political ones which left a profound mark on the twentieth century and its inheritance.

Modern architecture is motivated by both aspirations, and tends to reconcile the opposites in a superior synthesis.

While we must agree with Edoardo Persico's affirmation that "European architecture is born as a reaction to the environment, as the opposition of the individual to society…"[9] we must also acknowledge that at the same time this "demands that the twentieth-century architect must fully adapt to the spirit of necessity that now regulates all contemporary activities."[10]

The propensity to reconcile a high spiritual tension with the objective demands required of modernity is an inclination inherent in the Modern Movement.

For example, Marcel Breuer maintained that "the force of persuasion of the truly inspiring constructions is generated by a persistence, almost a passion, that is by itself beyond logic,"[11] and that "with pure logic one cannot define the spirit of the time in its most profound orientations."[12] At the same time, he declared himself convinced of the possibility of using "the most easily understood part of the modern will, the practical and technical one, to serve as a bridge to the other part, the one that, not precisely expressed, has an artistic and spiritual nature."[13]

The descent into the realm of utility and necessity was led by the eighteenth-century engineers who demonstrated how in the beauty of the machine (and in bridges and buildings) "the line of strength and beauty are one and the same line."[14] The conquest of the "purity" of the modern machine was seen as an indispensable step towards access to essentiality and therefore to the truth of architectural forms. Le Corbusier dared to go even further, at least in words, declaring himself convinced that "science and its works derive from the prescriptions of a primal will" that is manifest in "the criterion of harmony." In such a criterion he saw, in fact, "the indefinable trace of the absolute preexistent to the foundation of our being."[15] Furthermore, for him, more than "organisms tending to purity and subject to the same evolutionary rules of objects of nature that provoke our admiration,"[16] "creations of the machine aesthetic" were unequivocally manifestations of the divine.

Although in general, modern architectural masters have adopted less prophetic tones, they are no less inclined to a mysticism that is both religious and scientific, and they are, no less than Le Corbusier, convinced of the possibility of architecture synthesizing the absolute spirit and the spirit of time. When the freest subjectivity approached the highest objectivity, the creative act of the architect, and modernity itself, were seen as manifestations of the divine. This is a philosophy, more or less implicit in modern architecture, for which Julius Evola delineated the essential terms in 1933: "In the order of such construction there is a reversal of the usual notion itself, romantic/bourgeois, of beauty. In fact, the beautiful was previously derived from the fantasy, taste, and personality of the individual artist—now the beautiful becomes a dominion dependent in the strictest sense on science and power...it corresponds to the kind of *necessity* to which the exact form of a modern machine obeys....Where the person disappears, there remains a method and a style of *pure objectivity*."[17]

There are certainly some theoretical differences concerning the relationships between architecture and function. For example, between Sartoris, for whom "we cannot stand by indifferent to the utilitarian power of the machine without transposing, in architecture, not the forms themselves of the machine, but that exact notion of utility which constitutes its entire functional value,"[18] and Mies van der Rohe, who did not believe in a direct and immediate discovery of the architectural form in compliance to functional demands. Mies pointed out that such a discovery lies elsewhere, in the arduous passage "from function to worth."[19] This conviction, Peter Blake wrote, "finally persuaded [Mies]—at least for a little while—that, in reality, functionalism is the enemy of beauty..."[20] However, similar differences do not prevent a more profound community of intentions that work to make the spirit a reality, to render manifest the absolute in modernity.

The Modern Movement consumed itself with the tension between function and beauty, and eventually clarified its greatness and its limitations.

Modern architecture reached high levels of expression through the synthesis between a clarity[21] obtained by the most rigorous exercise of subtraction, and a "harmony of contrasts"[22] as mimesis, in the self-sufficient and detached form of architecture as the conflict engaged by the spirit-creator and chaos. However, that same experience has completely failed in its endeavor to reestablish the city. Nevertheless, this failure is a fact of epochal importance, and the responsibility for it falls to society as a whole. This does not mean, however, that the Modern Movement is not, in its own way, also partly responsible.

At the base of such a co-responsibility there is, above all, the absence of a critical attitude with regard to modernity, in scientific, technological and economic fields, as well as in the political and social arenas. Among the many testimonies to this responsibility is a passage from the previously cited writings of Breuer, in which one can trace the tragic civic profile of an entire generation. "What good does it serve to know for example whether Stalin and the creators of the Soviet Palace are communists, and what good is it to know their reasons? The important thing is that their arguments are the same as those of an automobile maker who thinks in a symbolic and primitive way, whether he is a capitalist, a democrat, a fascist or a conservative."[23]

With this I do not intend at all to interpret the theoretical and practical production of modern architecture in the light of political or ideological orientations. I would instead like to point out how much already has emerged in projects to redevelop or expand the city: the essential similarity between the concept of order underlying those proposals and the concepts of order underlying the Fordist model on one side, and modern political totalitarianism on the other.

This similarity is not solely reliant on the fact that all these models of order are based on the work of a single creator,[24] but also from the imposition of order itself and by the promotion of order as sole and exclusive meaning.

There are certainly rare exceptions[25] which repropose the founding spirit of the European city, that is, the centrality of social places as reinterpretations of the "common hearth" at the origin of the polis and as expression of collective living. In general though, the urban designs of the Modern Movement organized spaces on the basis of abstract and monotonous rhythms which lacked a discursive interaction with the past from which the historic city had taken its complex order and its density of meanings and sense (although the rational layout minutely complies with the principles of hygiene and efficiency—thus the influence of medicine and industrialism).

The desire to "modernize" cities was a great flaw of the Modern Movement. Blind to the interdependent layers of richness, reinterpretation, and invention, "modern" cities ignored the tradition of existence on a simultaneously individual and collective scale. Derived from a similar lack of consciousness are both the battle against the historical city—the Corbusian "il faut tuer la rue corridor" arrives emblematically at the assassination—and the choice to subject the organization of space to a univocal temporality, the same temporality of modernity, in full adherence to the Fordist model. With the failure of discourse, order faced an excess with respect to human presence, resulting in designs for neighborhoods and cities in which the architectural objects were isolated, cut off from one another, to adhere to an abstract, randomly imposed rhythm, from which surprise and wonder were precluded, as well as every receptivity to desire. Far from evoking the divine, that order showed itself incapable of continuing the narration which I have discussed. And from here are generated designs which the irony of fate makes us call urban, and which are instead a faithful mirror of the poverty of meaning which modernity faces.

What does all of this have to do with a book that deals with an architect like Albert Kahn, removed from, when not in open conflict with, the theoretical approach and the practice of the very architecture of the Modern Movement?

It is worth asking, in the first place, the reasons for the lack of renown that Albert Kahn had among architectural scholars in the postwar period. We must take into account that in general, his works, or those produced under his direction, did not achieve the levels of the great masters of modern architecture, although some of his projects have attracted quite a bit of attention (for example, the Half-Ton Truck plant for the Chrysler Corporation in Warren and the Lady Esther plant). It should also be added that the prolific nature of Albert Kahn, Inc. renders the reconstruction of a complete repertory difficult, and the firm's disconcerting eclecticism defies formulation of a global interpretation, since this would also necessitate an enumeration of the specific contributions of the many collaborators. Lastly, one cannot disregard Kahn's practice of adhering—like Henry Ford—to his past experiences: this led Albert Kahn to construct a theoretical apparatus that did not go beyond the principles delineated by the evidence of facts. His "architecture is 90% business and 10% art" demonstrated in no uncertain terms a completely set personality, exempt from idealization and romanticism, but also exempt from the aspirations to universal theories prevalent in the Modern Movement. While all of this surely does not create attention and fascination for this figure, the disinterest also reveals the limits of an architectural historiography and criticism accustomed to discussing single personalities and movements and interpreting them against enunciated programs and not instead in the framework of the complex evolution of landscapes and cultures of construction, and therefore of societies.

It is this approach which believes it possible to attend to the *parole* without attending also to the *langue*, and thus loses sight of the effective course of the individual who reveals the potential of the *langue*. *Langue* preexists creative work, *langue* is modified, and *langue* is pushed to new developments, even if they are imperceptibly slight. In other words, this is an approach that separates the architecture produced by single personalities from the complex, and from the more general mode of organizing, living and feeling space (and time).

It is within this more vast horizon of the study of the figures in the modern landscape that the work of Albert Kahn presents an interest. This interest derives not only from his direct and intense involvement in the events of the Ford industries and from his contribution to the enunciation of solutions adequate for new production demands, but also and above all, because Kahn was a person who knew how to interpret in architectural terms that perception of time and space as obstacles of which we spoke at the beginning of this introduction.

With the Packard Building no. 10 of 1905, Kahn accomplished a double revolution: on the one hand, he carried to its extreme developments the search for wide covered spaces liberated from weight-supporting features: a fact which—as Federico Bucci explains—precedes and makes possible the adoption of the production line system (which occurred eight years later in the Highland Park complex). On the other hand, he constructed a building whose structure was exposed and entirely glazed and which needed only to raise itself on its *pilotis* to display the five features that Le Corbusier later enumerated as the innovations of the modern architectural revolution. "The system of independent structure, which allows the maximum freedom in the composition and distribution of floor plans, logically fused with the facades..." was a system which Sartoris, in the footsteps of Le Corbusier, numbered among the "major achievements of the rationalist tendency."[26] In reality, it had a very long gestation and reached mature expression in the Packard Building at the beginning of the century.

In fact, the Packard Building responded to the archetypal ideal of space toward which modernity had been moving since the eighteenth century.[27] It was universal space as close as possible to the purity and abstraction of Cartesian space, in which the absence of obstacles (supporting elements) reached the greatest freedom of movement and the most flexible adaptation to functional changes.

This spatial archetype constituted the ideal theater in which modernity demonstrated its restrictions and its freedoms. Thanks to that type of space it was possible to both accommodate Fordist production, engendering a totalitarian concatenation of space and time, and to attain freedom from spatial and temporal conditions. Not incidentally, in taking this second aspect to the extreme, Mies van der Rohe theorized the reduction of the structure to "almost nothing," consistent with the aspiration to a "universal architecture" understood as "the highest possible degree of freedom."[28]

As we have seen, the utopia and the drama of the Modern Movement lie in the conviction that these two courses—the one towards the full implementation of the Fordist model, and the other towards the liberation of the human condition from spatial/temporal obstacles—can be followed simultaneously and with mutual enrichment. In reality these paths go in opposite directions, just as Ildefonso Cerdá intuited early on in his *Teoria general de l'urbanización* (1867). He indicated that the central issue of urban design was the discovery of an equilibrium between motion and rest, in the sense of the necessity of a defense of the latter from the former.

The same principle is symbolically clear in the design of the concert hall by Mies van der Rohe in 1942. The hall was an adaptation of the interior of the Martin bomber factory built three years earlier by Albert Kahn.[29]

In that construction—which, according to Franz Schulze, summed up the "essence of building,"[30] Mies accomplished a work of subtraction and limitation. The monotonous seriality of the container conceived of so as to accommodate the uniform and accelerated production flow, became for Mies a musical score in which he could perform a solo: free variations on a theme which, in architectural terms, configured a space-time which harmonized with the pre-established rhythm of the spans. The result is an exemplary representation of the richness of meaning that springs from the coexistence of motion and rest and from their interactive rhythms. Architecture, while it gathers the anxiety of freedom in the permeability of spaces, delimits them so as to better unite them in the necessary complementariness of rest and motion. Action can coexist with contemplation, and the theatricality which results from this becomes a founding quality of the habitability of the place: exactly that which is missing from a great part of city and neighborhood designs based on rational layout or on the principles of the Charter of Athens.

Likewise, the enormous containers of the huge plants for Ford production designed by Albert Kahn barely escape the monotonous rhythm of simplified music. Certainly this order lacking surprise and desire is better than the absence of any rhythm. But if it is reductive to see reflected in these that which Gramsci called the engaged battle of industrialism for the "subjugation of natural instincts...to ever more complex and rigid norms and habits of order, exactness and precision..."[31] it is surely too generous an interpretation that assimilates that order to the "reconciliation of mechanism and spirituality, necessity and freedom,"[32] which sees in Albert Kahn the consumption of a drama which is totally foreign to him and which is instead that of the Modern Movement.

One must instead acknowledge that this order takes its monotony from its perfect adherence to the unfolding pattern of modernity, and from the "absence of meaning"[33] which characterized modernity. The incapacity to refer to the interior and to produce cities is the most evident manifestation of this. The fact that the Modern Movement often relied on impotent analogy is reason for further inquiry and reflection for which this research on "Ford's architect" offers material and starting points for productive comparisons.

Federico Bucci's inquiry into the production of Albert Kahn, Inc. has the merit of offering itself not only as a basis for useful comparisons with the events of the Modern Movement, but also allows complex considerations on the building industry in the twentieth century. In fact it presents the social significance of design work, without neglecting the influence on its outcomes of the methods of labor management within large firms. This book provides ground-breaking work on this subject.

Giancarlo Consonni

NOTES

1 K. Marx, *Das Kapital*, Dietz, Berlin 1947, Book I (Hamburg 1867), p. 1. Marx had already used the expression in *Zur Kritik der politicischen okonomie*, Berlin 1859.

2 W.J. Cameron, "Il decentramento dell'industria," in *Tecnica e organizzazione*, annal I, no. 6, November 1937, p. 61.

3 A. Gramsci, *Quaderni dal carcere* [Notebook 22, 1934. Americanism and Fordism], V. Gerratana (ed.), Einaudi, Turin 1975, p. 2164.

4 W. Schivelbusch, *Geschichte der Eisenbahnreise*, Hanser, Munich-Wein 1977; S. Kern, *The Culture of Time and Space 1880–1918*, Harvard University Press, Cambridge, MA 1983.

5 Michel Foucault's affirmation in the conversation with J.P. Barou and M. Perrot collected in *L'occhio del potere* carried in the introduction to J. Bentham's *Panopticon ovvero la casa d'ispezione*, M. Foucault and M. Perrot (ed.), Marsilio, Venice 1983, p. 18.

6 F.W. Taylor (1856–1915) undertook his studies in the field of production when he was still quite young, but he concentrated his attention on the experts of production management only in 1895 when at the American Society of Mechanical Engineers he presented the paper 'A Piéce-Rate System, Being a Step Towards a Partial Solution of the Labor Problem.' Afterwards with his books *Shop Management* (1903) and *The Principles of Scientific Management* (1911), he arrived at an organic formulization of his theories. These and other important writing are collected in F.W. Taylor, *Scientific Management*, Harper and Brothers, New York and London 1947.

7 D.H. Lawrence, *Women in Love*, 1917, Heinemann, London 1957.

8 Ibid., p. 300.

9 E. Persico, "L'architettura mondiale," in *L'Italia Letteraria*, July 2, 1933.

10 A. Sartoris, *Introduzione alla architettura moderna*, Hoepli, Milan 1949 (3rd) (1943).

11 M. Breuer, "Wo stehen wir?" in *Casabella*, annal VIII, no. 87, March 1935, p. 7.

12 Ibid., p. 6.

13 Ibid.

14 This statement is taken from a lecture by Oscar Wilde in 1882, cited in N. Pevsner, *Pioneers of Modern Design*, Penguin Books, Harmondsworth 1960 (3rd).

15 Le Corbusier, *Vers une Architecture*, 1923, Vincent, Fréal & C., Paris 1958, p. 165.

16 Ibid., p. 80.

17 J. Evola, "Realismo, architettura nuova e fascismo," in *Regime fascista*, March 3, 1933.

18 A. Sartoris, *Introduzione alla architettura moderna*, p. 202.

19 See A. Monestiroli, "Le forme e il tempo," introduction to L. Hilberseimer, *Mies van der Rohe*, Theobald, Chicago 1956, It. trans. Clup, Milan 1984, pp. 7–17.

20 P. Blake, *The Master Builders*, Gollancz, London 1960, chapter "Mies van der Rohe."

21 On the roots of "clarity" in modern thought, I refer the reader to F. De Faveri, *Sublimità e bellezza. Alle basi della nuova estetica architettonica*, CittàStudi, Milan 1992.

22 M. Breuer, "Wo stehen wir?" p. 7.

23 Ibid., p. 5.

24 Significantly, one of the philosophies which has laid the basis of modern thought introduced its reflection by the "verification" that "works constituted by more parts and realized by the contribution of different artists do not reach that level of perfection which have instead those works wrought by the hand of a single master." R. Descartes, *Discours de la Méthode pour bien conduire sa raison et chercher la vérité dans les sciences*, 1637, in Idem, *Oeuvres et lettres*, A. Bridoux (ed.), Bibliotheque de la Pléiade, Paris 1949. See the author's "Scientismo e morfologia nello studio dei passaggi. Per una critica," in *Urbanistica*, no. 96, October 1989, pp. 63–67.

25 Among these exceptions, the author cites Siedlung the Iron Horse, by Berlin Britz, built in 1925–1926 according to the design by Bruno Taut and Martin Wagner.

26 A. Sartoris, *Introduzione alla architettura moderna*, p. 6.

27 S. Giedion, *Space, Time and Architecture*, Harvard University Press, Cambridge, MA 1941.

28 P. Blake, *The Master Builders*, p. 212.

29 F. Schulze, *Mies van der Rohe. A Critical Biography*, The University of Chicago Press, Chicago-London 1985, pp. 231–232.

30 Ibid., p. 231.

31 A. Gramsci, pp. 2160–2161.

32 A. Tilgher, *Homo Faber*, Rome 1929, p. 142.

33 U. Galimberti, "La religione dei nostalgici senza Dio," in *Il Sole-24 ore*, October 27, 1991.

PREFACE

This book began as a Master's thesis: *"Organizzazione scientifica del lavoro e razionalizzazione dello spazio negli anni tra le due guerre: il modello di Taylor e di Ford e le particolarità del caso italiano"* [The Scientific Management of Labor and the Rationalization of Space in the period between the World Wars: the Models of Taylor and Ford and the Details of the Italian Case], defended by Pierluigi Tavecchio and myself—with our advisor Giancarlo Consonni, on March 19, 1984 at the School of Architecture at the Milan Politecnico. This research explored in depth the relations between the world of industrial production and the architectural and urban planning communities within a historical period which had witnessed, on the one hand, the affirmation of Taylorist theories and Fordist practice and, on the other hand, the growing interest on the part of the architectural avant-garde for the novelties introduced by the new systems of production organization. Within this framework, the work of Albert Kahn for the Ford Motor Company was one of the case studies included in the part dedicated to North America. Specifically, the subject of Fordist space had been previously discussed in the article *"La macchina totale. La razionalizzazione fordista dello spazio,"* [The Total Machine. The Fordist Rationalization of Space] published in *Classe*, no. 22, December 1982. This article treated subjects raised in *Urban Planning I* which then were developed into this thesis. Subsequently, the first specific inquiries into the work of Albert Kahn, conducted by Pierluigi Tavecchio and myself, took the form of the piece *"Organizzazione scientifica del lavoro intellettuale e progettazione architettonica dello spazio di fabbrica: il caso della Albert Kahn, Inc. 1896–1945"* [The Scientific Management and Architectural Design of the Factory Space: the Case Study of Albert Kahn, Inc. 1896–1945] (in *Annali di storia dell'impresa*, no. 2, 1986) and in the simple guide "Albert

Kahn and Detroit," (in *Domus*, 670, September 1986) which signaled a new point of departure.

In addition to this research, I then began a more detailed study on the work of Albert Kahn. I greatly benefitted by the opportunity to consult the archives of Albert Kahn Associates Inc. Architects and Engineers of Detroit, the firm established by Albert Kahn in 1895 and which is still today a great presence in the field of large building design. With the Albert Kahn, Inc. archives, I was faced with the problem of a great bulk of heterogeneous material—designs, photographs, newspaper reviews, writings—conserved for the needs of the company and not at all organized for historical research. The greatest difficulty was maneuvering within an iconographic documentation which included an overwhelming number of buildings constructed: around two thousand between 1895 and 1945. Another obstacle was the fact that the industrial buildings in Detroit (the most consistent part of Albert Kahn's production) had in general undergone modifications due to production needs which made it difficult to recognize the original design, or they had been demolished to make room for other installations or abandoned after the automobile industry crisis. For this reason I have tried to use photographs of the buildings immediately after construction.

The access to the archival material allowed me to focus on the various facets of the work of Albert Kahn and his firm. The principle aim of this book is to investigate the relationship inherent in the subtitle (*The Architect of Ford*), rather than to present a monograph on a little-studied architect. The objective was to explore the influence exercised by the scientific management of labor and of the modern factory on the architecture of this century, primarily the points of contact, but also the points of divergence with the theoretical elaborations of the Modern Movement.

My hope is that this book may also stimulate interest concerning the timeliness of the subject of the organization of design work and large professional firms involved in the field of architecture.

PREFACE

Many people devoted their attention to the preparation of this book. In the first place, I would like to express my gratitude to Joseph Bedway who faithfully assisted me in the archival research and who always went beyond the usual tasks required of his position. At Albert Kahn Associates, Inc. I found a welcoming and hospitable environment; for this I thank the president, Edgar E. Parks, the vice-president, William Demiene, and David Barczys, with whom I profitably and enjoyably discussed American architecture.

In addition, I am grateful to Antonio Monestiroli, director of the Dipartimento di Progettazione dell'Architettura [Department of Architectural Design] of the Milan Politecnico who, along with the scientific committee of the series *Studi e progetti* believed in this research.

Special thanks to Kevin Harrington for his helpful comments after a careful reading of the text. Furthermore, for their invaluable help I want to thank Claudio Camponogara, Paola Montagna, Gianmario Andreani, Franco Riva, George Danforth, Elaine Harrington, John Pratt, Augusto Rossari, Duccio Bigazzi, Raffaella Poletti, Allison Saltzman, Carmen Di Cinque, Luigi Viola, the personnel of the Libraries of the School of Architecture of the Milan Politecnico, of the Usis in Milan, the University of Detroit, the University of Michigan at Ann Arbor, and especially my parents and my wife Emanuela who, along with our child Lorenzo, daily supported the presence of Albert Kahn in our life.

Last, but not least, my work could not have taken place without the irreplaceable guidance of Giancarlo Consonni, a patient and attentive *tutor* for this type of research.

Obviously, I alone am responsible for the final result.

Milan, February 7, 1994

to Emanuela and Lorenzo

Albert Kahn in his office: Detroit, 1940

FROM SELF-EDUCATION TO PIONEER WORK WITH FORD
From Rhaunen to Detroit: The Birth of a Self-Made Man

Albert Kahn was born in Rhaunen, Germany (near Frankfurt) on March 21, 1869, the first son of Rosalie and Rabbi Joseph Kahn. The precarious economic conditions of the family were such that, after a brief stay in Luxembourg, the Kahns decided to try their luck in the United States, and settled in Detroit in 1881. While Detroit was not a large city, it was well-located for industrial development. Between Lake Erie and Lake Huron, it was near the source of raw materials and joined to a major means of transportation.

Nevertheless, Joseph Kahn's various enterprises in Detroit were unsuccessful, and the invitations that he received from the Jewish community for posts in isolated towns did not provide adequate family income. Therefore, at a very young age, Albert was forced to interrupt his studies in order to help alleviate the economic difficulties in which the family, by now quite large, had fallen.[1]

Thanks to his aptitude for design, after some private lessons, Albert was taken on by the architectural firm of Mason & Rice, among the best in the city. In 1884, at the age of fifteen, Albert began his professional apprenticeship. He spent his entire day at the drafting table but in his free time would slip into the firm's library to look through the architecture books and magazines.

Albert's self-education received a boost when, at age twenty-one, he was awarded a scholarship from *The American Architect and Building News* to spend one year in Europe. For young American architects of that period, the study of historical architectural styles was considered an obligatory step in the formative journey: compositional structures and decorative details of the principal monuments of European cities were scrupulously redesigned as a nutritive element for the planning of buildings in America.[2]

Albert Kahn traveled throughout England, France, Belgium, Germany and, above all, Italy, where he met Henry Bacon, the future architect of the Lincoln Memorial, the masterpiece of American eclecticism. When he returned to Detroit, Albert produced a wide repertory of designs and sketches, revealing a mastery that earned him the title of chief designer in the firm of Mason & Rice. Thirty years later in *Pencil Points*, an article dedicated to Albert Kahn in a series on master draftsmen, read: "The European sketches originally made for *The American Architect* show Mr. Kahn's style of draftsmanship in its first full development....They are purely architectural records, faithfully and brilliantly made."[3]

Albert Kahn's career reached a turning point in 1895, when he refused an enticing offer from Louis Sullivan[4] and established his own firm with associates George W.

Nettleton and Alexander B. Trowbridge, colleagues of Mason. "Both," remembered Albert Kahn, "G.W.N., the senior, and A.B.T., the junior, had had training at Cornell and a number of years in an office, while I had only the training of the office where I started as an office boy—having left school when eleven years old upon emigrating from Luxembourg to this country."[5] The firm of Nettleton, Kahn & Trowbridge was short-lived: Trowbridge accepted a teaching position at Cornell University, and Nettleton died tragically in 1900.

Nevertheless, Albert did not abandon his enterprise. First with his mentor George D. Mason (until 1902), then with the architect Ernest Wilby (until 1918), and finally as Albert Kahn Incorporated Architects and Engineers, he established a career destined to leave its decisive mark on North American industrial architecture.

Reinforced Concrete and Typological Invention

From the beginning, the career of Albert Kahn was linked to the automobile industry which had established plants in Detroit in the beginning of the twentieth century. The rapid rate of growth in the industrial sector required research for new solutions for production space: traditional factory plans proved inadequate in providing the flexibility and safety needed for the new management of labor.

The new solutions experimented with innovations in construction techniques and structural concepts. In working this terrain, Kahn counted on the invaluable help of his brother Julius, an engineer involved in experimentation with the uses of reinforced concrete.

Julius Kahn, younger than Albert by five years (he was born in Germany in 1874), had been able to graduate from the University of Michigan with a degree in engineering in 1896, thanks to the financial help of his brother. As a junior associate of the American Society of Civil Engineers, he immediately distinguished himself in January 1899 in the Society's assembly periodicals, with skillful analyses of the new copper mining plants of Calumet and Hecla Mining Company, located in the vast mining area along the American shore of Lake Superior.[6]

Two years later, returning to Detroit after a work experience in Japan, Julius joined Albert. "This was the beginning of a lifetime team in America's construction era: Julius Kahn, the inventor and manufacturer, and Albert Kahn, the artist and architect, both specializing in industrial construction."[7]

It didn't take Julius Kahn long to prove his talent. He took out a patent on reinforced concrete, the Kahn System of Reinforced Concrete, which was the end result of studies and experiments on American construction techniques since the second half of the nineteenth century.[8]

The system of reinforcement was composed of a steel skeleton supported by soldered wings angled upwards, which, positioned according to the direction of the principal forces of compression, had the advantage of offering greater resistance while also simplifying the construction.[9] With typical American pioneer style, Albert Kahn attested to the decisive importance of the Kahn System: "And then there came a turn in the use of reinforced concrete which meant much in the future of my career. My brother Julius, a graduate engineer, who had spent several years in Japan, returned to join me. He quickly saw the weak spots in the empirical system of reinforcement being used and promptly designed a form of reinforcement along scientific principles. We made tests which were conclusive, confirming his theories...the so-called "Kahn" system quickly became established and popular throughout the country and while heartaches during the first years were many, the system won out finally."[10]

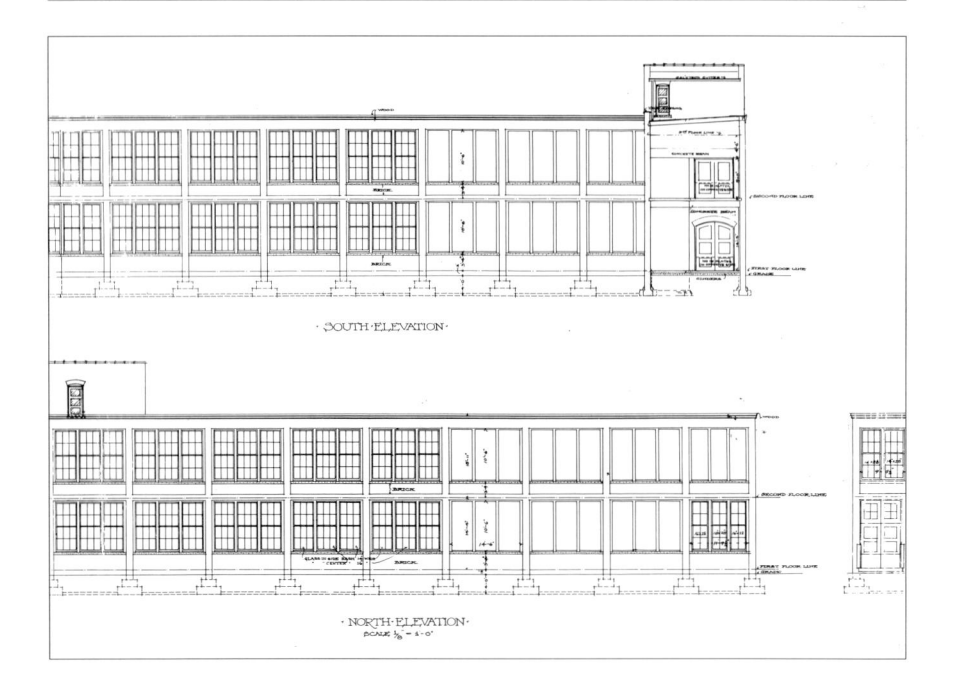

THE PACKARD MOTOR CAR COMPANY, BUILDING NO. 10: DETROIT, MICHIGAN; ALBERT KAHN, ERNEST WILBY, 1905
Elevations

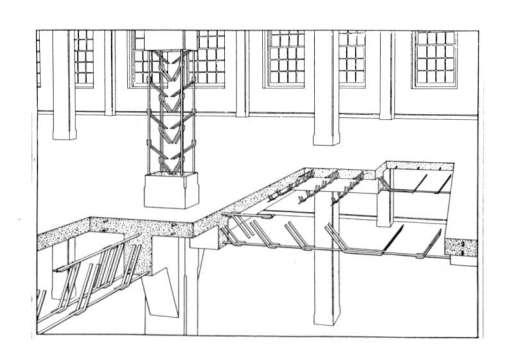

THE KAHN SYSTEM OF REINFORCED CONCRETE
Detail

The system met with notable success among specialized technicians in both the United States and Europe.[11]

The rapid and enduring success of the Kahn System of Reinforced Concrete is related to the brilliant commercial management of the patent awarded to Trussed Concrete Steel Company. The Detroit company, founded by Julius Kahn, extended its activities through a network of affiliates in many American and European cities, and even in Japan.

In 1914 the central headquarters of the company, which had assumed the name of the Truscon Steel Company, was transferred to Youngstown, Ohio, nearer the source of raw materials. In 1935, after more than thirty years of intense activity, it became part of the stock package of the Republican Steel Corporation, of which Julius Kahn was vice-president.[12]

The Kahn System was first used in the Engineering Building at the University of Michigan in Ann Arbor, which Albert and Julius Kahn (with the collaboration of Ernest Wilby) completed in 1903. Its first real success came when Henry B. Joy, president of the Packard Motor Car Company, commissioned Albert Kahn to design a new plant in Detroit. The assignment of this first industrial commission was purely fortuitous: as Albert himself later admitted, he had "practically no experience in factory building,"[13] and had been chosen because of the trust inspired by his remodeling of Joy's home.

While the first nine buildings of the Packard plant were constructed according to contemporary models of the American building trade, the 1905 design of Building no. 10 offered the opportunity for a decisive turn: reinforced concrete (according to the methods of the Kahn System of Reinforced Concrete) replaced traditional structural materials of iron, stone, and brick.[14]

And so the Kahns created a two-story building (about 18.2 x 98.1 meters, 60 x 322 feet) that may have been one of the first factories for automobile production in Detroit.

There were two requirements for which the use of reinforced concrete was optimal: to guarantee the structure's stability and to protect the structure from the frequent risk of fire. But what fully demonstrated the advantages of a reinforced concrete structure was its capacity to define very large, covered spaces, and free the floor plan from the encumbrance of weight-bearing structures. Referring to Building no. 10 in an article in 1931, Albert Kahn remembered with pride his "spans [of] thirty feet [nine meters] in each direction."[15]

The Packard Building no. 10 thus introduced a new definition of factory space. Architectural design was no longer merely the study of a shell to dress the underlying structure or the production function, but was the creation of a building which expressed the complete harmony of these two elements.

PACKARD MOTOR CAR COMPANY: DETROIT, MICHIGAN; ALBERT KAHN, ERNEST WILBY, 1903–1910
General view of the complex in a watercolor by Jules Guerin

Building no. 10 had important implications for the budding American automobile industry, regarding both the adoption of reinforced concrete structures, and the flexibility of internal space for experimentation in the organization of the production process.[16] Referring to this accomplishment, Reyner Banham in *A Concrete Atlantis* (1986), used expressions such as "the air of grudging meanness," "the zero-term of architecture."[17] However accurate these observations may have been, Albert and Julius Kahn had, in designing Building no. 10, aimed for the establishment of a laboratory for the research of new construction techniques and new systems for the management of labor; they were less concerned with exterior design. Yet, the resolution of the internal-external relationship corresponded to the manifestation of the construction principle, and set an early precedent for the Modern Movement to follow.

opposite page:
PACKARD MOTOR CAR COMPANY, BUILDING NO. 10: DETROIT, MICHIGAN; ALBERT KAHN, ERNEST WILBY, 1905
View of the building, 1950s (with two stories added after 1905)
Interior

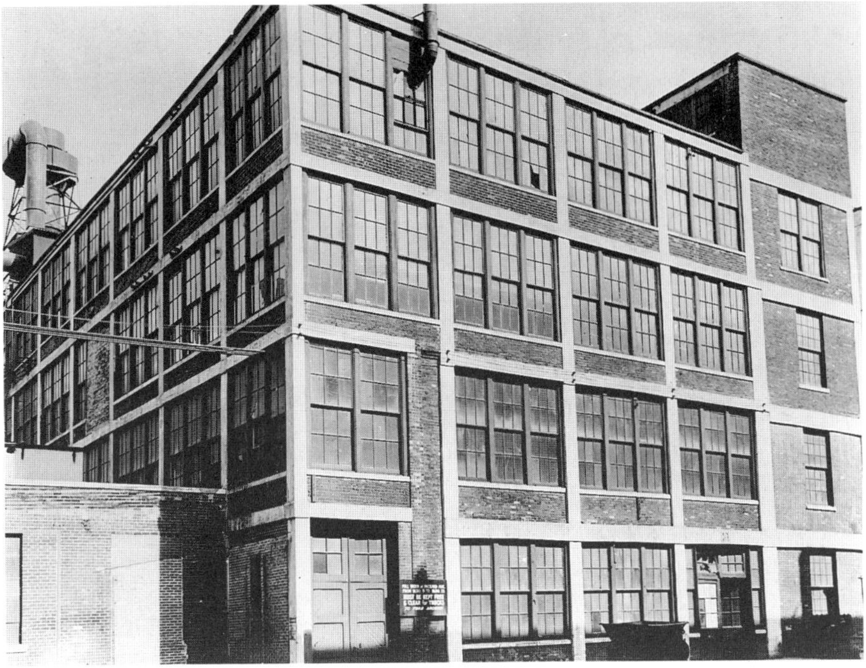

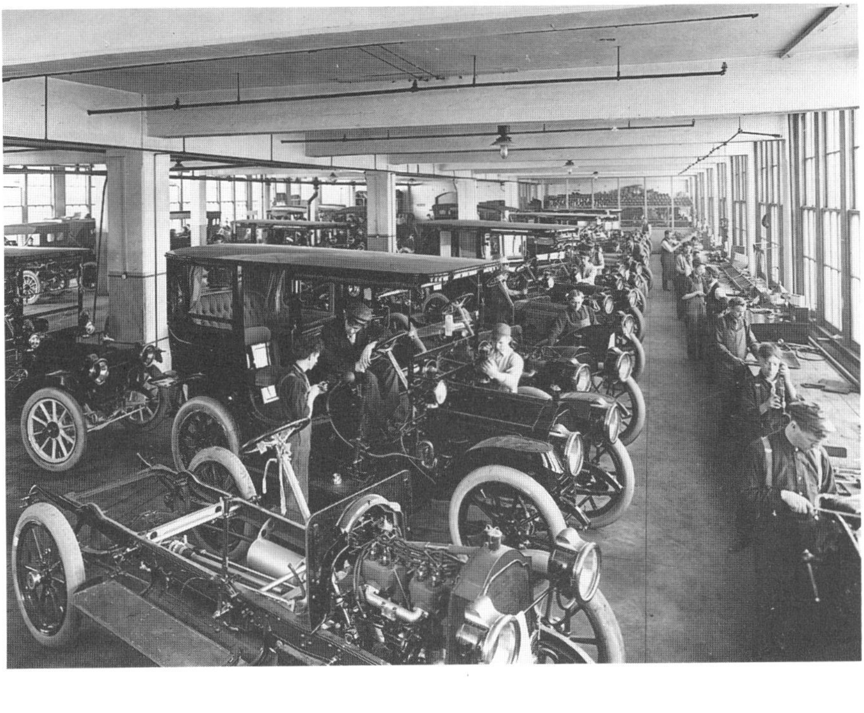

BURROUGHS ADDING MACHINE COMPANY: DETROIT, MICHIGAN; ALBERT KAHN, ERNEST WILBY, 1907–1912

BROWN LIPE CHAPIN COMPANY: SYRACUSE, NEW YORK; ALBERT KAHN, ERNEST WILBY, 1907

MERGENTHALER LINOTYPE COMPANY: BROOKLYN, NEW YORK; ALBERT KAHN, ERNEST WILBY, 1907

CONTINENTAL MOTOR COMPANY: DETROIT, MICHIGAN; ALBERT KAHN, ERNEST WILBY, 1911
A one-story factory modeled after the George N. Pierce plant in Buffalo, New York

After the Packard Building no. 10, Albert Kahn employed this model of the generously fenestrated, brick-supported, reinforced concrete assembly plant for two other factories built in Detroit in 1907: the plants of the Burroughs Adding Machine Company and the Chalmers Motor Car Company. A variation was introduced with the buildings for the Mergenthaler Linotype Company in Brooklyn (1907) and the Brown Lipe Chapin Company in Syracuse (1907–1909), which were built entirely of reinforced concrete without tiled roofs; between the horizontal and vertical links of the structure there were only iron window frames.[18]

During these years, there was experimentation with an alternative arrangement of the automobile factory: an articulated organism in one-story structures corresponding to the various divisions of labor. The plans for the Pierce Great Arrow Automobile Plant (Buffalo, 1906) were designed according to this criterion. The construction of the Pierce plant called for the cooperation of Albert and Julius Kahn with the firm of Lockwood, Green & Martin of Boston, and with a local architect. While who actually played which role in this project is a source of debate,[19] the tendency to assign a preeminent contribution to the Kahn brothers stems from a brochure of Julius Kahn's Trussed Concrete Steel Company, that featured the Pierce plant. On one occasion, speaking of his first industrial buildings, Albert Kahn remembered that "They had employed a firm of Eastern architects and engineers, experienced in mill building and totally inexperienced in reinforced concrete.... Then one night, while bids were being taken on the new plant, the old—a mill building—went up in smoke.... We consequently had a hurry call from the owners, and agreed to design, for the architects then employed, the new plant in reinforced concrete."[20] With that "we," Kahn implied his firm and his brother's company.

The novelty of the Pierce plant lay in the organization of the entire work cycle on the same floor. The layout was articulated in seven one-story buildings of reinforced concrete with shed roofs, each corresponding to one segment of the production process: Garage, Manufacturing Building, Assembly Building, Body Building, Brazing Building, Motor Testing Building and Power House. The raw materials arrived via railroad to the Brazing Building; from there they proceeded towards the Manufacturing Building (that produced motors and frames) and the Body Building. The Assembly Building was located in the center of the plant where the three parts of the car were assembled (the motors first passed through the Motor Testing Building for inspection); once completed, the vehicles were sent to the Garage to be equipped.

This model of organization of the production flow, one that moved the piece work through the single buildings, anticipated the concept of assembly-line production that would be more extensively and systematically employed in the Ford industry: "This plant," wrote Grant Hildebrand, "seems so ideally suited to assembly line operations that it is almost startling to realize that they were not used there when the plant was completed and in fact were not used in automobile production until 1913, nearly seven years after the Pierce design."[21]

Albert Kahn, without ever losing sight of the demands of production, had in some way anticipated the typological characteristics of the modern factory. More importantly, Kahn accomplished this independently of the definitive systematization of the Fordist organizational model of production.

The two models of industrial buildings in reinforced concrete—the Packard Motor Car Company in Detroit and the Pierce Great Arrow in Buffalo—possessed the essence of the character of factory space which was to be fully displayed during Kahn's years with Ford.

The Packard Building no. 10 anticipated that which would be applied in the Ford Motor Company plant in Highland Park (1909), where from one floor to the next, the vertical production flow would develop into the famous assembly line. And the Pierce Great Arrow building became the experimental model for the organization of horizontal production, perfected in the twenties by Henry Ford in his enormous plant on the Rouge River, a model unequaled in industrial centralization.

Highland Park: A Space Made to Order for the Assembly Line

The prestige accorded the firm of Albert Kahn following these first accomplishments convinced Henry Ford to avail himself of Kahn's services. They began a long and productive friendship that would result in the construction of great plants for the Ford Motor Company in Detroit and around the world.

It is useful to explore the common traits in the biographies of the two men,[22] to understand the motivations and characteristics of a partnership that left its indelible mark on industrial architectural history.

Ford and Kahn were both born in the 1860s, as were several other leaders of architectural and industrial culture. In America as well as in Europe, during the first years of the century, these men reestablished the relationship between the worlds of production and art.[23]

Additionally, both Kahn and Ford were self-made men. Ford, son of an Irish farmer, began his career building automobiles of his own invention in a small mechanic's shop in Detroit.[24] Kahn, son of a German rabbi, did not attend college or art school, but at fifteen years of age was sent to work in an architecture firm, also in Detroit.

Two parallel lives, two men raised in the same urban setting, with shared faith in the guiding principles of the heroes of American capitalism: complete dedication to work, courage, initiative and the spirit of sacrifice.[25]

"Architecture is 90% business and 10% art," the phrase often spoken by Albert Kahn,[26] synthesized a way of conceiving design work that was surely closer to the practical sense of industrialists than to the intellectual labors of architects.

The long collaboration between Henry Ford and Albert Kahn had, as a starting point, this unity of vision. With the same ideas and with the same methods, one produced automobiles and the other, architectural designs. The friendship was strong enough to survive even Henry Ford's clamorous anti-Semitic campaign in the columns of *The Dearborn Independent*, between 1920 and 1921: he never considered the possibility of offending Albert Kahn, a Jew, who was at that time designing the colossal plants of the Ford Motor Company on the Rouge River.[27]

In their case, the relationship between architect and entrepreneur distinguished itself from other American experiences—the works of Hunt for the Vanderbilts or of Beman for Pullman—as well as from the European model of Behrens and the A.E.G.[28]

Ford was not in search of an artist who would build him a celebrative image of achieved economic potential, nor was he interested in paving the way for a new ten-

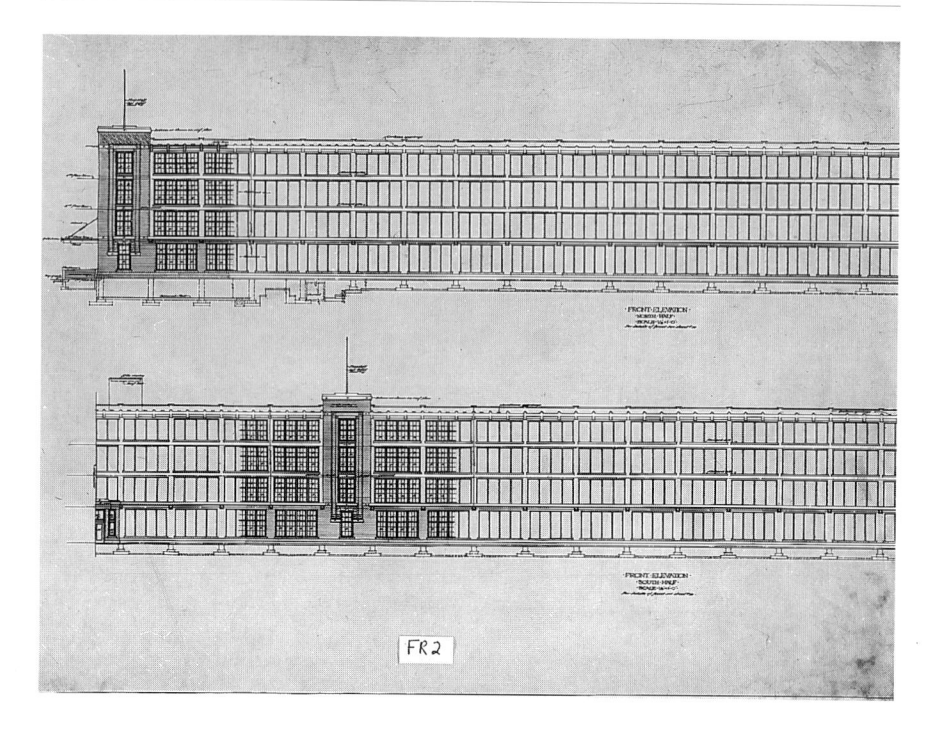

FORD MOTOR COMPANY, ORIGINAL FACTORY BUILDING: HIGHLAND PARK, MICHIGAN;
ALBERT KAHN, ERNEST WILBY, 1909
Elevations

dency in industrial aesthetics; he wanted only a designer capable of responding concretely to the specific demands of mass production. As perfect "business architect,"[29] Albert Kahn immediately understood this need and, above all, intuited the possibility of establishing a design enterprise that was based on an efficient organizational structure and that was capable of proposing avant-garde solutions in the construction sector.

The first product of the collaboration between Ford and Kahn was the Automobile Assembly Building, built in 1909 in the Highland Park suburb of Detroit. This factory served as a laboratory in which new principles of labor management and new construction methods could be tested and improved.

Until then—the Ford Motor Company was started in 1903—the craftsman-like production of automobiles had been carried out in buildings that met the requirements of workmanship based on the traditional criteria of the mechanics industry. After the first shop on Mack Avenue had been begun, Ford, in 1904, transferred production to the new Piquette Avenue plant. This three-story structure with references to eigh-

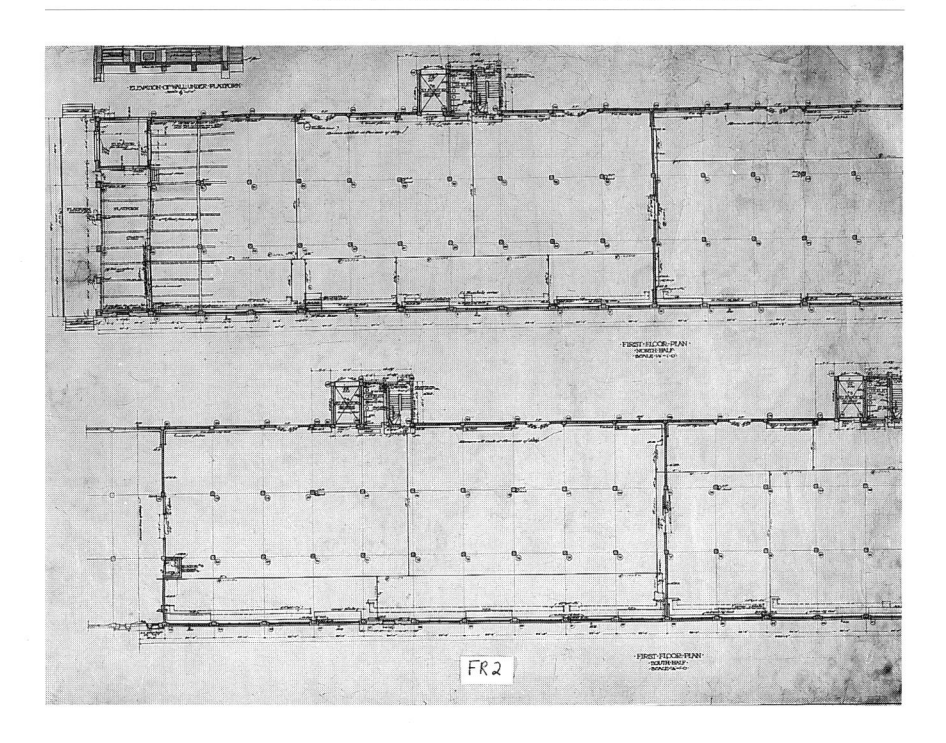

FORD MOTOR COMPANY, ORIGINAL FACTORY BUILDING: HIGHLAND PARK, MICHIGAN; ALBERT KAHN, ERNEST WILBY, 1909
Floor plan

teenth-century industrial architecture, soon proved to be inadequate, and in 1908, it was adapted to house a rudimentary continuous assembly line for the production of the first model T.[30]

The new assembly workshop in Highland Park was a four-story factory, with a relatively reduced width in relationship to the exceptional total length (about 22.8 x 262.1 meters, or 75 x 860 feet). While the building was based on the Packard Building no. 10 and the Mergenthaler Linotype Company, it was not without significant innovations: the great dimension, the distribution characteristics, the attention to construction details (in particular, the brick-covered towers for vertical communications), and the total formal design itself.[31]

The weight-bearing structure was reinforced concrete with six-meter spans (20 feet) between the columns: there were no interior dividing walls. The vertical communication structures, pushed to the exterior of the workshop, rose up at regular intervals along the longer side of the building. They housed all of the auxiliary facilities (changing rooms, bathrooms, etc.), as well as the hydraulic freight elevators which transported materials to the work floor.

The resulting open space was ideal for continual changes in the placement of machinery, and above all, made possible the completion of experiments on the continuous assembly line for standardized production, which was finally implemented on October 7, 1913.

The elementary arrangement of the Highland Park plant was the solution for the assembly line production of the Model T: well-lit floors laid out horizontally and joined effectively. Thanks to an integrated system of conveyors,[32] the piece-work underwent different operations in various departments on the top floors; the assembled parts, by way of numerous openings in the floors, were then transferred to the body assembly lines (on the second floor) and to the chassis assembly (on the first floor). At a station outside of the factory, the frame was lowered and mounted on the chassis: the car was then complete and ready for testing.

The fundamental principles of Fordist labor management were applied in this building. It was Ford himself who summarized them for the *Encyclopedia Britannica* in 1929, enumerating three essential points: "a) the methodical and planned advancement of the goods through the workshop; b) the consignment of work rather than reliance on the worker's own initiative; c) an analysis of the operations in their constituent parts."[33]

The possibility of continual experimentation and eventual perfection of the production process (guaranteed by such an ideal workspace) inaugurated a new age in the history of industrial architecture.

The actual implementation of Kahn's designs involved the same process of planning. To meet Ford's orders, it was necessary to have cohesion between the work of the production engineers, who concentrated on the technical definition of the product, the lines of labor and the tool machines, and that of the designers who designed the physical space.

The interaction of the two processes of conceptualizing resulted in a precise method of labor management within the firm of Albert Kahn itself.

The Highland Park factory presented a very long front along Woodward Avenue (the cross street that today, still cuts metropolitan Detroit in two), with its structural links of reinforced concrete, interspersed with great glass walls (metal-framed windows, imported from England).[34] "The windows extended from practically the floor line to the ceiling," wrote Albert Kahn.[35]

In this way, Henry Ford's exacting prescriptions for lighting, cleanliness, ventilation and the economy of interior space—the mandatory conditions for the scientific management of labor—found full accommodation in Albert Kahn's architectural solutions.

To quote Ford himself on this subject: "One point that is absolutely essential to high capacity, as well as to humane production, is a clean, well-lighted and well-ventilated factory. Our machines are placed very close together—every foot of floor space in the factory carries, of course, the same overhead charge.... We measure on each job the exact amount of room that a man needs; he must not be cramped—that would be waste. But if he and his machine occupy more space than is required, that is also waste. This brings our machines closer together than in probably any other factory in the world.... Our factory buildings are not intended to be used as strolling parks.... Something like seven hundred men are detailed especially to keeping the shops clean, the windows washed, and all of the paint fresh.... We tolerate makeshift cleanliness no more than makeshift methods."[36]

The economy of time and space, and the insistence upon cleanliness, lighting and ventilation—expressed with characteristic succinctness, these were the fundamental principles of the Fordist rationale of space.

This coherent development of principles related to labor management was fully applied in the architecture of Albert Kahn.

It should be noted, nevertheless, that the severe mass of glass and reinforced concrete of the Highland Park factory had several decorative concessions. For example, there is a delicate pediment along the top of the building, and a compositional design in the support bricks of the vertical facility towers.

This subtle ornamentation, probably the work of Kahn's partner, Ernest Wilby, did not indicate a desire to repropose the monumental figurations of European proto-rationalism for industrial architecture. It was not in Kahn's nature, nor in that of his client, to concede space to costly decoration. He wanted only to claim the right to build a factory by employing elements of the traditional, local construction. In this was evident the willingness to anticipate and interpret the expectations of the client, an attitude present in all of Kahn's work. He did not limit himself to designing a modern and rational productive machine in glass and reinforced concrete; he catered to his personal memory as well, the memory of the old brick architecture of Michigan.[37]

The Highland Park plant, opened on January 1, 1910, was located in a concentrated industrial zone of which Ford tried to take advantage. This anticipated the union of internal and external economics that were fully realized in the construction of the River Rouge plants in Dearborn.

In this first, early phase, production activities were linked to the urban area by limitations in the transportation network, and Ford did not explore any geographical alternatives.[38] Only when it became advantageous to the expansion needs of the industry, would autonomous administrations be installed beyond the confines of Detroit.[39]

FORD MOTOR COMPANY: HIGHLAND PARK, MICHIGAN; ALBERT KAHN, ERNEST WILBY, 1909–1918
Aerial view of the plant, 1915

Inherent in the Fordist conception is an idea of industrial production as a point susceptible to continuous, necessary revisions. This open-mindedness towards unhesitatingly discarding less successful means and materials involved the entire assembly line, and even a minimal change in the product could cause a new working order for machinery, a redefinition of the labor process, as well as adaptations of the work place.

Just a few years after its completion, the Highland Park plant underwent a radical functional transformation that demonstrated the extraordinary flexibility of its spatial organization. It became an integral part of a vast complex composed of an assemblage of structures, each of which specialized in a single work operation. At that point, the factory under one roof had become obsolete. This was the phase in which Henry Ford applied the assembly line conception to complexes as a whole, joining together single buildings that accommodated specific tasks. Albert Kahn had intuited this need in

opposite page:
FORD MOTOR COMPANY: HIGHLAND PARK, MICHIGAN; ALBERT KAHN, ERNEST WILBY, 1909–1918
Two views of the original factory building

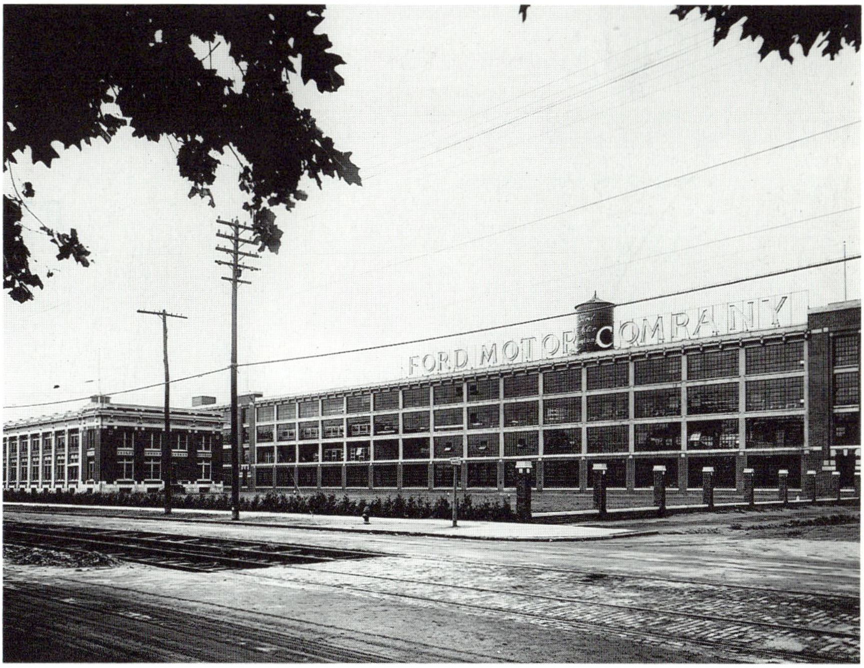
FORD MOTOR COMPANY

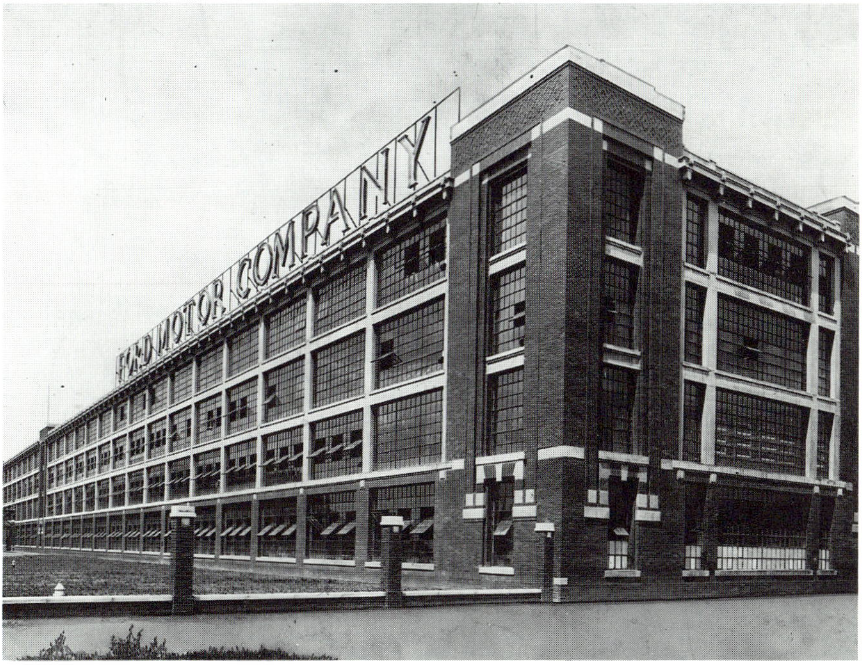
FORD MOTOR COMPANY

FORD MOTOR COMPANY: HIGHLAND PARK, MICHIGAN; ALBERT KAHN, ERNEST WILBY, 1918
The building annexed to the original factory, exterior view

designing the Pierce Great Arrow factory in Buffalo, and again with the construction of the River Rouge plants.

With these refinements, the plan used for the Highland Park plant held its own for yet another decade, even in sectors outside the automobile industry.

Albert Kahn reproposed the Highland Park model, with some variations, for the Dodge Brothers Corporation plants in Hamtramck (another urban district of Detroit) and for the Fisher Body Company plant in Cleveland (1921).[40]

Albert Kahn's revolutionary new experience with the Fordist industrial universe also had a precise correspondence with theoretical production, with which Moritz Kahn, the third of the five Kahn brothers, was involved.

Moritz Kahn was born in 1880 in Echterbach (Luxembourg), and after graduating from the University of Michigan with an engineering degree, he worked at the Trussed Concrete Steel Company. In 1905, Julius entrusted him with the organization of its London headquarters. In 1923, Moritz returned to Detroit and became an associate of Albert Kahn, Inc. and from 1928 to 1932, he assumed the delicate task of managing the Soviet affiliate of the company.[41]

In 1917, for the Technical Journal of London, Moritz Kahn published *The Design and Construction of Industrial Buildings*, a text that, due to his familiarity with the works of the firm of Albert Kahn, was a contribution to the vanguard of technical man-

FORD MOTOR COMPANY: HIGHLAND PARK, MICHIGAN; ALBERT KAHN, ERNEST WILBY, 1918
The building annexed to the original factory, interior view

uals for the building industry.[42]

Moritz's text highlights some fundamental theoretical principles in the work of Albert Kahn and his group, and forms a complete analysis of a manualistic systematization of that work experience. To wit, the parts of the text that deal with the theme of business image, with the question of costs, design schedules, and construction of buildings, as well as the group's rich iconographic repertory, were mostly a product of the firm itself.[43]

The text insisted that among the wide-ranging demands to which the industrial architect must respond, there was a series of conditions dictated by the specific layout of every labor cycle. Taylorist rigidity was overcome through the assumption of an innovative conceptualization of the labor industry as being in a state of continuous flux, with as few stagnant moments and interruptions as possible.

While industry's debt to Henry Ford's experimentation is clear, it is also interesting to observe his influence on architectural design.

The distributive schemes proposed, the attention to compositional elements and the construction particulars came together in a layout whose design was a flow of production. In this framework, innovations of construction techniques were understood as variables that, once unified and properly applied, resulted in a reduction of time, both in conceptualizing and executing ideas.

DODGE MOTOR COMPANY: DETROIT, MICHIGAN; ALBERT KAHN, ERNEST WILBY, 1911

FISHER BODY COMPANY: CLEVELAND, OHIO; ALBERT KAHN, INC., 1920

There was also considerable attention given to the men.

According to Moritz Kahn, industrial buildings not only had to meet hygienic requirements, but could induce a positive mental attitude on the part of the workers towards their own work, through an improvement in the overall quality of the working environment.

It is significant that this premise, seemingly exclusively based on functional and economic prerequisites, was also a commentary on the aesthetic characteristics of production buildings. The chapter "Architectural Treatment of the Factory Building" described the extent to which the Highland Park plant succeeded in this endeavor: "With the simplest materials and the simplest forms of treatment a capable architect can produce pleasing results."[44] Moritz Kahn, in fact, insisted on the secondary importance of the aesthetic treatment of the organization of interior space as it conformed to the cycle of production. The use of decoration, he maintained, had to be limited to a few particulars for advertising only—for example, the main entrance of a building.

Another novel aspect of the manual was its definition of a new professional figure: the factory designer, a designer capable of combining "with his knowledge of architecture that of the civil, the mechanical, and the electrical engineer."[45] In short, a role that recalled all that had been achieved in Albert Kahn's firm.

These explications by Moritz were to become instrumental in the education of one of the most prestigious names in modern English architecture: Owen Williams. After graduating with an engineering degree, Williams began work as a designer in reinforced concrete at the Trussed Concrete Steel Company of England, managed by Moritz Kahn. Williams produced some of the most important monuments to British functionalism: the Boots Wets Factory in Nottingham during the thirties, and the Boac hangar of the London airport in the fifties.[46]

River Rouge: The Second Fordist Revolution

"It's been a few years now," wrote Ford in *Today and Tomorrow* (1926), "since the Rouge River (which feeds into the Detroit River and thus is connected to the Great Lakes) was simply a shallow, windy current of water about thirty meters [98 feet] wide, on which nine hundred ton boats could not reach the factory docks.... Now we have a direct canal which reduces the distance between the lake and our reservoir by three to five miles. The canal and the river are ninety meters [295 feet] wide and have an average depth of 6.6 meters [21 feet], sufficient for our needs."[47] The construction of the canal was a prerequisite for the construction of the gigantic River Rouge complex, central headquarters for the Ford empire and prototype for a new way of conceptualizing industrial localization and production organization.

Construction of Albert Kahn's design for the River Rouge installation had already begun in 1917, when Ford decided to build a submarine factory for the American Navy. He commissioned Kahn to design Eagle Plant, a steel structure of exceptional dimensions (about 30.4 meters high, 91.4 wide and 518.1 long, or 100 x 300 x 1,700 feet). After World War I, Eagle Plant was converted to support the production cycle of the Fordson tractor, which began at Highland Park.

Due to years of experience in industrial architecture and to internal reorganization of the firm (that provided for specialized sectors in the designing of various construction elements), Albert Kahn, Inc. had no trouble in designing the buildings for the new installation.

The various structures were designed to create a self-sufficient plant for the production of subassemblies and components. The plant was composed of sawmills, blast furnaces, foundries, body and glass departments, a power house, a considerable number of auxiliary activities, and a scraps dump. Foundry Building (1921), Glass Plant (1922), Cement Plant (1923), Power House (1925), Open Hearth Building (1925), Tire Plant (1931), and Press Shop (1939) occupied a total surface area of about five square kilometers (1.9 square miles); the engineers' workshops, the hospital, and the airport were added later.[48]

More than in its formation, the true innovation of River Rouge lay in its organization of the flow of materials from the inside to the outside of the complex. The organizational models first tried in single buildings were extended to the entire production cycle, including not only every aspect of the internal organizational space of the factory compound, but also the territorial expansion of the supply and distribution flows.

In this area Albert Kahn and Henry Ford had a reciprocal influence on one another. The architect brought his mature experience with one-story factories (such as Pierce

FROM SELF-EDUCATION TO PIONEER WORK WITH FORD 51

FORD MOTOR COMPANY, B BUILDING, RIVER ROUGE PLANT: DEARBORN, MICHIGAN;
ALBERT KAHN, ERNEST WILBY, 1917
Exterior view

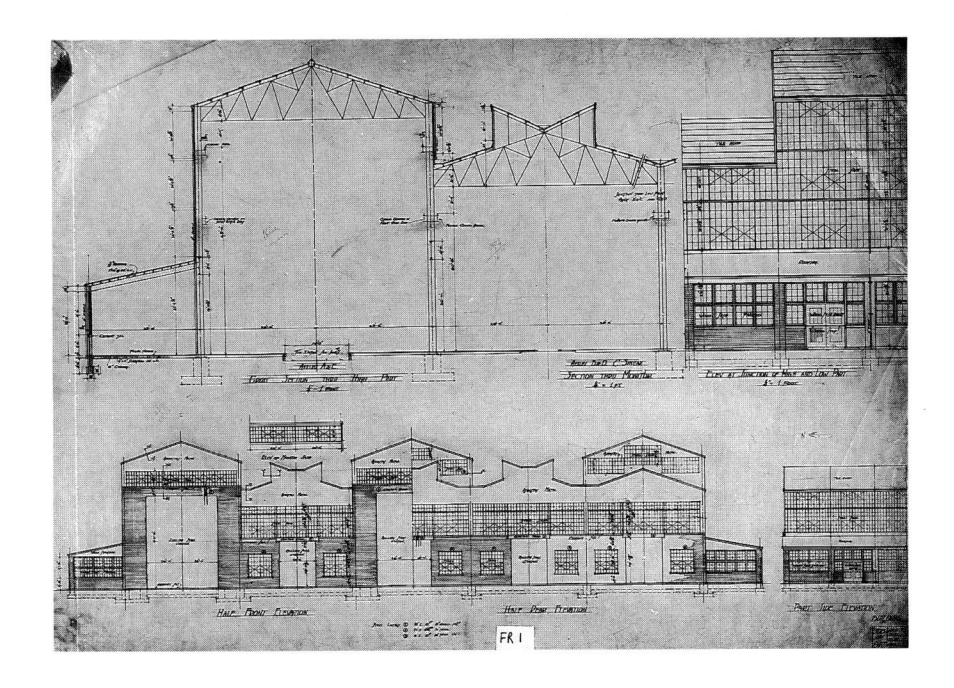

FORD MOTOR COMPANY, B BUILDING, RIVER ROUGE PLANT: DEARBORN, MICHIGAN;
ALBERT KAHN, ERNEST WILBY, 1917
Section and elevations

following pages:
FORD MOTOR COMPANY, OPEN HEARTH MILLS, RIVER ROUGE PLANT: DEARBORN, MICHIGAN;
ALBERT KAHN, INC., 1925

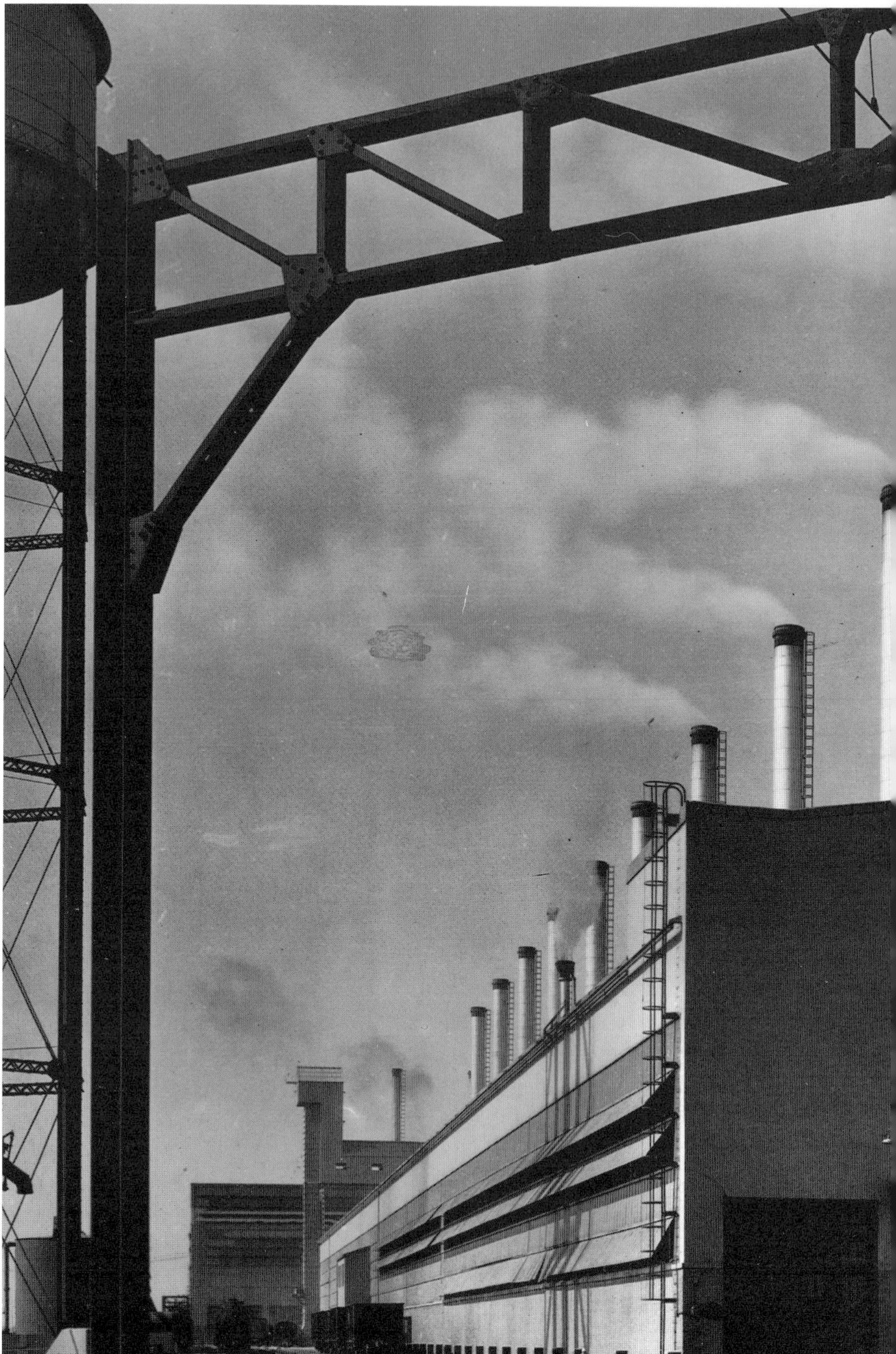

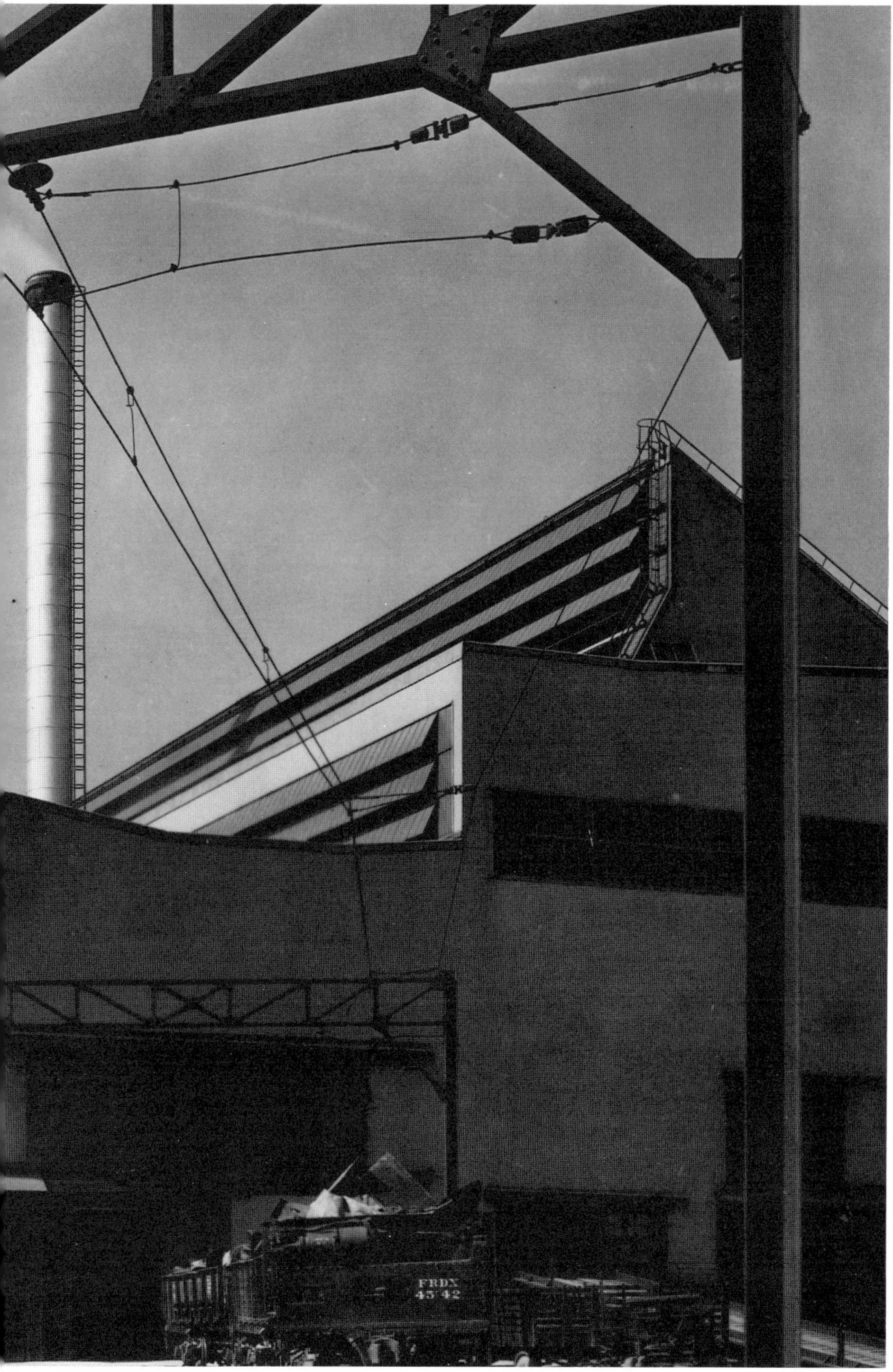
FRDX
4542

Great Arrow of 1906 and Paige Motor Company of 1914), and the industrialist made the obtained results possible with his perfection of the production process.

The underlying principle was that of maximum economy of time and space accomplished through the continuous movement of the raw materials and piece work. "The entire complex," wrote Ford, "was constructed according to a single idea of simplification of the flow of materials."[49] The entire plant, then, had the configuration of a giant assembly chain, whose fulcrum was the High Line, a concrete structure twelve meters high (40 feet) and three-quarters of a mile long, with five sets of tracks and two elevated walkways for pedestrians[50] which crossed the entire industrial area, sorting the raw materials from the point of arrival (the canal) to the different work areas.

The exceptional infrastructural setup that lined the River Rouge area was made even more efficient by the development of an internal railroad network that increased from thirty-eight kilometers (23.5 miles) of track in 1920 to one hundred and fifty kilometers (93 miles) in 1926.

"This gray city of factories,"[51] as Luigi Barzini, Jr., the 1934 correspondent of the Milan newspaper *Corriere della sera* defined it, "was born of a total programmatization that included the cycle of production from the extraction of raw materials to the finished product and depended on the utilization of all territorial resources."

The fundamental principle that inspired the Ford model—synchronic linkage of operations—was well summarized in the brochure that was distributed to visitors to the River Rouge complex:

> *Monday 8 AM:* After a trip of approximately 48 hours from Marquette the ore boat docks at the River Rouge plant. Hulett unloaders start removing the cargo, which is transferred to the High Line, and from there to the skip car which charges the blast furnace. By continuous process this takes 10 minutes.
>
> *Tuesday 12:10 AM:* Sixteen hours later the ore has been reduced to foundry iron. It is then cast into pigs and sent to the foundry, where, mixed with certain proportions of scrap, it is remelted. This takes about four hours in all. Blast furnace metal is also cast direct, in which case four hours are saved.
>
> *Tuesday 4:10 PM:* As the conveyor brings the molds past the pouring station the hot metal is cast into cylinder blocks. These then go to the shake-out station and are taken away to cool and be cleaned. The cooling and cleaning process requires several hours.
>
> *Tuesday 12:20 PM:* The casting now goes to its first machining operation. There are 58 operations in all, all of which are done in approximately 55 minutes.
>
> *Tuesday 1:15 PM:* About 3:30 the motor block is ready for the assembly line.

FORD MOTOR COMPANY, RIVER ROUGE PLANT: DEARBORN, MICHIGAN; ALBERT KAHN, INC., 1938
Aerial view

> Ford mechanics have reduced the time required for motor assembly to an average of 97 minutes.
>
> *Tuesday 3:00 PM:* The finished motor coming out over a trunk line conveyor is loaded into a freight car...and shipped to a branch for assembly into a finished car.
>
> *Wednesday 8:00 AM:* Arriving at the branch plant the motor is unloaded and sent to its station on the final assembly line.
>
> *Wednesday 12 NOON:* Long before noon the dealer will have taken delivery of the car and paid for it."[52]

One important feature of this organizational model was the perfection of labor control. The foreman, the typical figure in the Taylor model, was substituted by a timing gear composed of synchronized mechanical apparatuses that signaled and prevented noncompliance on the part of the worker with respect to assigned tasks and work rhythms.

FORD MOTOR COMPANY, GLASS PLANT, RIVER ROUGE PLANT: DEARBORN, MICHIGAN; ALBERT KAHN, INC., 1922

While the layout—the diagram—of pre-established manufacturing,[53] was assumed as a basic plan for the definition of physical work space, Albert Kahn did not see the planning of industrial architecture as a simple response to the changes of labor management, but as an element that must be able to permit such changes. This way of proceeding, which implied continuous exchanges with the Ford Motor Company techniques, suggested the overcoming of the concept of a building univocally set on a unique, complex gear.

The search for maximum flexibility in the building plan led Albert Kahn to repropose the one-story building type, in a revised version suitable for very extended surface areas.

The adoption of metal roof beams for the grid, and the use of industrially produced and standardized construction materials reduced assembly time, and allowed for very wide surface areas of roof supported by very slender columns. The end result was a building shell that allowed maximum freedom of action to the engineers responsible for defining the organization of the work cycle.

It is therefore rather difficult to establish, after the fact, the role played by the different specialists in defining the industrial architecture of complexes like those of River Rouge. It should be remembered that Albert Kahn, in his public interviews, never failed to underline the fundamental role of Henry Ford in regard to the definition of the architecture itself.

FORD MOTOR COMPANY, ADMINISTRATION BUILDING, RIVER ROUGE PLANT: DEARBORN, MICHIGAN; ALBERT KAHN, INC., 1927

In the case of one of the most well-known buildings of the River Rouge plants, the Engineering Laboratory (1925), Ford's influence is very clear, which testifies to Kahn's complete willingness to adhere to the expectations of the client.

The structure was meant to house functions not strictly related to the means of production. Therefore, while on the inside, the most modern criteria for construction of factory space were employed. "Externally," wrote Albert Kahn, "the building is designed to express Mr. Ford's idea of a plant of the kind." This meant the implementation of elegant tympanums modeled on the Secessionist school of Viennese architecture.[54]

Albert Kahn's intense exchange of ideas with Henry Ford and his profound commitment to playing the role of designer at the service of industry, were well synthesized in the following reflection that Kahn included, with little variation, in many of his numerous writings dedicated to industrial architecture. In this case, the quote, in a more elongated form, is taken from a conference held on October 16, 1941 at a meeting of architects and engineers in St. Louis. For the occasion, Albert Kahn spoke of his thirty year collaboration with the automobile industry magnate: "It was he who first insisted on having practically all departments under one roof, with no courts of any kind and no dividing walls—it being his conviction that supervision was thereby simplified and economy in manufacture effected....It was Mr. Ford who first used steel sash so commonly employed now. It was he, also, who, after building hundreds of acres of floor space in multiple story buildings, concluded that raising materials to upper floors by elevators was an economic waste because of the time consumed by men and the cost of transporting materials. He had built six- and eight-story buildings in Detroit and many other cities. But once convinced that multiple story buildings were uneconomical for the manufacture of his product, he abandoned one after the other, replacing them with one-story structures, top lighted, with columns spaced some forty feet apart as against twenty-five in the earlier buildings. That the one-story plant is, at least for the major part, the proper solution for the manufacture of certain products is proven by the adoption of such since by so many other companies. The courage of Mr Ford, as shown in the development of the motor car, has been evidenced equally in his factory buildings. Who but he would have had the courage to practically abandon the enormous Highland Park plant for the River Rouge development where he had adequate room for one-story structures, and opportunity for more economical production as well as for bettering working conditions for his men. Proper sanitation, ventilation, air and light, safety appliances, first aid stations, all have had his close and thorough consideration. Other innovations of Mr Ford's are his plants along waterways, making possible water shipments, and his placing of numerous smaller plants in rural districts in attractive settings, giving employment to farmers during the winter months, which has proven of great economic help to the respective communities and his business as well. It was also Mr Ford who proved the advantages of decentralization now so generally adopted."[55]

FROM SELF-EDUCATION TO PIONEER WORK WITH FORD

FORD MOTOR COMPANY, ENGINEERING LABORATORY, POWER HOUSE, RIVER ROUGE PLANT:
DEARBORN, MICHIGAN; ALBERT KAHN, INC., 1925

FORD MOTOR COMPANY, ENGINEERING LABORATORY: DEARBORN, MICHIGAN; ALBERT KAHN, INC., 1925

Manufacturing Decentralization: The Third Fordist Revolution

The new manufacturing reality at which Albert Kahn had hinted was another of Ford's widely publicized self-criticisms: a criticism of the scaled economies that supported enormous constructions like the one at River Rouge. After having built the River Rouge plant, the largest industrial plant in the world, and after having attracted 1000 workers to Detroit's urban area, Ford coined a new phrase: anti-urbanism. "There is something about a city of a million people which is untamed and threatening. Thirty miles away, happy and contented villages read of the ravings of the citiy. A great city is really a helpless mass. Everything it uses is carried to it. Stop transport and the city stops. It lives off the shelves of stores. The shelves produce nothing. The city cannot feed, clothe, warm, or house itself. City conditions of work and living are so artificial that instincts sometimes rebel against their unnaturalness. And finally, the overhead expense of living or doing business in the great cities is becoming so large as to be unbearable." The condemnation of urban concentration concluded in prophetic tones:

"The modern city has been prodigal, it is to-day bankrupt, and to-morrow it will cease to be."[56]

Having foreseen this crisis, Ford came to insist on the integration of agricultural work and industrial labor. The new strategic direction constituted a response to problems deriving from the exceptional industrial concentration of River Rouge—in 1929, about 100,000 workers were employed, and the six-dollars-a-day wage was not enough to justify the harsh conditions of the assembly chain. It was also part of the great wave of North American anti-urbanism, whose advocates included farmers as well as a considerable number of intellectuals.[57]

When, from this perspective, Ford proposed the construction of many small factories in bucolic environments along waterways and green areas, the design task again fell to Albert Kahn. For the new plant in Northville, several kilometers from Detroit, Kahn radically changed the aesthetic, from that of an urban factory to one that recalled more traditional brick industrial buildings.

The nearly thirty years of collaboration between Albert Kahn and Henry Ford were based on a relationship of mutual exchange: with Highland Park, River Rouge and the buildings of decentralization, "Ford's architect" never once thought to create monuments. He instead insisted on rendering a service to his client, having made the organization of space assume the fundamental role in affirming the principles of scientific management of labor.

This was a service that touched on promotion of Ford's ideas. When Albert Kahn, in his addresses, emphasized "Mr. Ford's idea," "the courage demonstrated by Mr. Ford," or "the innovations of Mr. Ford," he was carefully complying with the line of thought dictated by the Ford Company press office.

The following comment by William J. Cameron is indicative as to the role Henry Ford's public image played in establishing his line of business politics. As head of the public relations department of the Ford Motor Company from 1918 on, Cameron was responsible for shaping the Fordist image.[58] In an address given at the American Society of Mechanical Engineers in 1937, Cameron spoke of the decentralization experience in these terms: "It's been twenty years now since Ford has been actively involved with decentralization. I could also add that he is personally involved, because every problem, from the choosing of location to the progress of construction of the plants, and everything that follows; everything has always received his personal attention…

following pages:
FORD MOTOR COMPANY, ENGINEERING LABORATORY: DEARBORN, MICHIGAN; ALBERT KAHN, INC., 1925
Interior

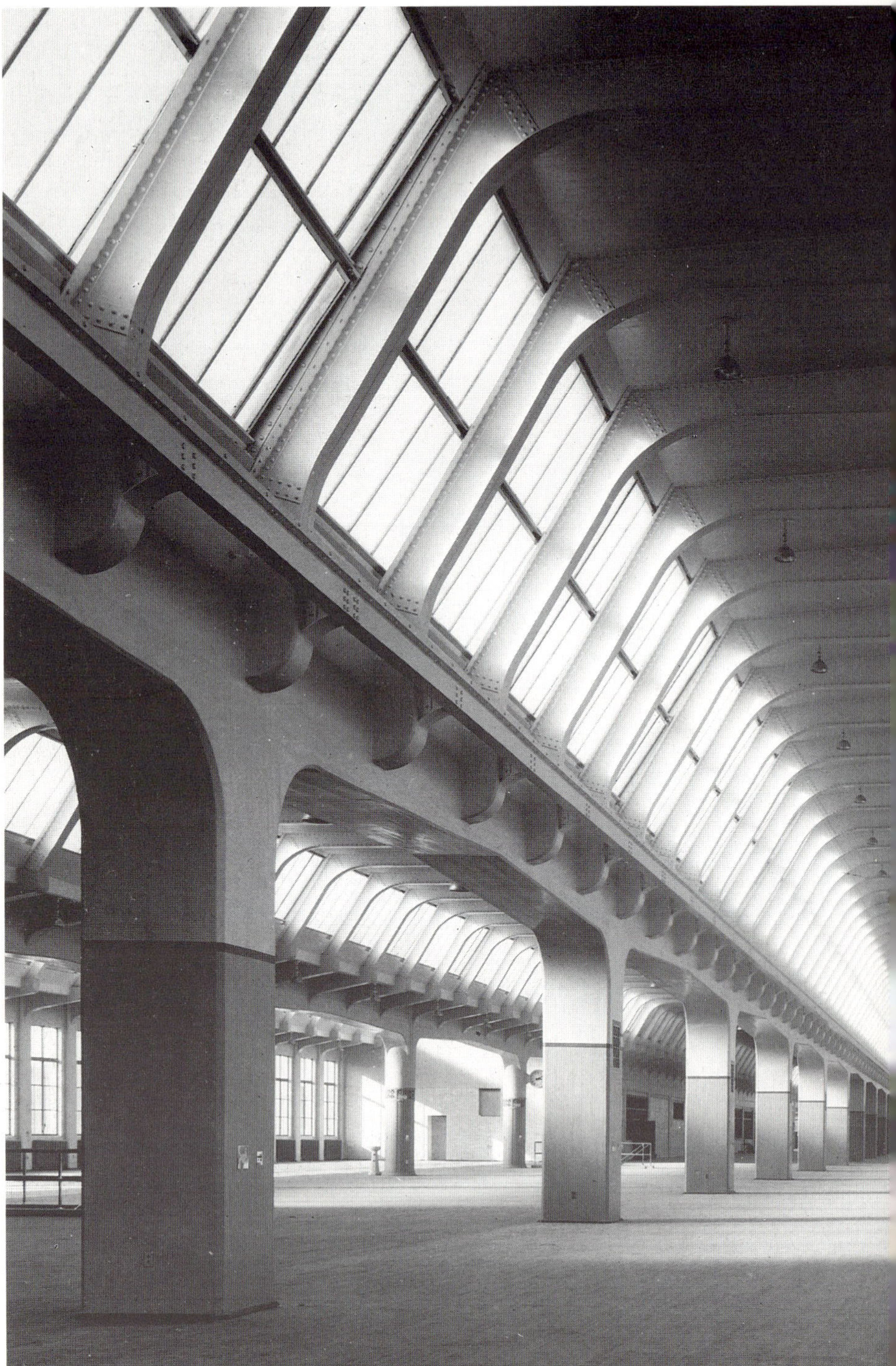

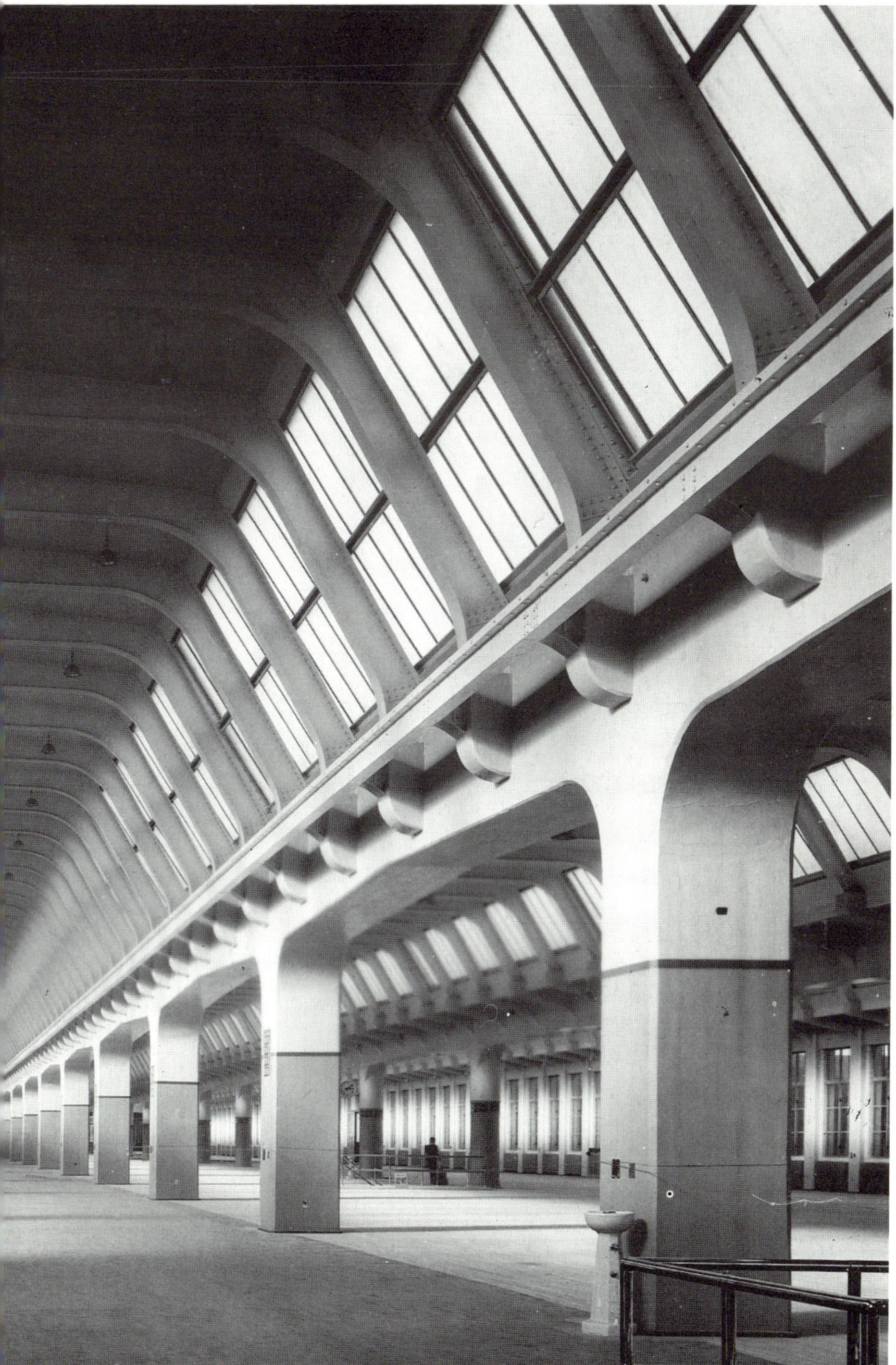

FORD MOTOR COMPANY, ASSEMBLY BUILDING: LONG BEACH, CALIFORNIA; ALBERT KAHN, INC., 1926

FORD MOTOR COMPANY, ASSEMBLY PLANT: EDGEWATER, NEW JERSEY; ALBERT KAHN, INC., 1929

His first experiments began in 1918 with an old gristmill known as Wankin's Mill, situated on the Rouge River, which farther North is still quite small. Since that time, he has founded along the Rouge eight industries that employ from fifteen to four hundred workers: most in modern plants that, instead of bringing a contrasting note to the areas, totally harmonize with the countryside's landscape. These plants in little country towns are beautiful."[59]

Northville, Waterford, and Wankin are all pleasant areas around Detroit where Ford experimented with the small, rural plant model that had been unsuccessful along the Tennessee River. The Muscle Shoals project (1922), in the Tennessee Valley, had been conceived of as a powerful publicity vehicle against the alarming figures of the growth of industrial cities in the North and the consequential abandonment of agricultural areas in the South.

According to Henry Ford's plans, as described in the pages of preeminent American periodicals, Muscle Shoals was to be organized as a technologically advanced form of farming, in conjunction with the fertilizing industry and the production of electricity. But Ford went beyond a generalized plan of economic development, designing an entire urban installation. Muscle Shoals was a linear city of about 120 kilometers (74 miles) founded on the utilization of the local natural water resources, organized manufacturing in small factories, and the integration of farming and industry, all supported by a great program of territorial infrastructure. In practice, this should have meant the employment of about 200,000 men: a great drawing point for the South.[60] "If Ford is permitted to expand all the ideas he has in the back of his head for Muscle Shoals," wrote a journalist of *Automotive Industries* in 1922, "the vision the people of Alabama see of a great industrial city on the banks of the Tennessee, which will rival Detroit, will become a reality."[61]

George Norris, a staunch opponent of Ford's, maintained that even if the Muscle Shoals project had been successful, it would have served only as an enormous electricity source for Detroit factories.[62]

The Muscle Shoals project therefore, was seen as a paternalistic facade which masked the reality of Ford's industrial empire.

In fact, since the twenties and contemporaneous to the building of the River Rouge plants, the Ford Company was composed of specialized wholes, scattered over the northern United States and joined together by a tight network of transportation infrastructure, but inevitably attached to metropolitan areas. Ford recognized the fragility of the gigantic-scale model and proposed manufacturing installations that were of average size, and that specialized in single operations, but did not forfeit the advantages offered by urban concentration.

Once again it was Albert Kahn who translated Henry Ford's new program to built form, in plants in numerous American and European cities. Chicago, Philadelphia, Cleveland, Dallas, Seattle, Kansas City, Charlotte (North Carolina), St. Paul, Jacksonville, Memphis, Long Beach (California), Edgewater (New Jersey), Toronto, Mexico City, Copenhagen, and Dagenham (England) were the cities in which, between 1925 and 1935, Albert Kahn created installations for the Ford Motor Company.

Ford's invective against large cities and his claims to favor manufacturing decentralization and the integration of farming and manufacturing industries were useful publicity vehicles and reference models for urban utopias.[63] The revolutionary construction of a network of single-specialty production entities at River Rouge confirmed Ford's empire as a formidable international affirmation of metropolitan logic.

NOTES

1. After Albert came Gustave, Julius, Mollie, Paula, Moritz, Felix and Louis. Julius, Moritz and Louis eventually played decisive roles in Albert Kahn's career. On the formative years of Albert Kahn, see W.H. Ferry, *The Buildings of Detroit. A History*, Wayne State University Press, Detroit 1968, p. 131; S. King, *Creative-Responsive-Pragmatic. 75 Years of Professional Practice Albert Kahn & Associates Architects-Engineers*, The Newcomen Society in North America, New York 1970, pp. 8–15; G. Hildebrand, *Designing for Industry. The Architecture of Albert Kahn*, MIT Press, Cambridge (MA)–London 1974, pp. 5–24; L. Robinson, "Albert Kahn," in *The Architectural Review*, vol. CLVII, no. 940, June 1975. p. 349; R. Conot, *American Odyssey*, Wayne State University Press, Detroit 1986, p. 128.

2. On the structure of American architecture schools and on the influence of the teaching of the Beaux-Arts, see J.B. Robinson, *Architectural Composition*, Architectural Record, New York 1899; J.V. Van Pelt, *A Discussion of Composition, Especially Applied to Architecture*, MacMillan, New York 1902; N.C. Curtis, *Architectural Composition*, Jansen, Cleveland 1923; J.F. Harbeson, *The Study of Architectural Design with Special Reference to the Program of the Beaux-Arts Institute of Design*, Pencil Points Press, New York 1927; and for a critical analysis, J.P. Noffsinger, *Influence of the Ecole des Beaux-Arts on the Architecture of the United States*, Catholic University Press, Washington, D.C. 1955.

3. F.S. Swales, "Master Draftsmen, XIII, Albert Kahn," in *Pencil Points*, vol. VI, no. 6, June 1925, p. 58.

4. This item is reported by G. Nelson, *Industrial Architecture of Albert Kahn, Inc.*, Architectural Book Publishing Company, New York 1939, p. 16.

5. A. Kahn, "Architect Pioneers in Development of Industrial Buildings," in *The Anchora of Delta Gamma*, vol. LIII, no. 4, May 1937, p. 376.

6. See J. Kahn, "The Coal Hoists of the Calumet and Hecla Mining Company," in *Transactions of the American Society of Civil Engineers*, vol. XLI, 1899, pp. 271–292.

7. O.W. Irwin, "Julius Kahn, M. Am. Soc. C.E.," (obituary) in *Transactions of the American Society of Civil Engineers*, 1942, p. 2.

8. On the diffusion of reinforced concrete in Europe and America, see P. Collins, *Concrete. The Vision of a New Architecture*, London 1959; C.W. Condit, "The First Reinforced-Concrete Skyscraper: the Ingalls Building in Cincinnati and Its Place in Structural History," in *Technology and Culture*, vol. 9, no. 1, January 1968, (pp. 24–33 for the "Kahn System"); A.L. Huxtable, "Reinforced-Concrete Construction. The work of Ernest L. Ransome, Engineer. 1884–1911," in *Progressive Architecture*, vol. XXXVIII, no. 9, September 1957, pp. 139–142.

9. A complete technical description of the patent is found in *The Kahn System of Reinforced Concrete*, Trussed Concrete Steel Co., Detroit, undated (in the Albert Kahn Associates, Inc. Architects and Engineers Archive, Detroit henceforth AKA). See also G.A. Hool, *Reinforced Concrete Construction*, vol. II, McGraw-Hill, New York–London 1913, p. 517.

10. A. Kahn, "Industrial Architecture," in *Weekly Bulletin of the Michigan Society of Architects*, vol. 12, no. 52, December 27, 1938, p. 6. This article (also published in a shorter version in *The Architectural Forum*, vol. 70, no. 2, February 1939, pp. 131–132) is the text from a conference held at the Detroit Leland Hotel on the evening of December 21, 1938 on the occasion of the Building Industry Luncheon.

11. In Italy, for example, it was presented at the International Exposition of Turin in 1911. But some years before, in a manual by Luigi Mazzocchi, one of the first Italian volumes concerned with the applications of reinforced concrete, we find this: "Kahn's reinforced bar, with its rigidly connected diagonals, is apt to resist every force and ensure the following advantages: economy of man

power, since it is quite easier to work with a Kahn bar than with a round bar with detached bindings: perfect security of the binding, since in this system the disposition of the brackets is guaranteed, something which in all the other systems is left to chance.: complete savings, as the brackets are included with the bars, and they have a higher market value than the current base prices....The Kahn bar has revolutionized the use of iron in reinforced concrete and has simplified its system of calculations....In Italy, the Kahn bar has already been adopted by the State Railroad." L. Mazzocchi, *Calci e cementi*, Hoepli, Milan 1909.

[12] On the life of Julius Kahn, see O.W. Irwin, "Julius Kahn, M. Am. Soc. C.E.," In particular, for his experience in the military engineering corp, see L. Fine, J.A. Remington, *United States Army in World War I. The Technical Services. The Corp of Engineers Construction in the United States*, United States Army, Washington D.C. 1972, pp. 36–37. A list of the "Kahn System Engineers," the agent engineers of the patents of the Trussed Concrete Steel Co., is found in *The American Magazine*, August 1910, where, for the city of San Francisco, Felix Kahn is listed. Felix (1882–1958), the second youngest of the Kahn brothers, moved to California at the age of twenty, spread the "Kahn System," and founded MacDonald and Kahn, Inc., which became one of the most important construction companies on the West coast (See "Felix Kahn, S.F. Builder, dies at 76" in *The San Francisco Examiner*, June 6, 1958). The commercial structure of Julius Kahn's company can be compared with what was being done on a similar level in Europe: François Hennebique had organized a tight network of small businesses across Europe, using his patent (see J. Gubler, "Prolegomeni a Hennebique," in *Casabella*, no. 458, 1982, pp. 40–47). Regarding Italy, there is the interesting case of the Anonymous Ferrobeton Society (see *Ferrobeton. Impresa generale di costruzioni. Roma. 1908–1933*, Archetipografica, Milan 1933).

[13] A. Kahn, "Architect Pioneers in Development of Industrial Buildings," p. 377. On Henry B. Joy and the Packard Motor Car Company, see R. Conot, *American Odyssey*, pp. 116–117 and 127–128.

[14] On this accomplishment see A.L. Huxtable, "Factory for Packard Motor Car Company. 1905," in *Progressive Architecture*, vol. XXXVII, no. 10, October 1957, pp. 121–122; W.H. Ferry, *The Buildings of Detroit. A History*, pp. 182–183; S. King, *Creative-Responsive-Pragmatic. 75 Years of Professional Practice Albert Kahn & Associates Architects-Engineers*, pp. 13–15; *The Legacy of Albert Kahn*, The Detroit Institute of Arts, Detroit 1970 (catalogue of the exhibit held from September 15 to November 15, 1970 and curated by W.H. Ferry), p. 11; G. Hildebrand, *Designing for Industry. The Architecture of Albert Kahn*, pp. 28–34; L. Robinson, "Albert Kahn," pp. 351–352; C.K. Hyde, *Detroit: An Industrial History Guide*, Detroit Historical Society, Detroit, undated [1980], pp. 16–17.

[15] A. Kahn, *Article on Industrial Architecture for Collier Encyclopedia*, typewritten, August 1931, p. 3 (AKA), published in part for the entry "Factory Building," in *National Encyclopedia*, Collier and Sons, New York 1932.

[16] In 1909, Frederick W. Taylor, father of "scientific management," held one of his first public conferences at the Packard Motor Company of Detroit, in front of "600 shop foremen and supervisors of Detroit automobile plants." See D. Nelson, *Frederick W. Taylor and the Rise of Scientific Management*, The University of Wisconsin Press, Madison 1980.

[17] R. Banham, *A Concrete Atlantis. U.S. Industrial Building and European Modern Architecture 1900–1925*, MIT Press, Cambridge (MA) 1986, p. 86.

[18] For these projects, see *The Legacy of Albert Kahn*, p. 12.

[19] See R. Banham, *A Concrete Atlantis*, pp. 86–88, and G. Hildebrand, "New Factory for the Geo. N. Pierce Company, Buffalo, New York. 1906," in *Journal of the Society of Architectural Historians*, vol. XXIX, no.1, March 1970, pp. 48–56 (article reproduced in part in the book *Designing for Industry. The Architecture of Albert Kahn*).

[20] A. Kahn, "Industrial Architecture," in *Weekly Bulletin for the Michigan Society of Architects*, p. 7. The brochure for the Trussed Concrete Steel Company, *The Typical Factory: the Factory behind the Car*, Detroit 1907, is cited by G. Hildebrand (*Designing for Industry. The Architecture*

of Albert Kahn, p. 69 and "New Factory for the Geo. N. Pierce Company, Buffalo, New York. 1906," p. 48) which consulted the copy of Albert Kahn's daughter, Lydia Kahn Winston, a great collector of art, who died recently. In the firm's archives there are no copies of this publication, although the work for the Pierce Great Arrow plant of Buffalo is included in the general list of accomplishments in no. 297.

21 G. Hildebrand, "New Factory for the Geo. N. Pierce Company, Buffalo, New York. 1906," pp. 54–55.

22 For specifics on the relationship between Henry Ford and Albert Kahn, see D.L. Lewis, "Ford and Kahn," in *Michigan History*, vol. 64, no. 5, September–October 1980, pp. 17–28.

23 Among the industrialists were Henry Ford (b. 1863), and Walter Rathenau (b. 1867); among the architects, we can cite Hermann Muthesius (1861), Hans Poelzig (1869) and Albert Kahn (1869), each in his own way a impassioned researcher of a new relationship between architecture and industry. For the generational element as possible interpretive key of some of the subtle connections between modern and contemporary architects, see G. Canella, "Circuiti generazionali," in *Hinterland*, VI, no. 27, 1983, pp. 1–3.

24 For Ford's beginnings, see A. Nevins (with the collaboration of F.E. Hill), *Ford. The Times, the Man, the Company*, C. Scribner's Sons, New York 1954, in particular, chapters 1–11 describe—in laudatory tones—the period preceding the establishment of the Ford Motor Company. For an autobiographical account (with the collaboration of S. Crowther), see *My Life and Work*, Doubleday, Page & Company, Garden City 1922, particularly chapters 1–3.

25 Descriptions of "capitalist America" before World War I in W. Sombart, *Der Bourgeois*, Munich–Leipzig 1913, and T. Dreiser, *The Financier*, New York 1912; the first in a sociological context and the second in a literary one, help explain the motivations and actions of Henry Ford and Albert Kahn.

26 This saying is found in almost all of Albert Kahn's contributions on industrial architecture. See also G. Nelson, *Industrial Architecture of Albert Kahn, Inc.*, p. 21 and in particular V.H. Hosking, "Ninety Percent Business, Ten Percent Art," in *Automotive Industries*, August 20, 1938.

27 The articles are collected in the volume by H. Ford, *The International Jew*, Garden City 1921. On Ford's anti-semitism, see A. Lee, *Henry Ford and the Jews*, Stein and Day, New York 1980. Ironically, Albert Kahn was considered instead one of the most representative figures of the Jewish community of Detroit; see A. Caplan, "A Man Who Modernized American Architecture," in *The Jewish Tribune*, January 24, 1930, pp. 5–7.

28 For Hunt's work, see P.R. Baker, *Richard Morris Hunt*, MIT Press, Cambridge (MA)–London 1980. For Beman's work for Pullman, see T.J. Schlereth, "Solon Spencer Beman, Pullman, and the European Influence on and Interest in his Chicago Architecture," in J. Zukowsky (ed.), *Chicago Architecture. 1872–1922. Birth of a Metropolis*, The Art Institute of Chicago and Prestel–Verlag, Munich 1987, pp. 173–187. On Behrens, Rathenau and the A.E.G. experience, see the historical monograph of F. Hoeber, *Peter Behrens*, Georg Muller und Eugen Rentch, Munich 1913, which in particular documents the designs for industrial architecture; T. Buddensieg, H. Rogge, *Industriekultur. Peter Behrens und die A.E.G. 1907–1914*. Gebr. Mann, Berlin 1979. Finally, for a general picture of German culture of that period and its relationships with industrial development, see T. Maldonado (ed), *Tecnica e cultura. Il dibattito tedesco fra Bismarck e Weimar*, Feltrinelli, Milano 1979.

29 This is G. Nelson's definition, *Industrial Architecture of Albert Kahn, Inc.*, p. 15.

30 The Mack Avenue building was reconstructed in Greenfield Village in Dearborn, the museum founded by Ford to collect testimonies of American life. For a description of the Piquette Avenue building, designed by the firm of Field, Hinchman & Smith, see C.K. Hyde, *Detroit: An Industrial History Guide*, p. 17, and site 11. For eighteenth-century American industrial architecture, see A.L. Huxtable, "New England Mill Village. Harrisville, New Hampshire," in *Progressive Architecture*, vol. XXXVIII, no. 7, July 1957, pp. 139–140 and S. Kostof, *America by Design*, Oxford University Press, New York–Oxford 1987, pp. 80–101.

31 On the Highland Park plant, see A.L. Huxtable, "Factory for Ford Motor Company 1909–1914," in *Progressive Architecture*, vol. XXXVIII, no. 11, November 1957, pp. 181–182; *The Legacy of Albert Kahn*, pp. 12–13; W.H. Ferry, *The Buildings of Detroit. A History*, pp. 182–183; L. Robinson, "Albert Kahn," pp. 352–354; G. Hildebrand, *Designing for Industry. The Architecture of Albert Kahn*, pp. 43–54; S. King, *Creative-Responsive-Pragmatic. 75 Years of Professional Practice Albert Kahn & Associates Architects-Engineers*, pp. 15–16; C.K. Hyde, *Detroit: An Industrial History Guide*, p. 21 and site 6; S. Kostof, *America by Design*, pp. 108–110; for organizational methods, see H.L. Arnold, F.L. Faurote, *Ford Methods and the Ford Shops*, Arno Press, New York 1972 [1919] and S. Kaskovich, "Ford celebrates 75 years on assembly line," in *The Detroit News*, October 1, 1988.

32 For the importance of conveyor belts in rational American production, see H. Dubreuil, *Standards. Le travail américain vu par un ouvrier français*, Grasset, Paris 1929.

33 H. Ford's entry, "Mass Production," in *Encyclopedia Britannica*, vol. 15, London–New York, 1929, p. 40.

34 Today, along Woodward Avenue, the standing part of the original Highland Park building can be seen as a symbol of the fate of industrial Detroit. The plaque indicating "National Historical Landmark" is rather anachronistic in the middle of the overwhelming degradation of the area.

35 A. Kahn, *Article for Architectural Book Publishing Co.*, typewritten, September 4, 1931 (AKA), p. 9.

36 H. Ford, *My Life and Work*, pp. 113–114.

37 "The Old Shop," writes Reyner Banham, "was not just a production facility; with its immensely long facade running parallel with Woodward Avenue for a whole city block and clearly visible in spite of three smaller structures in front, it was also part of the public face of Ford. It therefore had to be "architecture," as the term would be understood by Kahn and Edward Grey (his collaborator inside the company):" R. Banham, *A Concrete Atlantis*, p. 98. In his analysis of the building, Banham further attributed much importance to a "decorative motif" that is barely visible in the building, not taking into account Michigan construction tradition. The pattern in which the bricks are laid for the towers of Highland Park recalls the first laboratory of Thomas Alva Edison that Ford had reconstructed at Greenfield Village. Banham's essay, even in the context of a very personal interpretation, nevertheless served to open discussion on the relationships between American industrial buildings and the European avant-garde, surmounting old historical interpretations. The debate is referred to in this comment by Pevsner on Behrens's turbine factories for the A.E.G.: "A similar project has nothing in common with the usual factories of the time, not even those most functional ones of Albert Kahn, which also have a visible steel structure. Here, for the first time, were visualized the creative possibilities of industrial architecture." N. Pevsner, *Pioneers of Modern Design. From William Morris to Walter Gropius*, Penguin Books, Harmondsworth 1960 (3rd), chapter 7. For a criticism of the theses expressed by Banham in the work *A Concrete Atlantis*, see the author's review in *Domus*, no. 721, November 1990.

38 For industrial/territorial relationships in the United States over the past two centuries, the ground-breaking work of A.R. Pred remains unsurpassed: *The Spatial Dynamics of U.S. Urban-Industrial Growth, 1800–1914. Interpretive and Theoretical Essays*, MIT Press, Cambridge (MA) 1966.

39 For the urban development of Detroit, see the excellent study by R. Conot: *American Odyssey*.

40 For a in-depth historical reconstruction of the Dodge installation at Hamtramck, see C.K. Hyde, *Dodge Brothers Motor Car Company*, 1981, research commissioned by the City of Detroit, Michigan State Historic Preservation Officer, Federal Advisory Council on Historic Preservation, held at the State of Michigan Archives and Detroit Public Library (Burton Historical Collection). An abridged version was published in Detroit in *Perspective. A Journal of Regional History*, vol. 6 no. 1, Spring 1982, pp. 1–21. A description of the Fisher plant in Cleveland is found in A. Kahn, *Description of Fisher Body Ohio Company's Plant, Cleveland,*

Ohio, typewritten, undated (AKA) and "Air View of Fisher Body Plant," in *The Detroit Free Press*, March 14, 1926.

41 For biographical information on Moritz Kahn (1880–1939), see the obituary published in *Weekly Bulletin of the Michigan Society of Architects*, January 24, 1939.

42 M. Kahn, *The Design & Construction of Industrial Buildings*, Technical Journal Ltd., London 1917. This volume played a fundamental role in the international reknown of the industrial architecture of Albert Kahn: see H.R. Hitchcock, "American Influence Abroad," in AA.VV., *The Rise of an American Architecture*, The Metropolitan Museum of Art, New York and Praeger Publishers, New York–London, 1970, p. 45.

43 The section entitled "Examples of Industrial Buildings" speaks of a series of cards which illustrate, never citing Albert Kahn, the Detroit installations of the Packard Motor Company, Ford Motor Company, Hudson Motor Car Company, Burroughs Adding Machine Company, Dodge Brothers Motor Car Company, Lozier Motor Company, and Continental Motor Company. Along with these works were some examples of English factories of reinforced concrete built by Wallis, Gilbert & Partners, Architects. See M. Kahn, *The Design & Construction of Industrial Buildings*, pl. XV–LXII.

44 Ibid., p. 49

45 Ibid., p. 52.

46 See F. Newby, D. Cottam, "The Engineer as Architect. Sir Owen Williams, 1890–1969," in *Casabella*, LI, no. 537, July–August 1987, pp. 404–53; and the thorough work by D. Cottam, S. Rosenberg, F. Newby, G. Crabb, *Owen Williams, 1890–1969*, Architectural Association, London 1986.

47 H. Ford, *Today and Tomorrow*, Doubleday, Page & Company, Garden City 1926, It. trans. *L'oggi e il domani*, Sit, Turin 1926, pp. 101–102.

48 In general, for the Rouge River plants, refer to *A Tour of the Remarkable Ford Industries During the Days When the End Product Was the Matchless Model A*, Ford Motor Company, Dearborn 1929 (reprint by Post Motor Books, Arcadia 1961); H.W. Barclay, *Ford Production Methods*, Harper & Brothers, New York–London 1936 (in praise of Fordism by the director of *Mill and Factory* magazine, with some interesting technical information); A. Nevins, F.E. Hill, *Ford. Expansion and Challenge 1915–1933*, C. Scribner's Sons, New York 1957, pp. 200–216 and 279–299 (a laudatory historical reconstruction, important for its rich archival documentation); A.L. Huxtable, "River Rouge Plant for Ford Motor Company 1917," in *Progressive Architecture*, vol. XXXIX, no. 12, December 1958, pp. 19–22; G. Hildebrand, *Designing for Industry*, pp. 91–128; *Legacy of Albert Kahn*, pp. 23–24; S. Kostof, *America by Design*, pp. 110–114.

49 H. Ford, *L'oggi e il domani*, p. 89.

50 Ibid.

51 L. Barzini, Jr., "Ford e la logica dell'assurdo," in *Corriere della sera*, April 27, 1934, p. 3.

52 The brochure is quoted in H.W. Barclay, *Ford Production Methods*, pp. 44–45.

53 See C.E. Bullinger, *Layout of Industrial Plants*, Edward Brothers, New York 1924; W.J. Hiscox, *Factory Layout, Planning and Progress*, Sir Isaac Pitman & Sons, London 1931; R.W. Mallick, A.T. Gaudreau, *Plant Layout, Planning and Practice*, J. Wiley & Sons, New York 1951.

54 See A. Kahn, *Ford Laboratory*, typewritten, undated (AKA). The building's elevations show elements reminiscent of the work of Julius Hoffmann. The project is presented in "Construction Begun on New Ford Engineering Laboratory, Dearborn," in *Ford News*, April 8, 1923, which published a perspectival illustration signed by Albert Kahn.

55 A. Kahn, *Speech at St. Louis Engineering Society and St. Louis A.I.A. Joint Meeting*, typewritten, October 16, 1941, pp. 5–6 (AKA).

56 H. Ford, *My Life and Work*, pp. 192–193.

57 For an in-depth study on Fordist anti-urbanism and on his proposals for production decentralization, see F. Bucci, P. Tavecchio, "La macchina totale. La razionalizzazione fordista dello spazio," in *Classe*, no. 22, December 1982, specifically pp. 223–233. For the anti-urban positions of American intellectuals, see M. and L. White, *The Intellectual and the City: from Thomas Jefferson to Frank Lloyd Wright*, Harvard University Press, Cambridge 1962, and on pastoral ideology, see L. Marx, *The Machine in the Garden. Technology and the Pastoral Ideal in America*, Oxford University Press, Oxford 1964. For the farmers' perspective, see R. Hofstadter, *Anti-intellectualism in American Life*, Knopf, New York 1962, and P. Boyer, *Urban Masses and Moral Order in America, 1820–1920*, Harvard University Press, Cambridge 1978.

58 In this regard, see the excellent work by D.L. Lewis, *The Public Image of Henry Ford. An American Folk Hero and His Company*, Wayne State University Press, Detroit 1987, which, in examining the management of Ford's image and his company's image until after the War, highlights the promotional function of industrial buildings since the construction of Highland Park (see particularly p. 53).

59 W.J. Cameron, "Il decentramento nell'industria," in *Tecnica e organizzazione*, annal I, no. 6, November 1937, p. 58.

60 On the Muscle Shoals Project, see R.M. Wik, *Henry Ford and Grass-roots America*, The University of Michigan Press, Ann Arbor 1972; and on his relationship with architecture and urban design, see G.R. Collins, "Broadacre City: Wright's Utopia Reconsidered," in AA.VV., *Four Great Makers of Modern Architecture. Gropius, Le Corbusier, Mies van der Rohe, Wright*, 1961, Da Capo Press, New York 1970, p. 64; G. Ciucci, "La città nell'ideologia agraria e Frank Lloyd Wright. Origini e sviluppi di Broadacre," in AA.VV., *La città americana dalla guerra civile al New Deal*, Laterza, Bari 1973, pp. 869–373; F. Dal Co, "Dalla Progressive Era al New Deal. La questione di Muscle Shoals," in *Casabella*, annal XLI, no. 425, May 1977, pp. 35–43.

61 J. Dalton, "Ford Tells What He Hopes to Do With Muscle Shoals," in *Automotive Industries*, vol. XLVII, no. 16, October 19, 1922, p. 752.

62 See G. W. Norris, *Fighting Liberal*, MacMillan, New York 1945, pp. 245–259. Norris was the promoter of the Tennessee Valley Authority, the great planning operation of this area, the pride of the New Deal. See S. Potenza, "L'esperimento della Tennessee Valley Authority nella pianificazione delle risorse regionali: da tentativo di riforma delle istituzioni a intervento anticongiunturale," in AA.VV., *L'urbanistica del riformismo. U.S.A. 1890–1940*, Mazzotta, Milan 1975.

63 See L. Mumford, *Technics and Civilization*, Harcourt, Brace and Co., New York 1934, pp. 225–226. Also Ludwig Hilberseimer, from the 1920s to the American period, always refers to Ford in his studies on the city. See L. Hilberseimer, *Grozstadt Architektur*, Hoffmann, Stuttgart 1927; *The New City. Principles and Planning*, Theobald, Chicago 1944, and *New Regional Pattern*, Theobald, Chicago 1949. For the influence of the hypotheses of Fordist decentralization on Italian urban design, see R. Gabetti, "Fordismo e territorio in Italia durante il fascismo," in *Storia Urbana*, annal III, no. 8, May–August 1979, pp. 157–184.

PRODUCER OF PRODUCTION LINES 1929–1942
Theory and Practice of Industrial Architecture

Since 1910 in the United States, the debate on the planning of industrial cities has registered a complexity of positions that stem from two distinct disciplinary camps: organized engineers who promoted continuous study and experimentation on the principles of scientific management, and the advocates of architectural culture. The latter were then divided among those who affirmed the need for a strict coherence between the forms of industrial buildings and the simplification needed for mass production, and those who maintained that the appropriate aesthetic could be achieved only through the addition of ornamentation.[1] Despite the fact that since the 1920s, industrial building designers have been marginal figures in the American architectural scene and occupied a rather insignificant position in official vehicles of information, the debate is nevertheless interesting and shows a desire to create an autonomous body of knowledge.[2]

In two articles in *The Architectural Forum* of 1919, Fordist guidelines were enumerated for the industrial building designer:[3] 1) choose the site, giving priority to the parameters of the neighborhood, the sources of raw materials, and the proximity of final merchants; 2) design the layout of the plants, paying attention to ground infrastructure (railroads, roads, canals, electric lines, etc.); 3) choose the construction material on the basis of specific qualities and convenience (steel, reinforced concrete, brick); 4) establish adequate levels of illumination and ventilation by installing large windows, shed roofs, etc.; 5) know the manufacturing process; 6) apply a fire prevention system; 7) define the distance of the technical installations to avoid interference with the building; 8) proportion the buildings according to the demands of the production process.

While these articles did not discuss architectural treatment, the argument was debated in the magazine's subsequent issues on industrial buildings, in the 1920s.[4] The September 1923 issue of *The Architectural Forum* contained significant contributions by two influential figures in American architecture, also involved in the field of industrial construction: Cass Gilbert and Harold Field Kellogg.

Gilbert's article, "Industrial Architecture in Concrete," opened with a statement similar to the motto of a modern European architectural master: "the simpler the form the better the design."[5] Using his plan for the U.S. Army Supply Base in Brooklyn (1918) as an example, the architect insisted on the importance of the articulation of the volumes in industrial buildings, condemning the use of decoration extraneous to the "direct and practical goals of such structures."[6] Such a declaration may have seemed suspicious coming from one of the representatives of

American eclecticism and the architect of the Neo-Gothic Woolworth Building in New York. However, it did not represent a sudden change of attitude. While it is true that the internal space of the U.S. Army Supply Base manifested similarities to the Highland Park plants, Gilbert took pains to point out that such a choice was valid only if applied to architectural design. In this area, he maintained, the architect must know how to assign an adequate aesthetic value, giving the economic and manufacturing relationship absolute priority.[7] Kellogg too, in his writings on the collaboration between architect and builder, aligned himself with Gilbert: total expressive freedom conditioned only by economic factors. This would explain why Kellogg, when planning the shoe factory of A.M. Creighton in Lynn, did not consider the addition of a Gothic clock tower in the simple four-story concrete structure a contradiction.[8]

In addition to voicing these theoretical considerations, *The Architectural Forum* contained technical pieces on natural and artificial lighting, ventilation and heating. These articles were reprinted in the section appropriately entitled "Architectural Engineering and Business," in the second monograph issue of September 1929.[9]

The illustrated plans in these two issues showed extremely diverse approaches, often because of the regional origins of the designers. There was quite a range of designs, from the severe structures of The Ballinger Company and of Lockwood, Green & Company on the East Coast, to the rich floral ornamentation and colonial influence of Morgan, Walls & Clements's industrial buildings in California.

In this debate, Albert Kahn, Inc.'s position was defined in an article by Moritz Kahn that opened the 1929 issue of *The Architectural Forum*.[10] The firm's approach to industrial architecture was founded on a series of directive principles that Moritz, synthesizing what Albert would write in a subsequent and more in-depth article, summarized in two main points.

The first had to do with the need to limit, as much as possible, the costs of construction, which had an immediate reflection on the architecture. "The designer of the factory should continually bear in mind that every manufacturer is interested in dollars and cents first of all, and in appearances only secondly. A good appearance can be obtained without extra expense by the proper use of materials, by the general contour or shape of the building, by the accentuation of structural lines, by the proper proportioning of solids and voids or the massing of the structure. This form of decorative treatment does increase the cost of the building, whereas an attempt to make an indifferent building presentable by applying ornament with a lavish hand is bound to prove a failure."[11]

The second point dealt with the relationship between the form of the building shell and the manufacturing process. "Probably the first important point to emphasize in the design of an industrial building is the need of planning it in cooperation with the manufacturer in order that the building may be designed for the specific purpose to which it is to be put. The character of the product and the processes of its manufacture must govern the design and type of the building to be used.... In other words, the method of production should not be adjusted to the building, but the building should be adapted to the production."[12]

If we compare these simple delineations with the other articles, and with the illustrated examples in the issue of *The Architectural Forum*, it becomes immediately evident that not all designers of industrial architecture were concerned with problems of the scientific management of labor. Only a small circle of specialists adhered rigorously to these principles, while others were absorbed by the problem of defining a "machine aesthetic" based on the European model.

The economic crisis of 1929, which shaped the entire American construction market until the New Deal era, initiated a kind of meditative pause for American architecture after the euphoria of the 1920s. There was much writing and debating.[13]

In this new climate, *The Architectural Forum*, gauge of the United States architectural scene, presented theoretical reflections instead of the 1920s formula of the monograph issue dedicated to architecture of a specific purpose.[14] The magazine's August 1932 issue presented eight pieces on "the future of the architect."

The essays were by Franklin D. Roosevelt (then governor of the state of New York), Ernest J. Russell (president of the American Institute of Architects) and other influential men of the architectural world: Frank Lloyd Wright, Richard Buckminster Fuller, Albert Kahn, William O. Ludlow, and Edwin Bergstrom.

A sense of veiled optimism pervaded the debate, evident in the almost prophetic words of Roosevelt: "I feel that the present economic depression will prove a great boon to the architectural profession."[15] The architects seemed to share his hopes for the future of their profession. Russell coined the phrase "once more the master builder,"[16] calling for a close monitoring of construction problems. Wright, in his piece entitled "Caravel or Motorship," maintained that the architect had for too long "preferred to sail or tow a caravel, instead of investing in a streamlined motorship of the line" and that now the moment had arrived to "*insist* that the motorship is more natural to us, more native than the caravel."[17] Fuller reiterated the issue of the close relationship with standardized industrial manufacturing that would become a constant in his design interests,[18] while Ludlow pointed out the new directions to take in professional practice. "The architect of today is not only an artist, as in the days of George B. Post, but he is a businessman, an engineer, a man in command, an executive, and the possibilities held out now to the practicing architect for the doing of big things was never so great."[19]

Albert Kahn, in turn, underlined the need for substantial support from the Federal Government in planning the construction of state offices, administrative headquarters, courthouses, city halls, libraries, museums and other buildings for the public welfare. He also gave a harsh warning: "If architects cannot prove their service worth while, they deserve to be replaced by others."[20]

From the articles emerged an image of a designer who could boast a wide range of abilities in order to meet the new and increasingly complex demands of an industrial society in rapid formation. On the eve of the New Deal, art and reality were in close harmony, evoking Albert Kahn's formula for "more business and less art."

Meanwhile, the great economic crisis of 1929 had grave consequences for Albert Kahn, Inc. While the firm's activities abroad had lessened the effects of the crisis, Albert Kahn, Inc. was forced to drastically redimension its personnel. "Nevertheless," wrote Albert Kahn, "we were fortunate enough to keep all our key men together."[21] Actually, the interval proved beneficial: the relaunching phase and the success that the firm had in the second half of the 1930s with industrial buildings, was due in large part to Kahn's theoretical reflections on scientific management of design work and construction methods. He was offered the opportunity to organize these thoughts in 1931, with an invitation to write the entry "Factory Building" for the *National Encyclopedia*.[22] With this invitation, Kahn had a means for ordering his experience of defining a series of operations adapted to a systematic approach to a problem.

After a brief historical preface, in which he recounted the pioneer phase of the introduction of reinforced concrete, Albert Kahn focused on three decisive factors for the construction of the industrial building: choice of location, type of building, and exterior design.

The choice of location, according to Kahn, should not be dependent simply on the proximity of energy sources, but must also consider a complex web of factors, determined by the final product.

In a certain sense, the geographical factor would partially lose the importance that it had had in the past (and that it would have in other contexts) since optimization of the local resources could be obtained artificially through the company's infrastructure (as with the Ford Motor Company).

The definition of the kind of building to be constructed was closely related to the specific manufacturing process: "The designer of the building must have in mind the process of manufacture so that there may be continuous and direct flow from the receiving of the raw material to the shipping of the finished product."[23] According to Albert Kahn, the building structure must adapt to the layout, and must not create obstacles for the movement of the piece work. Here the reference to Ford is clear. The free floor plan was an essential principle: "Internal columns should be as few as possible compatible with economy of construction and so located as not to interfere with production."[24] Kahn also emphasized the importance of installing lights, ventilation and heating.

As for the external design, Albert Kahn affirmed the importance of the appearance of an industrial building for both the company's image and its influence on the productivity of the workers. He maintained that "the best results are generally the simplest, the most direct solutions of a problem in which a virtue has been made of the structural and functional requirements."[25]

To support this statement he cited the work of Peter Behrens and Tony Garnier. This was not a tribute to the Modern Movement, because after praising the proto-rationalists, Albert Kahn launched a sharp criticism of the modern European architects (Mendelsohn, Gropius, Taut, Le Corbusier, and Lurcat) who had imposed their own personal elaboration on industrial building design. Against this "ultra-modern" approach, he leveled a technical/functional charge. He criticized the European architects of excessive use of glazed surfaces. Such a use, according to his point of view, was not the product of precise responses of a functional nature, but was motivated merely by aesthetic demands, and resulted in an unjustifiable increase in heating costs. This was hardly a marginal observation; it reflected the new course of American industrial architecture, characterized by the replacement of the day-lit factory (like Highland Park) with structures with reduced fenestration that would effect a savings in operation costs. Albert Kahn insisted on the importance of conceiving industrial buildings as perfect manufacturing machines and not, as in the case of Le Corbusier, as "magnificent first fruits of the new age."[26]

While in the programmatic statement of *Vers une architecture*, Le Corbusier identified an engineer as the person capable of designing this kind of building, Albert Kahn concluded his text by underlining the possibilities offered by "properly organized architectural firms," prepared to meet the structural, mechanical, administrative and aesthetic problems, according to an articulated system of synergetically used, specialized expertise.[27]

The new image of industrial architecture was not, then, for Kahn, a generic engineering factotum, but the firm that encompassed a wide range of all necessary expertise. As in Ford's case, this was both a declaration of principle and a given, anchored to practical experience: the experience of Albert Kahn himself.

In the beginning of the 1930s, Albert Kahn and his partners implemented an elaborate system of labor management capable of coordinating all the design contributions necessary for completing an industrial building. It was a move that would prove to be key when, between 1935 and 1945, the Detroit firm would be flooded with jobs to design factories all across America.

The new work system was based on the profound commitment to manualistic manufacturing and on the desire to define a standardized design approach.

Calling on years of experience in industrial typology, the firm sought to set a building model for every production sector. The system proved worthwhile even in smaller complexes. Among the various writings on the subject was a brochure edited in 1933 by Albert Kahn, Inc.'s engineering department, entitled *Layout Design of the Modern Brewery for Economical Production*.[28]

The design of a brewery was certainly far simpler than a plant for automobile manufacturing, as the narrow framework of problems to be resolved allowed immediate verification of methodological innovations. Since the end of the nineteenth century, in American as in Europe, brewery designers had tried to retain regional traditions through strong decorative accents, resulting in easily identifiable building types.[29] Since the brochure of Albert Kahn, Inc. proposed a rationalization of small plants as well, particular attention was paid to the criteria of the layout design and economical production, according to a taxonomy already tried in the large plants. Additionally, the extension of such principles to small manufacturing entities reinforced the abandonment of industrial gigantism inaugurated by the Ford company in the first half of the 1920s. Thus, the brochure spoke of a methodology capable of adapting to any number of situations.

From the presupposition that "economical production does not necessarily imply a sacrifice in quality,"[30] some general principles were developed for all industrial manufacturing, from the automobile sector to the food industry. Reduced to the essentials, these principles can be summarized in three points: 1) the transport of material in the course of production must proceed without hindrance; 2) the raw materials must enter the factory from one end and exit from another, thus permitting a simple and continuous line of production; 3) all divisions used for production must be structured in adequate space and conceived of in such a way as to permit any kind of amplification.

These three points were the cornerstones of mature Fordism, translated into organizational principles for factory space.

From these theoretical premises followed a series of explicit technical and design details on the construction of a brewery, with emphasis on hygiene and sanitation, the frugal use of materials, the production cycle, and the systems for guaranteeing adequate ventilation and lighting of interior space.

In summary, the prospective design for the interior of the plant seemed to implement a principle important to European functionalists: the form of the building was determined by its floor plan; and in turn, the floor plan was determined by the manufacturing flow.

These concepts were systematically applied in the late 1930s, in a period of great productivity for Albert Kahn, Inc.

This was the period in which the firm began to receive official recognition from the North American architectural community.

To celebrate forty years of work, in August 1938, *The Architectural Forum* devoted an entire issue to "Industrial Buildings. Albert Kahn, Inc."[31] In 1939, George Nelson published a monograph which added to and elaborated on most of the materials published by the magazine.[32] The issue of *The Architectural Forum* and the Nelson book were both successful and well-received: "Albert Kahn featured in *Architectural Forum*" was the headline on the front page of *Weekly Bulletin of the Michigan Society of Architects*.[33]

In addition to highlighting the firm's innovative design methods similar to those of manufacturing organizations, the two publications presented the major works of 1935 to 1938. The projects attested to the high professional standards attained in the search for new solutions for the organization of work space.

Thanks to its specialization in different technical sectors, Albert Kahn, Inc. was able to solve the more diversified problems posed by the Lady Esther Ltd. cosmetic factory in Clearing, Illinois (1936), a typical small-scale installation.[34]

The company's previous plant was a multi-story building in which the production cycle followed a vertical course from the top floor to the ground floor, like in the Ford plant at Highland Park. The new labor management proposed by the design division of Albert Kahn, Inc. adopted instead a horizontal plan, modeled on the Pierce Great Arrow and River Rouge plants: a one-story building with separate sections for each type of production. The layout divided the rectangular plant into four parts. On one of the longer sides ran a covered railroad track which, from one end, was used for the arrival of the raw materials, and from the other, for the delivery of the finished product. Located symmetrically on the other side were the alleys used for the same operation with motor vehicles.

The raw materials arrived in a large room situated at the southern end of the building; from here they were sorted along five separate corridors. Each contained specific lines of operation and led to a large room used for stock and the shipment of finished products.

In front of the production plant itself were the offices, the general employee facilities, and the main entrance.

The roof of both the labor division and the product creation division were built with steel relief joists, a method that was widely used in industrial buildings of the period. This type of roof permitted the installation of large east- and west-facing windows which provided natural lighting to the work space, and overcame the characteristic inconveniences of the shed roof.

LADY ESTHER PLANT: CLEARING, ILLINOIS; ALBERT KAHN, INC., 1936
Entry to plant and offices

LADY ESTHER PLANT: CLEARING, ILLINOIS; ALBERT KAHN, INC., 1936
Interior of factory

The architectural definition of the external walls was standardized and adaptable for different needs: base and cornice in brickwork, divided by continuous glass. The offices and main entrance were located along the front of the plant, centered about the entrance.

Following new organizational principles (this was the epoch of Mayo's principles of human relations), the interior of the Lady Esther plant succeeded in rendering "as pleasant as possible" the manufacturing conditions: "employees, for instance, enter the building directly through the main lobby, and differentiation between categories of workers has been studiously avoided. The color scheme is bright and cheerful. Floors are highly finished so they can be kept thoroughly clean, and the various manufacturing departments are constantly kept in shipshape order. The atmosphere produced by such inexpensive amenities has a direct relation to increased quality of output."[35]

The look of industrial architecture had changed: no longer a dark nineteenth-century building, but instead, a factory space shaped by the production cycle and by the efficiency of human labor.[36]

One of the most famous works by Albert Kahn, Inc., presented in both *The Architectural Forum* and Nelson's monograph, was the Chrysler Corporation's Half-Ton Truck Plant in Warren (in metropolitan Detroit), for the production of heavy equipment.[37] This plant, built in 1937, was composed of two buildings. The first, the Assembly Building, had impressive dimensions: 122.5 meters wide by 384 meters long (402 x 1,260 feet), with twenty-one spans of about 18.2 meters (60 feet) each. On the inside, in a well-lit space free of obstacles (all of the service structures were suspended from the roof with an access stairway in the direction of the work cycle), were the assembly lines where the motors and the frames of seven hundred heavy equipment products were assembled daily. The roof was made of steel column-joist cantilevering (with operable windows) while the front of the building presented a previously employed solution: a brick base with a large, glass surface.

The second building, the Export Building, had much smaller dimensions (around 37.1 x 73.7 meters, 122 x 242 feet) and was used for product inspection before shipment. The floor plan was the same as in the main building, but its large, open space emphasized the relationship between the walled and glassed surface area. It was a composition of great formal purity that Albert Kahn used in later plants, the Ohio Steel Foundry Company in Lima, Ohio (1938), for one. A Hedrich-Blessing photograph centered on the building's front added to the fame of the Export Building. It is one of the most well-known specialized photographic studies of American architec-

following pages:
CHRYSLER CORP., DODGE DIVISION, HALF-TON TRUCK PLANT: WARREN, MICHIGAN; ALBERT KAHN, INC., 1937
Elevations of the Assembly Building

WEST ELEVATION OF MOTOR RECEIVING ROOM

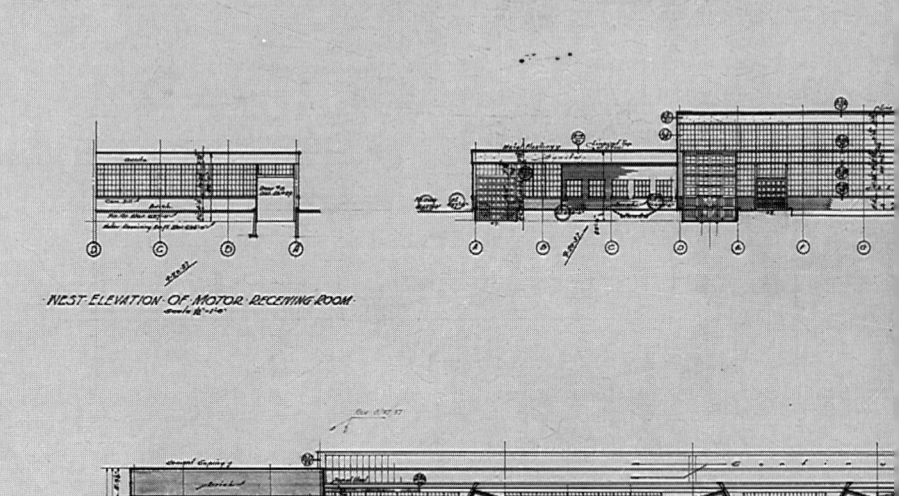

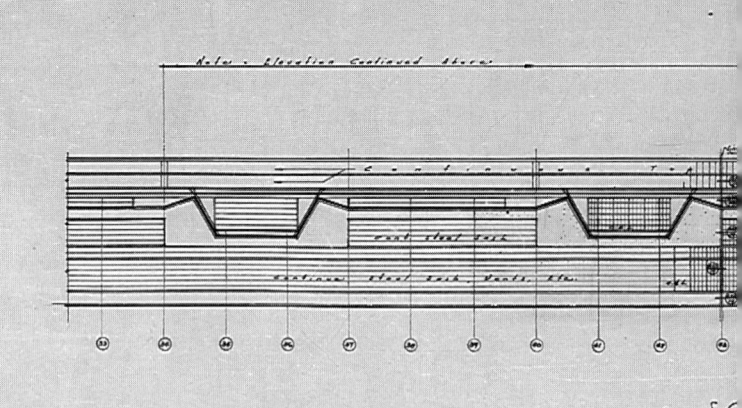

FR2

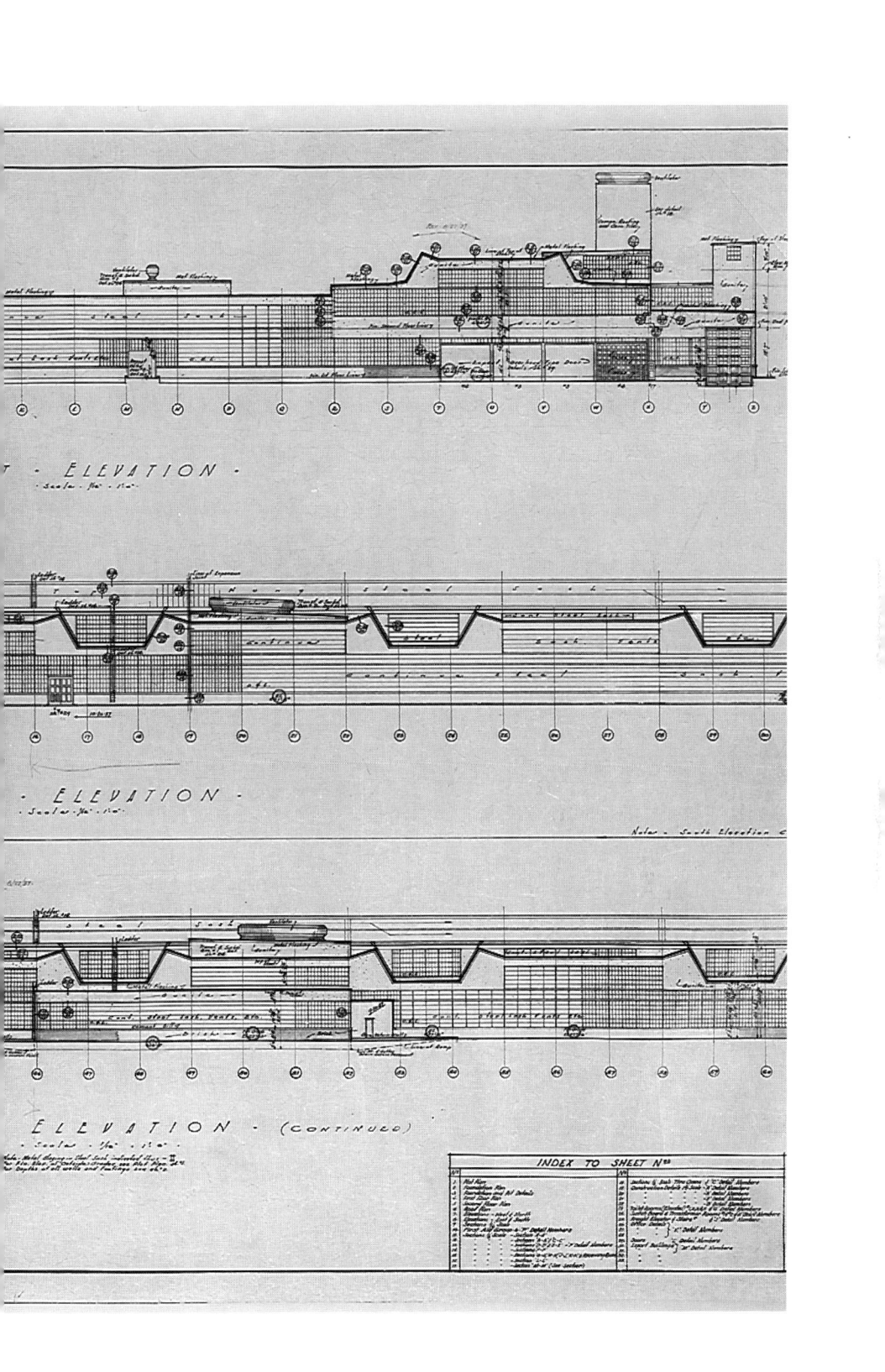

- ELEVATION -

- ELEVATION -

- ELEVATION - (CONTINUED)

ture, and it exalts the structure. The photo was also published in the catalog of the 1944 exhibit, *Built in USA 1932–1944*, organized by the Museum of Modern Art in New York. The photograph of the Half-Ton Truck Plant was hung near the photograph of Illinois Institute of Technology's Metallurgical Research Building, designed by Mies van der Rohe. The caption for both photographs read: "steel, brick and glass."[38]

In publications of 1938 and 1939 that focused on Kahn's work at that time, there were examples of other factories that also corresponded to specific functional needs.

Several published comments emphasized this aspect. The silos of the W.K. Kellogg Co. in Battle Creek elicited reactions on "the extraordinary purity of form of the most utilitarian structures...noted long ago by the first European modernists to visit this country;"[39] the Pratt & Whitney Engine Test House in Hartford, with its compact mass in reinforced concrete, and four towers with cells for motor testing, provided the basis for underlining the "purely functional design [that] has frequently more architectural quality than much so-called architecture."[40]

Finally, there are the buildings for the Ford Motor Company: the Tire Plant and the new Press Shop that completed the plant at River Rouge. The tire factory was the last testimony to Henry Ford's determination to be completely self-sufficient in producing all the materials for his automobiles. The factory, a structure of 73.1 x 243.8 meters (240 x 800 feet) with walls of special glass which filtered solar rays, produced tires using the rubber extracted from the Ford plantation in the Amazon Forest.[41] The Press Shop, "one of the largest industrial buildings ever built,"[42] was completed in 1939. L-shaped in plan, the building extends 505.9 meters (1,660 feet) along one leg and 284.6 meters (934 feet) along the other. The width varies from 73.1 meters (240 feet) to 119.4 meters (392 feet). The building's exterior was a testament to the new direction in "architectural treatment." The glassed areas were optimized and reduced, and were alternated with large groups of bricks. It was a preliminary test for solutions to safety problems in industrial plants, solutions that were to be widely employed during the war period.

The plants for the frame divisions of the General Motors Corporation in Indianapolis; Rochester, New York; Redford, Michigan; and Tonawanda, New York; for the Burroughs Adding Machine Company in Plymouth, Michigan; for the Chrysler Corporation in Detroit; and for the Republic Steel Company in Cleveland, are only a few other of Kahn's famous works which defined a path towards "modern architectural expression," "flexibility," and "simplicity of layout" in the organization of the production cycle. They were all buildings which paid careful attention to "working conditions" in the definition of interior space and they moved towards an architecture inspired by elementary principles: "simple mass, large glass areas and undecorated walls."[43]

CHRYSLER CORPORATION, DODGE DIVISION, HALF-TON TRUCK PLANT: WARREN, MICHIGAN;
ALBERT KAHN, INC., 1937
Export Building

CHRYSLER CORPORATION, DODGE DIVISION, HALF-TON TRUCK PLANT: WARREN, MICHIGAN;
ALBERT KAHN, INC., 1937
Boiler House

CHRYSLER CORPORATION, DODGE DIVISION, HALF-TON TRUCK PLANT: WARREN, MICHIGAN;
ALBERT KAHN, INC., 1937
Interior of the Export Building

W.K. KELLOGG COMPANY: BATTLE CREEK, MICHIGAN; ALBERT KAHN INC., 1936

UNITED AIRCRAFT CORPORATION, PRATT & WHITNEY DIVISION, TEST HOUSE: EAST HARTFORD, CONNECTICUT; ALBERT KAHN, INC., 1937

CHEVROLET MOTOR COMPANY, COMMERCIAL BODY
PLANT: INDIANAPOLIS, INDIANA;
ALBERT KAHN, INC., 1935

CHEVROLET MOTOR COMPANY,
MANUFACTURING BUILDING: TONAWANDA, NEW YORK;
ALBERT KAHN, INC., 1937

GENERAL MOTORS CORPORATION, DELCO APPLIANCE
DIVISION, MANUFACTURING BUILDING:
ROCHESTER, NEW YORK; ALBERT KAHN, INC., 1937

GENERAL MOTORS CORPORATION, ARGONAUT REALTY
DIVISION, DIESEL ENGINE: REDFORD TOWNSHIP,
MICHIGAN; ALBERT KAHN, INC., 1937

PRODUCER OF PRODUCTION LINES 1929–1942

The Soviet Adventure

The New York Times on May 7, 1929 read: "Albert Kahn, architect, of Detroit, has been engaged by the Soviet Government to plan and supervise the construction of a large group of manufacturing plants at Stalingrad, at the mouth of the Volga River in Southern Russia, it was made known yesterday. The buildings will be of American architecture and will cost about $4,000,000. The first one, to be erected for the manufacture of tractors, will employ about 2,000 men and have a capacity of 40,000 tractors annually. This plant will be followed by automobile factories, cotton mills and other industrial buildings."[44] Thus began Albert Kahn, Inc.'s Soviet adventure, with a deal that was part of American aid to the Soviet Union under the Fifteen Year Plan, and that played a role in the history of architecture and European urbanism of the period.

The contract between Albert Kahn, Inc. and the Soviet government led to the founding of Amtorg Trading Corporation, the Soviet international commerce liaison in New York that established agreements with major American enterprises to import advanced technologies under the developmental programs of the Fifteen Year Plan.

"Land of Communism Has to Use Resources of Biggest Anti-Communist Country," commented *The New York Evening Post*, speaking of the US companies involved in the modernization of the Soviet Union. *The Post* also added that "while American industry is responding to this call for assistance from revolutionized Russia, the people of the United States continue to feel utter antipathy for the Communist principles of the Soviet regime."[45]

Commercial bonds between the Soviet Union and the United States were not established immediately; they were preceded by years of cooperation between Henry Ford and the Soviet government. The first contacts between the Ford Motor Company and the new Soviet government began in 1919, with the acquisition of some American automobiles. In the 1920s, Henry Ford and "Fordizatsia" were already popular in the USSR. From 1922 to 1925, sales rose from about six hundred to eleven thousand vehicles—cars, heavy equipment, and tractors. Most successful was the Fordson tractor, a machine essential to the programs for the industrialization of farming.[46] "'Tractors! Tractors! Tractors!' they shouted all over the country. 'Civil progress! Cars! Literacy! ABCs! Radio! Darwin!' They despise America, that is, the great capitalism with a soul,

previous page:
BURROUGHS ADDING MACHINE COMPANY: PLYMOUTH, MICHIGAN; ALBERT KAHN, INC., 1936
CHRYSLER CORPORATION, DE SOTO DIVISION, PRESS BUILDING: DETROIT, MICHIGAN; ALBERT KAHN, INC., 1936

the land where gold is God. But they admired America, that is, progress, the electric iron, sanitation, aqueducts," commented Joseph Roth, the well-known writer, in *Frankfurter Zeitung* in 1926.[47]

Meanwhile, *Pravda* focused on the prospects of industrialization in the USSR—low cost, mass-produced American automobiles (the Model T). And the 1928 inauguration of the Fifteen Year Plan was met with a flurry of excitement and activity.[48]

The Russians proposed the construction of a Ford Motor Company tractor plant, and Henry Ford, who had just opened a similar facility in Cork, Ireland, agreed to provide machinery and methods of construction, and suggested Albert Kahn, Inc. as the firm to design the great structures.

And so, Ford, Kahn and the Soviets built the tractor factory in Stalingrad. Having seen the quality of the plant, the Soviet directors began to use Albert Kahn, Inc. for other projects. While the Stalingrad factory was being finished, in the first days of 1930 there was a new contract signed for the complete and expert advice of the firm for the construction of factories and for the training of Soviet engineers and architects. The January 11, 1930 issue of *The New York Times* described the details of the agreement: "The Soviet government proposes to construct four large motor-car, motor-truck, and motor-cycle factories, and nine plants to produce tractors and farm implements.... According to the present arrangement, Moritz Kahn will go to Russia shortly with a staff of twenty-five special assistants to organize a designing bureau which will comprise about 4,500 architectural and engineering designers, selected principally from Russia. This bureau will be directed by B.E. Barsky, who will be practically the dictator of building construction in Russia, according to Mr. Kahn."[49]

At this point the American press chose to portray Albert Kahn as a genius who knew how to conquer faraway lands. Their lofty tributes resulted in some dubious comparisons: "When Francis I of France wanted palaces designed, he summoned Leonardo da Vinci. George Washington, after the fever of a war, set out to build a capital in a wilderness. He employed a Frenchman, Pierre Charles L'Enfant....Just so, last week, the Supreme Economic Counsel of Soviet Russia, represented by Amtorg Trading Corp. in Manhattan, signed contracts to retain the Detroit architectural firm of Albert Kahn, Inc., as consulting architects for two years of Russia's famed five-year industrialization program..."[50]

Beyond concessions to rhetoric, the uncontested fact remained that the Moscow division of Albert Kahn, Inc., directed by Moritz Kahn, constituted a vanguard among those risen up between 1928 and 1932 to support the American presence in the Soviet Union. In the span of a just few years the company obtained surprising results. It implemented more than five hundred designs for industrial plants of large and medium size, with the help of about thirty people: American engineers and architects and numerous Soviet technicians in their professional apprenticeships.[51] Among the designs were those for the steel factories and foundries of Kharkov, Upper Tagil, Kuzniztsk, Kamenskoi, Kolomna, Lubertsk, Sormovo, Nihi Tagil, the automobile factory of Moscow, the aeronautic industries of Kramatorsk and Tomsk, and the chemical factory in Kalinin, up to the three great colossals of Cheliabinsk, Stalingrad and Magnitogorsk. Cheliabinsk and Stalingrad produced automobiles and tractors, and Magnitogorsk produced steel.[52]

Knickerbocker, a journalist who in 1930 visited the work in progress for the three plants, reported that "the dimensions of the [Cheliabinsk] plants are impressive. The assembly department is the largest, as far as area is concerned, in the entire world. It is 450 meters long and 135 wide [1,476 x 443 feet], and covers a surface area of 26 acres. The foundry is 235 meters long and 193 wide [771 x 633 feet]. The dimensions of the forge are 205 by 129 meters [672 x 423 feet]." In Stalingrad, he noted that "the assembly department...extends in length for 406 meters [1,332 feet], in width for 80 [262 feet], and it has been enclosed in glass walls, like a painter's studio....The conveyor belt, no longer an issue of disagreement between capitalists and socialists, has a chain about a kilometer [0.62 mile] long." And finally, in Magnitogorsk, Knickerbocker wrote that "in all, there must be eight blast furnaces, each one 33 meters [108 feet] high, with an internal capacity of 1180 cubic meters [41,654 cubic feet] and a daily production of 1000 tons of iron each. In America there are just eight blast furnaces so large."[53]

The Soviet adventure of Albert Kahn, Inc. was brief but intense. The design firm made use of all that it had learned in its long association with Ford, and reproduced the initial model founded on centralization and blind faith in the economic ladder. Naturally, they encountered numerous difficulties: the language, the climate, the customs, and above all, the scarcity of materials and the training of the work force.

"Many materials we consider standard here," wrote Albert Kahn, "are not to be had in Russia."[54]

What created worse problems was American public opinion. It was in this area that Albert Kahn found the most difficulty and risked unpopularity: initial enthusiasm and support waned when confronted with the inevitable political implications raised by the transfer of technology to a country whose political ideology threatened the West.

In 1931, William H. Bruss, an engineer at Albert Kahn, Inc., upon his return from the USSR, recounted to *The Border Cities Star* (a Detroit daily) his impressions of the Fifteen Year Plan. It was basically a series of denouncements: of the black market, the impossibility of leaving the country, the inadequacy of the judiciary system, the secret police, and the housing problem. But above all, and that which the American people

PRODUCER OF PRODUCTION LINES 1929–1942   93

TRACTOR PLANT: STALINGRAD, RUSSIA; ALBERT KAHN, INC., 1930

STEEL FABRICATING PLANT: NIHI TAGIL, RUSSIA; ALBERT KAHN, INC., 1932

DIESEL TRACTOR PLANT: CHELIABINSK, RUSSIA; ALBERT KAHN, INC., 1932

DIESEL TRACTOR PLANT: CHELIABINSK, RUSSIA; ALBERT KAHN, INC., 1932
Interior

feared—the reconversion of the plants into arms factories. Even more serious were the heavy accusations against Albert Kahn, Inc., as Bruss claimed that the contract with the Soviet government included a clause regarding the promotion of Communism in the United States.[55] Albert Kahn, Inc. responded immediately (on the same day) with a strongly worded letter from Moritz Kahn, denying everything. But the doubts and insinuations about American intervention in the USSR gave no hint of lessening.[56]

When the expiration date of the contract (March 1, 1932) drew near, Albert Kahn left for Moscow to negotiate a contract renewal. However, in spite of the positive beginning and the intention to start new affiliations in other cities, the negotiations crumbled over the issue of payment, for which the Russians wanted to use local currency. "Kahn breaks with Soviets," is how the March 26, 1932 *New York Times* announced the end of Albert Kahn, Inc.'s Soviet adventure.[57]

Considering the brevity of the association, the work of Albert Kahn left a decisive imprint on the technological and professional culture of the Soviet Union. This was attested to by, among other things, a telegram sent by the architect Viktor A. Vesnin to Ernestine Kahn after the death of her husband in December of 1942: "Soviet engineers builders architects send you their sincere sympathy in connection with the death of your husband, Mr. Albert Kahn, who rendered us great service in designing a number of large plants and helped us to assimilate the American experience in the sphere of building industry. Soviet engineers and architects will always warmly remember the name of the talented American engineer and architect, Albert Kahn."[58]

While Albert Kahn, Inc.'s partnership with the Soviets was the most publicized, it was not the only experience which involved American technicians in the planning of industrial buildings in the USSR. Among the other noteworthy projects was that of Niznij Novgorod, or Autostroy. Autostroy was an industrial complex for the manufacturing of automobiles, set up by the Ford Motor Company in 1929. Also in 1929, Albert Kahn, Inc. signed a contract with the Amtorg Trading Corporation to build a colossal plant based on the River Rouge model, for the production of automobiles (Model A) and trucks (Model AA). The chosen location was Niznij Novgorod along the Volga River, and the conditions were such that Ford would provide the complete supply of building projects, labor management systems, and technical assistance, in addition to a training session for the Soviet technicians in Dearborn.

Albert Kahn's firm quickly adapted the River Rouge model to the new context, and furnished all of the building plans for the industrial constructions.[59] The completed project was not entirely the work of Albert Kahn: the technical assistance in the undertaking was awarded by the Soviet government to the Austin Company of Cleveland, a company specialized in building industrial plants. To the same company also went the request to design the new industrial city of Niznij Novgorod. The choice surprised even the Soviet architectural community, which had entered numerous groups in the design competition for this commission. Evidently their proposals were deemed unworthy by the Soviet authorities, who decided to award the construction of the "typical Socialist city" to an American company.[60]

The design realized by the Austin Company for Niznij Novgorod reproposed an urban design inspired by the garden-city, which contrasted with the futuristic and untenable proposals of the Soviet architects.[61] There were polemics concerning this too, and *a posteriori*, the government itself judged the Austin project inadequate to the needs of the socialist city.

In 1935, Stalin put an end to technical collaboration programs with foreign countries: "we have already surpassed the period of drought in the field of technical equipment" he explained in a speech to the Academy of the Red Army.[62] While this was the official justification, the reality was quite different. Due to scarcity of means, the Stachanovistic fervor had been replaced by Taylorist science.

Chicago 1934, New York 1939: Architecture for the Expositions

The involvement of American companies in the USSR continued until the eve of the new American political course which marked the victory over the economic crisis begun in 1929. The investment in Soviet land had been a safety valve for some American companies. The Chicago Fair, opened in 1933, signaled the affirmation of a new course in the construction field. It was no coincidence that Franklin D. Roosevelt, still governor of New York, chose to promise a "new deal"[63] for the American people in Chicago, an industrial city hard-hit by the crisis. It was the fair's difficult task to sell the New Deal. The New Deal would exhibit a new America, and the exhibition pavilions assumed the responsibility of interpreting that new direction in an architectural language.

The coordinator of the fair, Joseph Urban—an architect who came from Austria in 1911—was well-known for having constructed the best theaters of New York.[64] This familiarity with scenography influenced all of the architecture of the exposition. From folklore of European villages to the futuristic pavilions of the major industries, the scenographic theme was the unifying factor in an otherwise diverse landscape. Such a theme created disagreements that culminated in the exclusion of Frank Lloyd Wright from the fair. In his autobiography, Wright remembers: "Because the only real interest I had in the Fair since first hearing of it, or any hope of it whatever, was to prevent any such catastrophe to our culture as occurred in 1893. Pro or con. I did hate to see the careful, devoted sacrifice of so many faithful years in building up a great cause again played up, and probably played out, down and out, by the clever pictorializing and current salesmanship that I knew would be snatching the great cause to feather the architectural offices of a few New York and Chicago plan-factories."[65] The reference to "plan-factories" was a very clear allusion to firms like Albert Kahn, Inc.

Kahn's firm was an important participant in the Chicago Fair, as its pavilions for General Motors and Ford were two of the fair's most popular attractions.

In response to Wright, Albert Kahn cut short the discussion, and declared that "comparison between the present fair and that of '93 is futile"[66] and he immediately accepted the responsibility of building the pavilions of the two great automobile companies. The opportunity interested him also because of the specific knowledge that the

following pages:
CHICAGO WORLD FAIR, GENERAL MOTORS BUILDING: ALBERT KAHN, INC., 1933
Interior

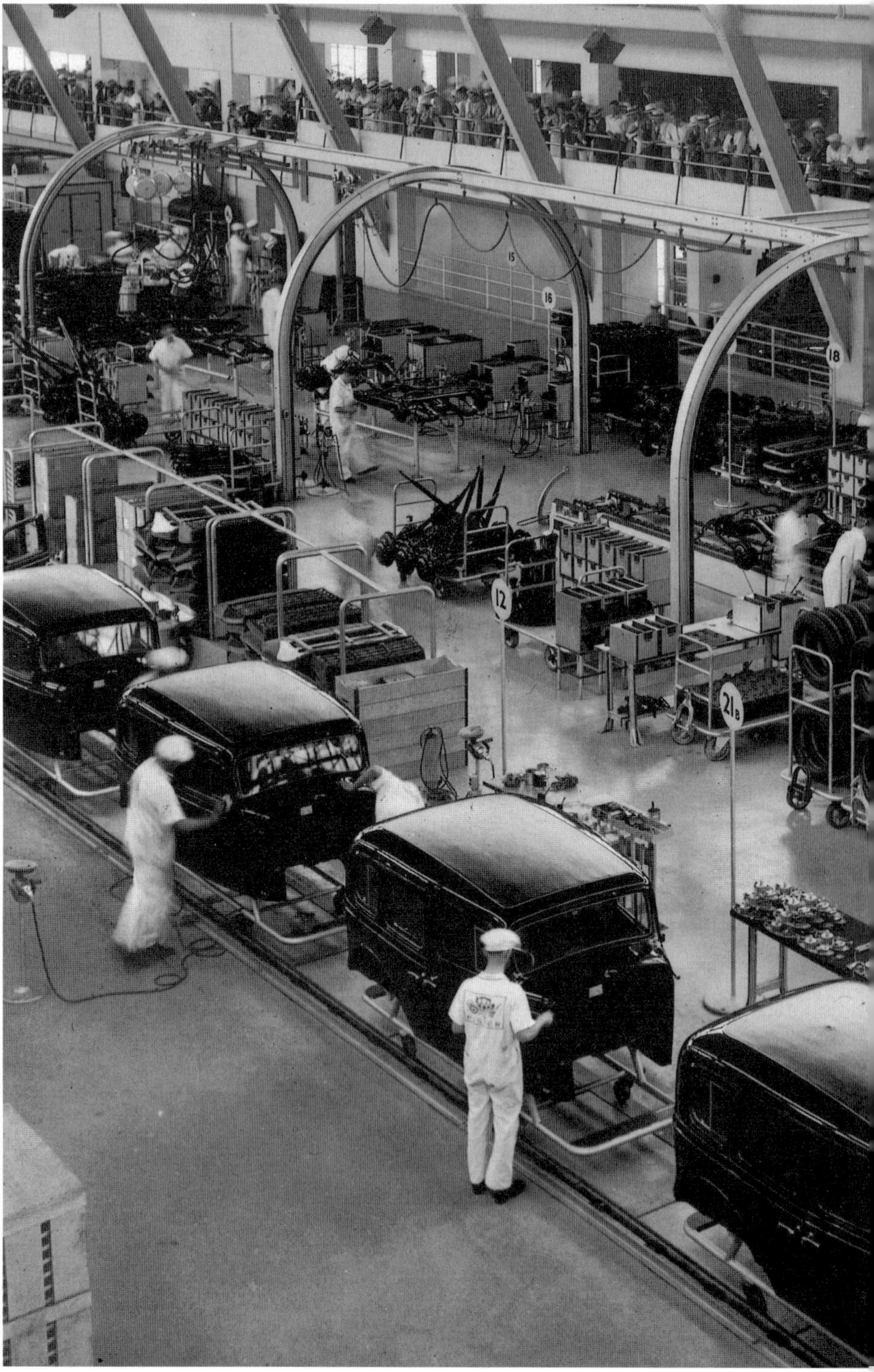
15
16
18
12
21e

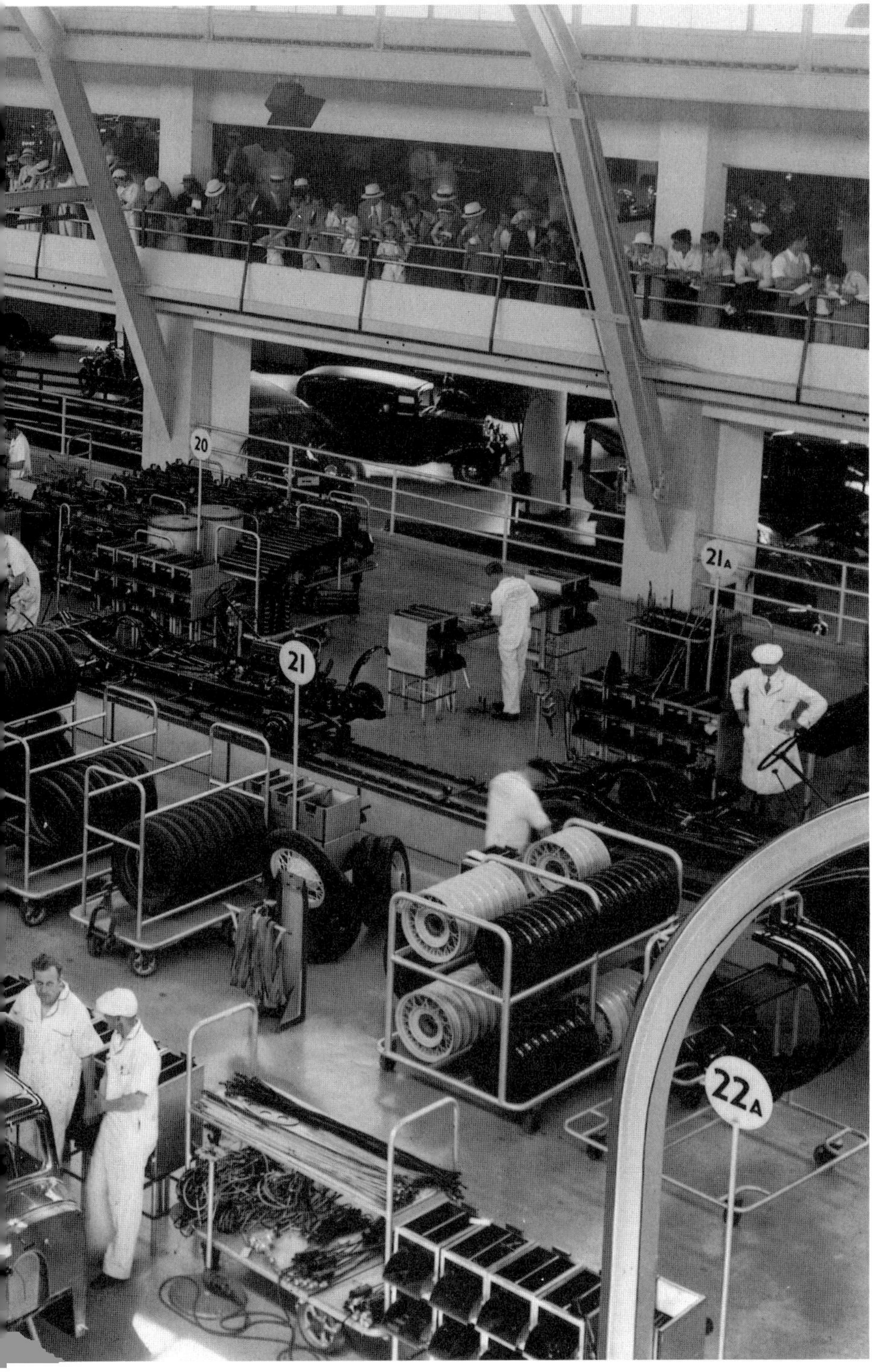
20
21
21A
22A

CHICAGO WORLD FAIR, GENERAL MOTORS BUILDING: ALBERT KAHN, INC., 1933
Aerial view

CHICAGO WORLD FAIR, FORD BUILDING: ALBERT KAHN, INC., 1934
Rendering by Hugh Ferris

FORD MOTOR COMPANY, ROTUNDA BUILDING: DEARBORN, MICHIGAN; ALBERT KAHN, INC., 1934

projects required, and because the designers were requested to display the tempos and the methods of labor organization inside a factory.

The General Motors pavilion, noted for "ultra-modern utilitarian design"[67] was composed of three elements: a central tower of about 60.9 meters (200 feet), a gigantic inside room where the cycle of production was displayed, and an auditorium for 250 persons. The colorful exterior invited one to visit the great murals of Diego Rivera which decorated the interior.[68]

The Ford pavilion, constructed the following year (the fair stretched from 1933 to 1934) perfected these distribution criteria, and used a different compositional solution. In a conference held at the Illinois Society of Architects in Chicago on March 20, 1934, Albert Kahn described in detail the structure of the building and the various phases of its construction, highlighting in particular the alacrity of the execution of all the work. From this emerged the idea of an undertaking organized according to the rules of the assembly line, and which had as its final result, a spectacular demonstration of "the Ford world empire."[69]

The Ford pavilion was also composed of three parts: a circular room called the "Rotunda" housed an exhibit on the history of transportation; a smaller space was occupied by the Ford Museum; finally, a large, rectangular space held the exhibition of the entire production cycle.[70]

The Rotunda was the fulcrum of the complex, and represented the "place of memory" in which the company celebrated its progress.

The Rotunda housed a museum that illustrated the pivotal role of the Ford industries in the production sector. The building was circular, with a blind front, unadorned except for modulating elements. It was open at the top to receive natural light. This widely-used dramatic lighting system was devised and developed by Hugh Ferris.[71]

At the close of the fair, the Rotunda Building was dissembled and transported to Dearborn, where it was placed at the entrance of the River Rouge plants to house a portion of the Ford Museum.[72]

Three years after the Chicago Fair, the Paris Expo took place. Here, in the middle of European culture, the triumph of reason signaled the defeat of the vanguards. While the pavilions of the Soviet Union and Germany displayed symbols of their respective regimes, France awarded the most prestigious buildings to the representatives of academic culture, and the work of the modern architectural masters was relegated to the back position.[73]

Albert Kahn visited the Exposition personally. He was invited by the French government, who had awarded him a gold medal of the Ministry of Commerce and Industry which dubbed him with the title of Knight of the Legion in honor of his services rendered during the First World War as designer of military bases.[74]

Aside from the serious criticism of the German pavilion, Kahn expressed a general admiration for this architecture. He declared that he appreciated everything "modern in spirit yet observant of classic principles, new but not revolutionary,"[75] and in doing so, he endorsed a public architecture of academic stamp, in open contrast to the innovative character of industrial buildings. It was a contradiction that surfaced in all of his work and which would be theorized in his later years.

Far from the unstable, pre-war European climate, New York hosted the World's Fair in 1939, which lasted about one year. America strove to exalt, once again not without rhetorical overtones, the possibilities of technology. It was to this aim that Trylon and Perisphere responded, with an enormous structure planned by Wallace Harrison that dominated the landscape of the Fair with its very high and slender pyramid flanked by a giant globe.[76]

Albert Kahn, Inc. collaborated with Norman Bel Geddes in designing the General Motors pavilion, and with Walter Dorwin Teague in designing the Ford pavilion. They gave the utmost demonstration of a capability to translate the Fordist culture into architectural form.

While the Ford pavilion echoed the style of the buildings of the Chicago Fair, the General Motors pavilion went beyond the simple didactic description of the techniques of modern industry, conveying imaginary visions of a city of a future dominated by the rhythm of automobile traffic.

The organization of the route through the fair was reconstructed in an Italian volume of 1954, dedicated to the architecture of the fairs: "the visitor embarks from the very beginning, in the comfortable armchairs of Futurama...and is led in this way to survey wonderful visions of a happy future world. At the end of the voyage, the passenger is deposited on the Street of the Future in which the circulation of the visitor pedestrians unfolds on an elevated platform dominating the lower carousel of General Motors cars."[77]

This was a real "mise-en-scène" of the wonders of technology; the successful advertising ability of designer and scenographer Bel Geddes converged quite well with Albert Kahn's experience in the field of industrial architecture. This way of conceiving the architecture of the fairs was very different from that which guided Alvar Aalto's Finnish pavilion, or of Niemeyer and Costa's Brazilian pavilion.[78]

While for them, architecture was the center of attention, in the case of the General Motors Building, the focus was on those aspects which involved the public, so as to impose social models conforming to the commercial strategies of the American companies. On the other hand, the great United States industry was prepared to support the war effort, and the General Motors pavilion was not only "an act of faith in Rooseveltian peace,"[79] but it symbolized the optimistic faith in technological innovations and it anticipated hypotheses of urban planning which characterized the postwar period.[80]

GLENN L. MARTIN COMPANY: BALTIMORE, MARYLAND; ALBERT KAHN, INC., 1937–1939
General view

GLENN L. MARTIN COMPANY: BALTIMORE, MARYLAND; ALBERT KAHN, INC., 1937–1939
Interior

AMERICAN STEEL FOUNDRIES, CAST ARMOR PLANT:
EAST CHICAGO, INDIANA;
ALBERT KAHN ASSOCIATED INC., 1942

AMERTORP CORPORATION, TORPEDO ORDANCE PLANT
CHICAGO, ILLINOIS;
ALBERT KAHN ASSOCIATED INC., 1942

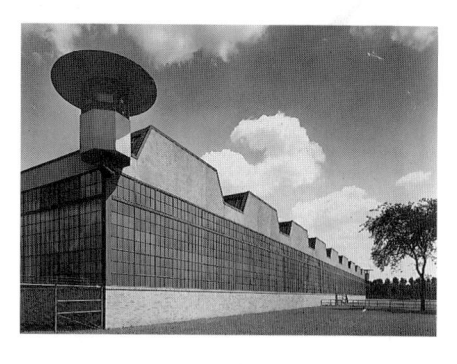

AMERICAN LOCOMOTIVE COMPANY, GUN SHOP:
SCHENECTADY, NEW YORK
ALBERT KAHN ASSOCIATED INC., 1942

CHRYSLER CORPORATION, DODGE CHICAGO PLANT,
OFFICE BUILDING: CHICAGO, ILLINOIS;
ALBERT KAHN ASSOCIATED INC., 1942

Plans for the Arsenal of Democracy

For Albert Kahn, Inc., the collaboration on the planning of the Exposition buildings was secondary to its concentration of all of its forces on industrial architecture.

In 1939, the enlarging of the Glenn L. Martin aeronautic plant in Baltimore provided an opportunity to try out new organizational systems of design work, and to implement new techniques of building construction. The original structure of the factory, built in 1937, was a great rectangular open space with a grid of columns (about 91.4 by 137.1 meters, 300 x 450 feet), with an enormous door that corresponded to the wing span of the airplanes[81] and occupied all of the smaller side of the building.

More than the construction characteristics, the new plant was distinctive for the record time in which it was completed: "An airplane factory built in eleven weeks," was the title of an article of *Engineering News Record* that reviewed the work.[82] It was an event on which specialized literature dwelled, and it became a famous reference among those in the field. "It was on Thursday, February 5, 1939," read *The Architectural Record*, "that Albert Kahn received a telephone call from the Glenn L. Martin company, Baltimore. 'Can you furnish plans quickly enough for us to put up a 440,000 sq. ft. building by May 1?' That was quite an order: a mammoth aircraft factory building to be ready for use in 84 days. But Kahn was prepared to answer, 'Yes.' Actually manufacturing began in that building on April 27, just 81 days after the call."[83]

Because of the exceptional swiftness of the design and execution, the construction of the Martin plant constituted a benchmark for the war industry. From 1940 to 1945, the United States was involved in an unprecedented production effort that involved all of the major automobile and aeronautic industries.

The need to assign government jobs to large private enterprises was emphasized by Albert Kahn at the Fifteenth International Congress of Architects in Washington, in September of 1939. In that session, the Detroit architect spoke of the efficiency of design firms and stated with satisfaction that the government could count on these firms without incurring the burden of assigning an inside technical office. Albert Kahn also let on that his firm was ready and willing to carry any consignment.[84]

Years of experience in mass production allowed the technicians of these firms to design, in very short time periods, assembly lines capable of producing great quantities of military equipment, even though they had no particular familiarity with the

following pages:
CHRYSLER CORPORATION, DODGE CHICAGO PLANT, TEST CELLS: CHICAGO, ILLINOIS;
ALBERT KAHN ASSOCIATED INC., 1942

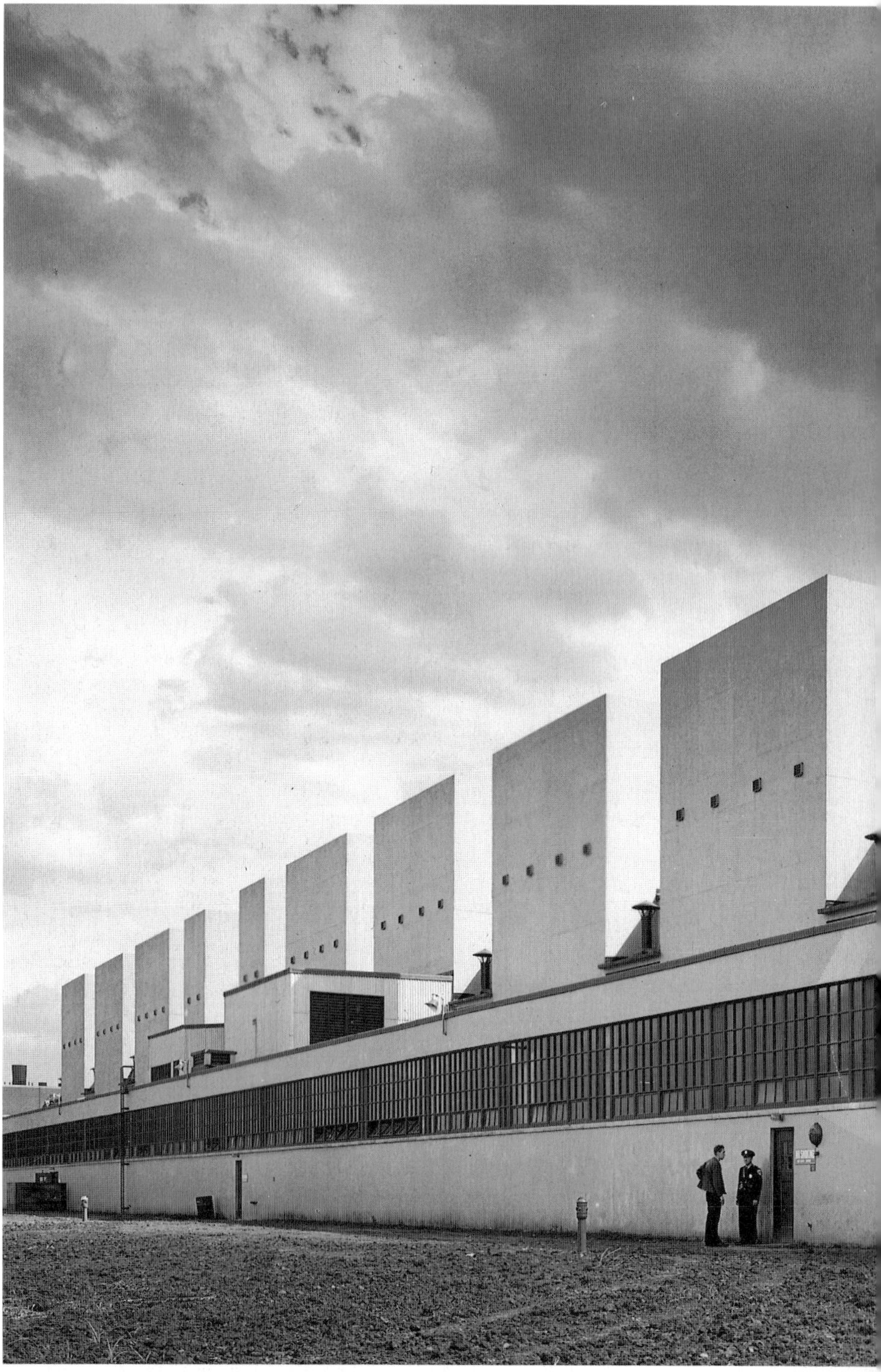

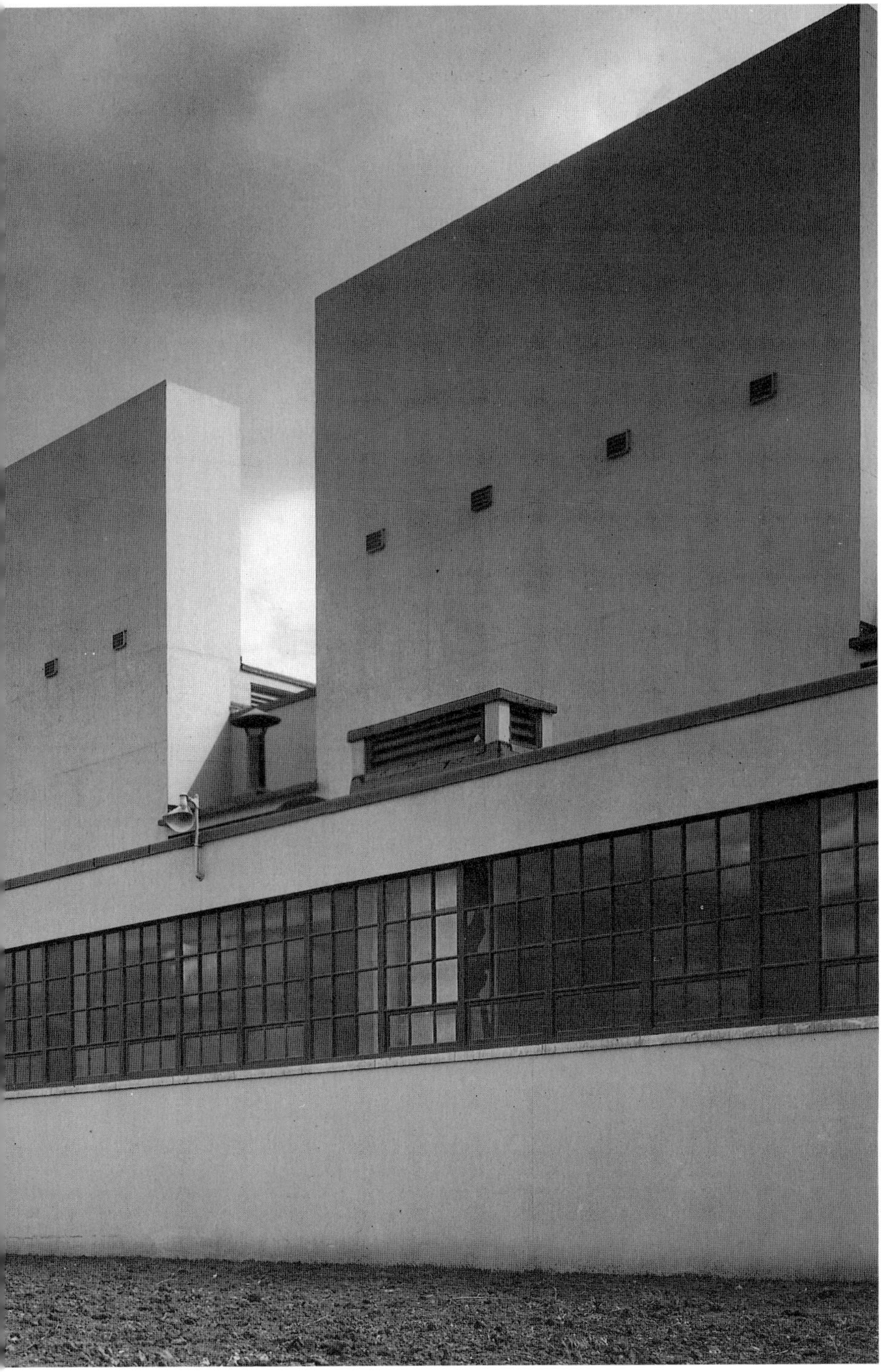

products. "Speed and more speed is the watchword of the Defense Program. Decisions to build or expand are made suddenly, and complete plans are expected of the architect 'immediately' if not sooner....There is no time for philosophizing, waiting for inspiration, or even considering the matter of aesthetics....Simplicity of design and construction is imperative. Every day counts and minutes must be saved. It is not only a matter of dollars and cents but, today, a matter of life and death."[85] But, besides the necessary swiftness, it was no less essential to ensure all the construction devices necessary to contend with aerial attacks, or sabotage. The issued regulations proposed by the War Department Board enumerated the location and the camouflage of the plants, the construction of anti-aerial shelters for workers, the adoption of appropriate technical solutions even in small construction details, and safety conditions to check the effects of fire or explosions. Furthermore, the need for frequent blackouts led to the use of special glass surfaces or, in some cases, to the study of systems of artificial illumination and ventilation: the famous windowless factories. Albert Kahn seemed to be rather skeptical about this particular solution. His critical arguments against it were of an economic and sanitary nature. On the one hand, he pointed out the difficulty of re-employing the industrial structures "after the emergency," in particular, on account of the cost of adding lighting and heat after the re-establishment of the regular eight-hour work day instead of the twenty-four hour schedule maintained during the war; on the other hand, he called attention to "the psychological effect of windowless plants on the workers."[86] For this reason, but also to stay ahead of the competition, Albert Kahn, Inc. devised a new system for covering glass surfaces during the night hours.

Albert Kahn returned to the theme of industrial constructions for the "national defense" in two articles that *Weekly Bulletin of the Michigan Society of Architects* published in their December 30, 1941 issue. Remembering the expansion of the Glenn L. Martin Company, Albert Kahn recalled that "speed is the password of the Defense Program. The decisions to construct or enlarge must be made quickly, and the architectural designs must be ready immediately....There is no time for philosophy, to wait for inspiration or to consider the aesthetic problems....Simplicity of design and construction is imperative. Every day counts and minutes must be saved. It's not only a question of dollars and cents but, today, it is a question of life or death."[87]

During the war climate, "standardization" of the architectural solutions acquired enormous importance. It was a practice that Albert Kahn, Inc. had refined and perfected during the Ford years. Kahn's considerable amount of accumulated technical knowledge justified the assuredness and the imperiousness of his specifications for the standardization of the industrial constructions: a "one-story structure of incombustible materials, with enormous uninterrupted floor spaces under one roof, with a minimum number of columns."[88] While he tended towards a single construction prin-

WRIGHT AERONAUTICAL CORPORATION,
AIRPLANE ENGINE PLANT: LOCKLAND, OHIO;
ALBERT KAHN ASSOCIATED INC., 1940

CONSOLIDATED AIRCRAFT CORPORATION,
FLIGHT HANGAR: NEW ORLEANS, LOUISIANA;
ALBERT KAHN ASSOCIATED INC., 1942

CURTISS WRIGHT CORPORATION, AIRPLANE DIVISION,
BUFFALO AIRPORT PLANT, BOILER HOUSE:
BUFFALO, NEW YORK;
ALBERT KAHN ASSOCIATED INC., 1940

CURTISS WRIGHT CORPORATION,
AIRPLANE DIVISION, ASSEMBLY PLANT:
LOUISVILLE, KENTUCKY;
ALBERT KAHN ASSOCIATED INC., 1942

CHRYSLER CORPORATION, TANK ARSENAL: DETROIT, MICHIGAN; ALBERT KAHN ASSOCIATED INC., 1940

ciple, the team he directed showed a great capacity for finding solutions for every conceivable problem.

The coexistence of these two principles—standardization and flexibility of solutions—made possible the perfect functioning of the design machine put in motion by Albert Kahn. "Tanks, plants, arsenals, airplane engine buildings and giant aircraft factories are all the same to Kahn when he sets his 450 architects and engineers to work. They turned out 1650 drawings in seven months when the Navy wanted Kahn to handle the construction drawings for the new Naval bases in the Pacific and Atlantic," Bernard Crandell, a journalist with the United Press, wrote as introduction to an interview with the seventy-two year old Detroit architect in March of 1941.[89] In this true assembly line for the production of factory designs (notwithstanding the declarations of Albert Kahn on the need to make speed of execution a top priority), the question of aesthetics remained. Albert Kahn himself, in one of his last interviews, did not fail to make a last clarification on the characteristics of industrial architecture. "Strictest economy must prevail in manufacturing buildings, especially in National Defense projects. Therefore elimination of non-essentials and of everything not purely utilitarian is imperative....Just as the mere clothing of the skeleton of a modern airplane by designers with an eye for line and a sense of fitness produces an object of beauty, so the frank expression of the functional, the structural, element of the industrial building makes for success....Occasionally a client is particularly solicitous about the appearance of his factory, and occasionally it proves difficult to dissuade him from building a classical temple."[90]

On December 8, 1942, six months after having received official recognition from the American Institute of Architects,[91] Albert Kahn died of a bronchial infection. Albert Kahn, Inc., however, was organized so as to be able to continue its activity even after the loss of its founder:[92] the presidency was immediately transferred to Louis, the youngest of the Kahn brothers.

The rest of the work completed during the war period was impressive. In addition to the military bases, the numerous projects included the American Steel Foundries Company plants in East Chicago (Indiana), the American Locomotive Company in Schenectady and Auburn (New York), the Amertorp Corporation in Chicago, the Chrysler Corporation, also in Chicago, as well as plants for the aeronautics industry: the Wright Aeronautical Corporation in Paterson (New Jersey) and Lockland (Ohio), the Consolidated Aircraft Corporation in New Orleans (Louisiana), and Curtiss Wright in Robertson (Missouri), Buffalo (New York), Columbus (Ohio) and Louisville (Kentucky).[93]

The best-known industrial buildings are undoubtably those of Chrysler and Ford, located not very far from Detroit. The Chrysler Corporation Tank Arsenal in Warren was a 158.4 x 420.6 meter (520 x 1,380 feet) rectangle in steel and glass, for the manufacturing of the M-3 and M-4 armored tanks. The Ford Willow Run Bomber plant at Ypsilanti (halfway between the River Rouge plants and the university town of Ann Arbor) was a gigantic structure (960.1 meters—3,150 feet—long, and varies in width from 213.3 meters—700 feet—to 396.2 meters—1,300 feet) completely self-sufficient, and was camouflaged by horizontal development and reduced fenestration. During the war period it produced about 8,500 B-24 bombers, and employed 42,000 workers.[94]

In all, during the war, Albert Kahn Associated, Inc. Architects and Engineers (the name assumed in 1940) designed about two hundred industrial buildings and military bases. Many of the factories built in this period were the famous five-year plants: that is, semi-permanent structures thus called because—as Louis Kahn explained—"five years was the maximum productive expected of them:"[95] a formula already thought-out for the post-war economy. A five-year plant, in fact, did not require excessive investment and its limited life span avoided the problems of overproduction.

following pages:
CURTISS WRIGHT CORPORATION, AIRPLANE DIVISION, ENGINEERING BUILDING INTERIOR: COLUMBUS, OHIO; ALBERT KAHN ASSOCIATED INC., 1940

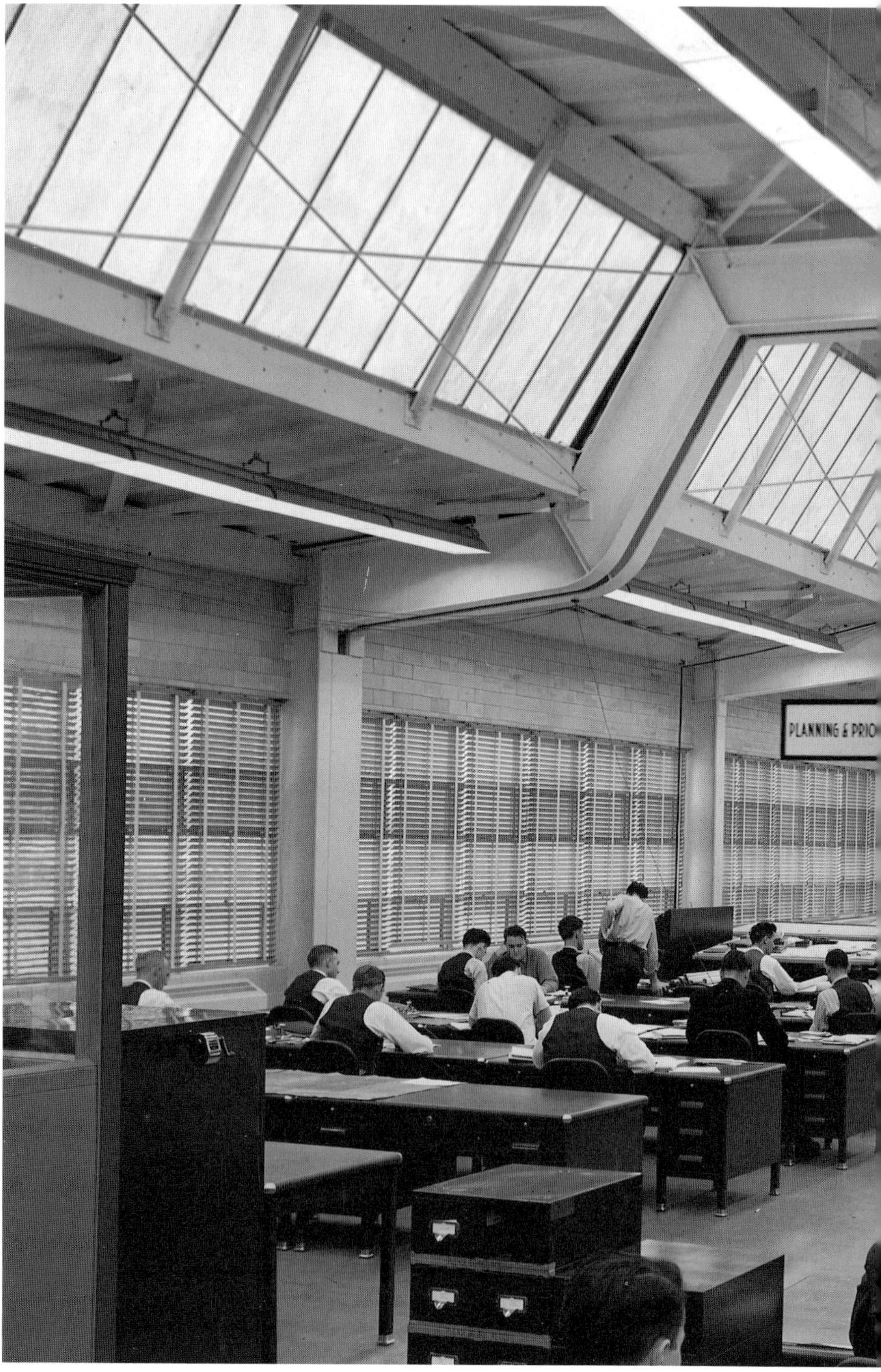
PLANNING & PRIO

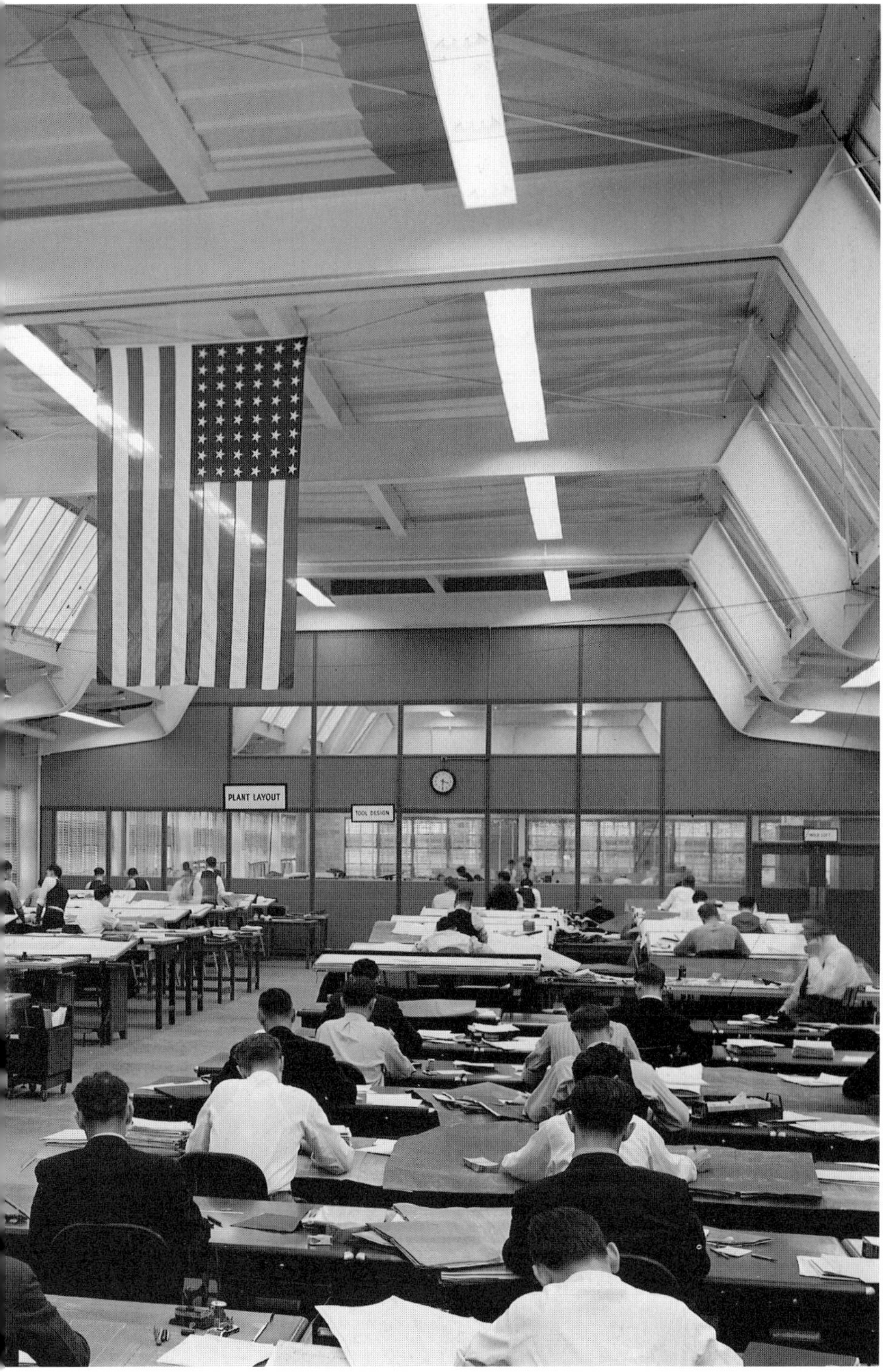
PLANT LAYOUT
TOOL DESIGN

CHRYSLER CORPORATION, JET ENGINE PLANT, TEST CELLS: MACOMB COUNTY, MICHIGAN;
ALBERT KAHN ASSOCIATED INC., 1948

As new president of the company, Louis Kahn, in 1944, was invited to the symposium *New Architecture and City Planning*, organized by Paul Zucker, which signalled a moment of fundamental reflection for the field of American architecture. The importance of the occasion could be measured by the interviews with other famous professionals who were registered: Richard Neutra, George Howe, Kenneth Reid, Serge Chermayeff, Henry Churchill, Jose Louis Sert, Lazlo Moholy-Nagy and, in the session entitled "The Problem of a New Monumentality," Sigfried Giedion, George Nelson and a Philadelphia architect then unknown but destined to occupy a leading role in the history of twentieth-century architecture: Louis Isidore Kahn.[96] The contribution by the homonymous new president of Albert Kahn Associated Inc., later collected in the essay "Industrial Architecture," was interesting because it constituted a synthesized and precise interpretation of the design philosophy carried out by his company, to the point that we can consider this writing the testimony of the firm's experience, as well as the basis on which future activity would be imposed.

In the first phrases of the article, there was a significant clarification on the role of the designer: "The industrial architect who can, by the skill of his physical arrangement of plant facilities and conveniences, lessen the tendency to costly labor dissension and strikes, is performing a needed and valuable service to his client."[97]

To the designer then are assigned precise prerogatives. In the industrial field, the architect is no longer called to "dress" the productive process, or to design the characteristics of an artificial monumentality, but must know how to interpret the wishes of the client so as to define a rational space suitable for rational manufacturing.

The architect "must consider himself an integral part of the organization he serves; he must understand the many and varied problems of the industrialist, and with his specialized skill, ingenuity and planning ability produce not buildings but a unit or series of units which will house a producing organization."[98] This effectively synthesized the direction pursued by Albert Kahn during his entire career; a different direction from the romantic American engineers "simplement guidés per les nécessités d'un programme impératif."[99] The so-called "necessities of an imperative demand" were in fact a complex system of factors which, arising from the translation of the needs of scientific management, was enriched by the relationships with the new theories of human relations and with urban planning.

For Louis Kahn, the factors that ordered the design of industrial buildings ranged from the location to the organization of the layout, from the workshop of the mechanical and electrical plants to the construction of adequate facilities for the workers, and, "last but important," the architectural design.

This was merely a further systematization of an ethic begun by Albert Kahn. The choice of location had to take into consideration the characteristics of the terrain, the foundry yield, and the transportation infrastructure present in the area. The needs of the layout ordered the entire building, creating a "simple, direct flow, in proper sequence, through the various phases of manufacture, assembly, inspection, and possible storage of the finished product before shipment."[100] The layout of the mechanical plants had to guarantee adequate levels of lighting, ventilation and heating within the plant, and the facilities for the workers had to satisfy the "human relations" aspect, as they determined the "psychological effect" of the industrial environment.

Louis Kahn, in conclusion, defined the role of the architect which closely followed one given by Albert in one of his final interviews: "The architectural design of the exterior will be rational, interpreting the function of the building and expressing in architectural proportion the romance of industry. Architectural beauty is largely a matter of proportion and requires no ornament to enhance it....The exterior design must be a direct, frank expression of the function—and straight-forward, as is characteristic in all fields of modern design. It need not be strained and expensive for the mere purpose of obtaining functional appearance, but direct and simple and honest."[101] In 1945, Louis Kahn died, but Albert Kahn Associated, Inc. Architects and Engineers continued to operate on the principles outlined by its founder.[102]

NOTES

1   In its November 1937 issue, *The Architectural Forum* (vol. 68, no. 11) carried an article entitled "Two Factories Which Pose the Question...is Architecture a Two- or a One-Way Street?" which illustrated and compared two types of industrial architecture: the traditional (Leo F. Caproni for Edwards and Co. in Norwalk) and the modern (Albert Kahn's design for General Motors in Linden). On the plant, see "G.M. Will Spend $5,575,000 on New Plant at Linden, N.J.," in *The New York Times*, August 28, 1936, which presented the design, and "General Motors Opens New Plant," in *The New York Times*, May 28, 1937, for a description of the completed work.

2   For a specific discussion on the themes debated in the American architectural community of that period, see T.F. Hamlin, *The American Spirit in Architecture*, Yale University Press, New Haven 1926; T. Tallmadge, *The Story of Architecture in America*, Norton & Co., New York 1927; F. Kimball, *American Architecture*, The Bobbs-Merrill Company, Indianapolis–New York 1928; G.H. Edgell, *The American Architecture of Today*, W.W. Norton and Company, New York 1936; and for a critical examination, dated but still basically accurate, see J. Burchard, A. Bush-Brown, *The Architecture of America. A Social and Cultural History*, Little, Brown and Company, Boston–Toronto 1961.

3   E.W. McMullen, "The Concrete Factory" and H.L. Gilman, "The Design of Industrial Plants," in *The Architectural Forum*, vol. XXXI, no. 1, July 1919, pp. 7–9 and 153–156, respectively. This issue also included some illustrations of Albert Kahn's work.

4   See *The Architectural Forum*, vol. XXXIX, no. 3, September 1923 and vol. LI, no. 3, September 1929.

5   C. Gilbert, "Architecture of Industrial Buildings in Concrete," in *The Architectural Forum*, September 1923, p. 83.

6   Ibid., p. 85.

7   On Cass Gilbert (1859–1934), see J.F. Gilbert, *Cass Gilbert, Reminiscences and Addresses*, Scribner Press, New York 1935; H.F. Withey, E.R. Withey, *Biographical Dictionary of American Architects (Deceased)*, Hennessey & Ingalls, Los Angeles 1956 (reprint 1970), pp. 233–235.

8   H.F. Kellogg, "Co-operation of Architect and Builder in Industrial Building," in *The Architectural Forum*, September 1923, pp. 96–98. On the urban microcosm of Lynn, the "shoe-factory city" where the Kellogg factory is located, see A. Dawley, *Class and Community. The Industrial Revolution in Lynn*, Harvard University Press, Cambridge 1976.

9   See, among the articles in *The Architectural Forum*, September 1929: C. De Moll, "Roof Types for Industrial Buildings," pp. 391–394; H.H. Fox, "Estimating the Costs of Industrial Buildings," pp. 395–398; W.R. Fogg, "Daylight Illumination of Industrial Buildings," pp. 405–410; A.L. Powell, "Artificial Illumination of Industrial Buildings," pp. 415–420.

10 M. Kahn, "Planning of Industrial Buildings," in *The Architectural Forum*, September 1929, pp. 265–272.

11 Ibid., p. 265.

12 Ibid., p. 266.

13 Concerning this subject, see the interesting volume by S. Cheney, *The New World Architecture*, Tudor Publishing Company, New York 1930, which delineates new developments in American architectural culture coming to grips with academic traditions, the national and international affirmation of Wrightian genius and the surfacing of the European avant-garde.

14 See the issues dedicated to banks (June 1928), hospitals (December 1928), churches (March 1928), stores (June 1929), industrial buildings (September 1929), and hotels (December 1929).

15 F.D. Roosevelt, "The Encouraging Economic Factors," in *The Architectural Forum*, vol. LVII, no. 2, August 1932, p. 93.

16 E.J. Russell, "Once More the Master Builder," Ibid., pp. 89–90.

17 F.L. Wright, "Caravel or Motorship?" Ibid., p. 90.

18 R.B. Fuller, "The Architect's Future is Now," Ibid., p. 92–93.

19 W.O. Ludlow, "To Organize, to Direct, to Design," Ibid., p. 91.

20 A. Kahn, "Federal Aid to the Social Welfare," Ibid., p. 94.

21 A. Kahn, "Architect Pioneers in Development of Industrial Buildings," in *The Anchora of Delta Gamma*, vol. LIII, no. 4, May 1937, p. 378.

22 A. Kahn, *Article on Industrial Architecture for Collier Encyclopedia*, typewritten, August 1931, (AKA), in part published in the entry "Factory Building," in *National Encyclopedia*, Collier and Sons, New York 1932.

23 Ibid., typewritten, pp. 5–6.

24 Ibid., p. 6.

25 Ibid., p. 11.

26 Le Corbusier, *Vers une Architecture*, 1923, Vincent, Fréal & C., Paris 1958, p. 20.

27 An affirmation maintained in A. Kahn, *Putting Architecture On a Business Basis*, text for the Cleveland Engineering Society conference held on December 15, 1930, typewritten (AKA).

28 Albert Kahn Engineering Corporation, *Layout Design of the Modern Brewery for Economical Production*, Detroit, undated [1933] (AKA); another manual by Albert Kahn Engineering Corporation is *Power Houses for Industrial Plants*, Detroit, 1932 (AKA).

29 On brewery architecture, see L. Utz, E.N. Campazzi, *Fabbricati ed impianti industriali moderni. Costruzione dei fabbricati. Distribuzione dei locali e del macchinario*, Hoepli, Milan 1926.

30 Albert Kahn Engineering Corporation, *Layout Design of the Modern Brewery for Economical Production*, unnumbered.

31 "Industrial Buildings. Albert Kahn, Inc.," in *The Architectural Forum*, vol. 69, no. 2. August 1938. This issue also contains numerous advertisements for the most famous American industrial companies. The ads glorify Kahn: "Albert Kahn, one of the greatest names in modern industrial architecture," (General Electric) or "Albert Kahn, the most famous factory designer in the world," while other advertising pages do not fail to mention that "Albert Kahn isn't just Big Business; he's also Big Architecture."

32 G. Nelson, *Industrial Architecture of Albert Kahn, Inc.*, Architectural Book Publishing Company, New York, 1939.

33 "Albert Kahn Featured in Architectural Forum," in *Weekly Bulletin of the Michigan Society of Architects*, vol. 12, no. 33, August 16, 1938, pp. 1, 5–6.

34 See *The Architectural Forum*, August 1938, pp. 97–101; "Lady Esther," in *The Glass Packer*, April 1939 and for the heating system, see F.O. Jordan, "One-Pipe Hot Water Plant for Modern Cosmetic Factory," in *Heating & Ventilation*, July 1938.

35 In *The Architectural Forum*, August 1938, p. 101.

36 For some historical delineations of industrial architecture, see C.L.M. (C.L. Banderslice Meeks),

H.M.M. (H.M. Millon): entry "Industrial Architecture," in *Encyclopedia Britannica*, vol. 12, Chicago–London 1963, pp. 288–290, which points out the "magnificent factories constructed in the United States by Albert Kahn" (p. 289); J.F. Munce, *Industrial Architecture*, F.W. Dodge Corp., New York 1960; J. Winter, *Industrial Architecture. A Survey of Factory Building*, Studio Vista, London 1970; O.W. Grube, *Industrial Buildings and Factories*, Praeger Publishers, New York 1971.

37 On this construction, see *Dodge Half-Ton Truck Plant, Detroit, Michigan*, typewritten, undated (AKA); "Chrysler to Build New Truck Plant Costing $2,500,000," in *Automotive Daily News*, August 21, 1937; "Dodge Truck Plant Opened," in *Iron Age*, November 3, 1938; "Dodge Completes Truck Plant in $6,000,000 Expansion," in *Michigan Manufacturer and Financial Record*, November 5, 1938; "Dodge Truck Division of Chrysler Corporation, Detroit," in *Factory Management and Maintenance*, April 1939; "Quarter-Mile-Long Assembly and Export Plant for Dodge Half-Ton Trucks," in *The Architectural Forum*, June 1939.

38 E. Mock (ed.), *Built in USA. 1932–1944*, The Museum of Modern Art, New York 1944, pp. 95 and 96. The same Mies had expressed admiration for Kahn's factories. As for Mies's design for the museum of a small city, Franz Schulze writes: "a photograph...captured his attention... The photo showed the interior of the Martin Bomber Plant near Baltimore, designed for the war effort by the American Albert Kahn. It was an immense space whose freedom from all interior supports depended on ranks of huge overhead trusses that spanned the entire room. One can imagine easily enough what Mies found to admire in it. It was an exercise in raw structure, not necessarily refined—Kahn was a no-nonsense builder of factories without frills—but clearly indicative of the unique capacity of modern engineering in steel to enclose a stupendous space. Steel technology might fulfill his deepest yearning for an architecture at once monumental yet dematerialized—in his much-quoted phrase *beinahe nichts* (almost nothing)—robustly structural yet, or thus, spatially most free. In its immensity, moreover, the space was maximally generalized, allowing a variety of specific functions to be acted out within it wherever or for as long as they seemed appropriate. The bomber plant, in short, was the essence of building, a limpid display of the grammar of an expressive language which, as Mies liked to put it, could be assembled into prose or elevated into poetry. Mies elected to design a serious project based on the photograph. He conceived the installation of a concert hall in the great Kahn factory space. Using his familiar collage-montage technique, he proposed a number of arrangements of wall and ceiling planes, horizontal and vertical, flat and curved, standing and hanging, all meant to define a space within the larger space, where groups of people could attend musical performances." F. Schulze, *Mies van der Rohe. A Critical Biography*, The University of Chicago Press, Chicago-London 1985, p. 231.

39 *The Architectural Forum*, August 1938, p. 112.

40 Ibid., p. 128. The photograph of the building was published in the article "Designed by Detroit Architect," in *The Detroit News*, April 3, 1938, with this caption: "these are not the ruins of some ancient temple, but a modern industrial building designed by Albert Kahn, Inc."

41 Fordlandia, 12,000 square kilometers acquired in 1927 from the Brazilian government, and Belterra were opened in 1934, close to which would be created an actual urban community. For Ford's Brazilian venture, see the brochure *The Ford Rubber Plantations*, Ford Motor Company, undated [1940]; V. Forbin, *Le caoutchouc dans le monde*, Payot, Paris 1943, pp. 117–185.

42 "Automobile Press Shop at Detroit," in *Engineering News Record*, October 26, 1939, p. 78. See also *Ford Press Shop*, typewritten, undated (AKA).

43 *The Architectural Forum*, August 1938: the quotes are taken from the texts on p. 97 and following pages.

44 "American to Build Soviet Auto Plants," in *The New York Times*, May 7, 1929.

45 "America's Best Brains Develop the New Russia," in *The New York Evening Post*, June 1, 1929.

46 See D.G. Dalrympe, "The American Tractor Comes to Soviet Agriculture: the Transfer of a Technology," in *Technology and Culture*, vol. V, no. 2, Summer 1964, pp. 191–214.

47 Roth's articles on the Soviet Union were published in the posthumous collection *Reise in Russland*, in *Joseph Roth Werke*, Kiepenheuer & Witsch, Köln 1976, vol. III.

48 See E.H. Carr, R.W. Davies, *A History of Soviet Russia. Foundations of a Planned Economy 1926–1929*, vol. I, MacMillan, London 1969.

49 "$1,900,000 Building by the Soviets in 1930," in *The New York Times*, January 11, 1930.

50 "Architects to Russia," in *Time*, January 12, 1930.

51 From the list of contracts and concessions between the USA and the USSR on January 1931 (quoted by F.A. Southard, Jr., *American Industry in Europe*, Houghton Mifflin Company, Boston–New York 1931): "Austin Company: Technical assistance in construction of the Nizhni Novgorod automobile plant...Ford Motor Company: Technical assistance in the construction and operation of the production of the Nizhni Novgorod automobile factory. Calls for purchase of $30 million of Ford cars and parts within four years; technical cooperation for nine years; building of 100,000 car factory at Nizhni Novgorod...Albert Kahn, Inc.: Designing of buildings for the Stalingrad tractor factory (40,000 capacity); also contract to render general consultation services to Supreme Economic Council as architects on industrial construction." pp. 203–204. More detailed information on these contracts are carried in *Handbook of the Soviet Union*, American-Russian Chamber of Commerce, New York 1936, pp. 375–376. Generally on the work of American technicians in Russia until the 1930s, see A.C. Sutton, *Western Technology and Soviet Economic Development*, Hoover Institution Press, Stanford University, Stanford 1968 (vol. I: *1917–1939*) and 1971 (vol. II: *1930–1945*). For references on technical magazines of that period which highlight the role of Albert Kahn, see "Detroit Engineers Direct Soviet Industrial Revival," in *Michigan Manufacturer and Financial Record*, April 19, 1930; A.L. Drabkin, "American Architects and Engineers in Russia," in *Pencil Points. The American Architect*, June 1930, (typewritten, AKA).

52 On the Stalingrad plant, see "The Stalingrad Tractor Plant," in *The Economic Review of the Soviet Union*, April 1, 1930, pp. 134–135. Also see the untitled typewritten record signed by Louis Kahn and dated February 7, 1944 (AKA).

53 H.R. Knickerbocker, *The Soviet Five-Year Plan and Its Effects on World Trade*, London 1931, It. trans. *Il piano quinquennale sovietico*, Bompiani, Milan 1932, p. 57. We have to consider these dimensions approximative, because we have not been able to find the original text.

54 A. Kahn, *Putting Architecture on a Business Basis*, typewritten, p. 24. For the part of this conference where Kahn speaks specifically about work in Russia, see also *Weekly Bulletin of the Michigan Society of Architects*, January 13, 1931, p. 2.

55 "World Revolt Ultimate Aim," in *Border Cities Star*, November 5, 1931.

56 "Kahn Firm Gives Reply," in *Border Cities Star*, November 9, 1931.

57 "Kahn Breaks With Soviets," in *The New York Times*, March 26, 1932.

58 Quoted in "Albert Kahn Memorial Issue," in *Weekly Bulletin of the Michigan Society of Architects*, vol. 17, no. 13, March 30, 1943, p. 91. On the work of European architects in Russia, see AA.VV., *Socialismo, città, architettura. Urrs 1917–1937. Il contributo degli architetti europei*, Officina, Rome 1976. The most complete study on the work of foreign architects in Russia is A. Kopp, *Foreign Architects in the Soviet Union During the Two First Five Year Plans*, Kennan Institute for Advanced Russian Studies, Woodrow Wilson International Center for Scholars, Colloquium Paper, May 14, 1987 (typewritten). For Albert Kahn's role, see pp. 44–57.

59 On the role of Albert Kahn, see M. Wilkins, F.E. Hill, *American Business Abroad. Ford on Six Continents*, Wayne State University Press, Detroit 1964, p. 220, and for a detailed analysis, based mainly on documents from the Ford Motor Company Archives, of Ford's relations with the Soviet Union in the 1920s and 1930s, see pp. 208–227. For Ford's Soviet adventure in general, see A. Nevins, F.E. Hill, *Ford. Expansion and Challenge 1915–1933*, Charles Scribner's Sons, New York 1957, pp. 673–684 (Appendix I. The Russian Adventures). Most helpful is P.G. Filene, *Americans and the Soviet experiment, 1917–1933*, Harvard University Press, Cambridge 1967, pp. 120–127.

60 See M. DeMichelis, E. Pasini, *La città sovietica 1925–1937*, Marsilio, Venice 1976, pp. 67–68.

61 The program for Niznij Novgorod—Autostroy, or Austingrad, as it was called in honor of the American company—provided for the construction of a residential community, schools, an "industrial kitchen," a cultural center, large department stores, a sports club, a movie theater, a library and a stadium. It was a city in the country, with water, sewer and electrical systems (novelties for the Soviet Union in the 1930s). The urban plan by the Cleveland firm provided a principal axis that led out of the city through the industrial zone. Directly off this street was a large plaza on which sat the Soviet House, the Cultural Palace, the Museum, the Hospital, the Hotel and the urban administration seat. Not far away was the athletic area and an avenue that led to the Volga River where a small port was planned. The city grid was geometrically developed on a checkerboard with cul de sacs, and the housing areas were located in rectangular lots. See Nikanorov, ["The Yard of Niznij Novgorod Automobile Plant,"] in *Revoljucija i kul'tura*, no. 1, 1930, for the Soviet plan; and M. Greif, *The New Industrial Landscape. The Story of the Austin Company*, The Main Street Press, Clinton, N.J., 1978, pp. 97–102 for the design by the American technicians.

62 J. Stalin, "Discorso pronunciato nel Palazzo del Cremlino il 4 maggio 1935 agli allievi dell'Accademia dell'Armata Rossa, in occasione della loro promozione," in *Lo Stato Operaio*, IX, no. 6, June 1935, p. 342. See also "A Conversation Between Stalin and Wells," in *The New Statesman and Nation*, October 27, 1934, pp. 601–603.

63 On this period of American history, the best source is still the chapter dedicated to Franklin Delano Roosevelt in R. Hofstadter, *The American Political Tradition and the Men Who Made It*, Knopf, New York 1951.

64 See D.P. Handlin, *American Architecture*, Thames and Hudson, London 1985, p. 194.

65 F.L. Wright, *An Autobiography*, New York 1943, Faber & Faber, London 1946, p. 311.

66 A. Kahn, *A Century of Progress*, typewritten, May 31, 1933 (AKA).

67 A. Kahn, *A Description of General Motors Exhibition Bldg. Century of Progress Exposition, Chicago*, typewritten and sent to the Publicity Department of General Motors, undated (AKA). See also F.E. Wilbur, "General Motors Building. A Century of Progress, Chicago 1933," in *Building Arts & Constructor*, September 1933.

68 "A House of Glass To Mark Automotive World," in *The Detroit News*, April 14, 1933. The building was featured in the same newspaper on May 21, 1932 in an article entitled "How General Motors Building at Chicago World's Fair Will Look," which showed two drawings of the building without the tower. The clipping of this article, conserved in AKA, carries a pen correction in which the tower has been inserted.

69 A. Kahn, *Speech Given at Illinois Society of Architects Chicago. March 20, 1934*, typewritten, (AKA).

70 On this project, see A. Kahn Inc., "Ford Exposition Building. Century of Progress," in *The Architectural Forum*, vol. LXI, no. 1, July 1934, pp. 2–10; A. Kahn, "A Pageant of Beauty," in *The Architectural Forum*, vol. LIX, no. 1, 1933, p. 26; L. Kirstein, "A Century of Progress. 1833–1934," in *The Nation*, June 20, 1934; "Ford To Have a Fair Building," in *The Detroit News*, February 14, 1934; M. McDowell, "Mile-High Torch, 200 Feet Through, To Be Thrill at Fair," in *The Chicago Tribune*, April 18, 1934; "Henry Ford's New Exhibit at World's Fair," in

Border Cities Star, May 16, 1934. The building was also advertised in Europe. See "Exposition de Chicago 1934. Batiment Ford. Albert Kahn, Architecte," in *La Construction Moderne*, annal 50, no. 4, October 28, 1934, p. 82, and "Rivista delle riviste. La Construction moderne, October 28, 1934," in *Rassegna di Architettura*, VI, no. 4, 1934, p. 510.

71   Hugh Ferris, an architect who specialized in futuristic perspectives, elaborated on previously designed projects (see H. Ferris, *The Metropolis of Tomorrow*, I. Washburn, New York 1929) and contributed his graphic skills to the best American architects (see H. Ferris, *Power in Buildings. An Artist's View of Contemporary Architecture*, Columbia University Press, New York 1953 which included a view of Albert Kahn's design for the Ohio Steel Foundry in Lima, Ohio). For a critical evaluation of Ferris's work, see M. Tafuri, "La montagna disincantata. Il grattacielo e la City," in G. Ciucci, F. Dal Co, M. Manieri-Elia, M. Tafuri, *La città americana dalla guerra civile al New Deal*, Laterza, Bari 1973, pp. 482–488.

72   On the transport of the building from Chicago to Dearborn, see: "Ford To Move Exhibit Here," in *The Detroit News*, November 22, 1934; "Ford Rotunda Open Saturday," in *The Detroit Free Press*, May 15, 1936. The Rotunda Building became a monumental entrance for visitors to the River Rouge plants. On this there is an interesting typewritten note by Albert Kahn on the Rotunda building from July 19, 1938 (AKA), carrying the following handwritten dedication: "for Mr. Giuseppe de Finetti, architect of Milan, Italy." In 1953, on the fiftieth anniversary of the foundation of the company, the Ford Company commissioned Richard B. Fuller to build a geodesic dome to protect the building, which was adapted to Albert Kahn's construction. See R.W. Marks, *The Dymaxion World of Buckminster Fuller*, Reinhold Publishing Corporation, New York 1960, pp. 58, 192–193.

73   On the Paris Exposition of 1937, see M. Tafuri, F. Dal Co, *Architettura contemporanea*, Electa, Milan 1988, p. 233.

74   See "Americans Get 41 First Prizes For Paris Exposition Exhibits," in *The New York Times*, June 21, 1937; "France Honors Detroiter," in *The Detroit News*, June 21, 1937.

75   A. Kahn, (record of the 1937 Paris Exposition), typewritten, April 3, 1938 (AKA), p. 3.

76   For a critical evaluation of Harrison's work, see V. Newhouse, *Wallace K. Harrison, Architect*, Rizzoli International, New York 1989.

77   L.C. Olivieri (ed.), *Documenti di architettura. Composizione e tecnica moderna. Mostre, esposizioni*, Vallardi, Milan 1954, p. 153.

78   For the New York Fair in general, see R. Wurts, S. Appelbaum, *The New York World's Fair. 1939–1940*, Dover Publications Inc., New York 1977. On the Ford Pavilion see "Ford Motor Company," in *The Architectural Forum*, vol. 70, no. 6, June 1939, pp. 412–413 (issue dedicated to the New York Fair); "Ford Building for N.Y. Fair," in *The Detroit News*, April 23, 1938 and "Elevated Highway To Be Fair Feature," in *The New York Times*, April 23, 1938. On Teague's role, see C.W. Ditchy, "Teague Traces Exhibit Trends," in *Weekly Bulletin of Michigan Society of Architects*, November 29, 1938 which underlines the architectural service of Albert Kahn, Inc. On the General Motors Pavilion, see "General Motors," in *The Architectural Forum*, June 1939, pp. 406–409 which indicated Norman Bel Geddes as designer and Albert Kahn, Inc. as architects; "General Motors Building at New York World's Fair," in *Monthly Bulletin of the Michigan Society of Architects*, July 1938; "General Motors Executives Look Over Model of Exhibit Building for Fair," in *The New York Herald Tribune*, July 24, 1938; G.M. Slocum, "Highways and Horizons!" in *Automotive News*, April 29, 1939; "General Motors Exhibit Voted Most Popular," in *Pearl River Searchlight*, June 23, 1939 which specified roles: "N.B. Geddes designed the exhibit. Albert Kahn is the architect;" "Motor Exhibit At Fair Begun," in *The New York Sun*, August 22, 1939, which covers the opening of the exhibit. In practice, as had already happened for other projects, Albert Kahn availed himself of Norman Bel Geddes's contribution to "dress" the building. On Norman Bel Geddes's work (his real name was Norman Melancton Geddes, born 1893, Adrian, Michigan, died 1958, New York), see N. Bel Geddes, *Horizons in*

Industrial Design, 1932, Dover Publications Inc., New York 1977.

79   M. Tafuri, F. Dal Co, *Architettura contemporanea*, p. 210.

80   See C.B. Coates, "The Industrial Town of Tomorrow," in *Factory Management and Maintenance*, no. 9, September 1939, pp. 38–48. For a critical evaluation of the General Motors Pavilion's role in the history of American urban design, see M. Scott, *American City Planning Since 1890*, University of California Press, Berkeley–Los Angeles–London 1969, pp. 361–365.

81   See A.K. [Albert Kahn], "Plants To Keep Peace with Clippers," in *Scientific American*, August 1938; and on the plants, see F.O. Jordan, "Factory Building with Three-Story Door Heated Without Boilers," in *Heating and Ventilating*, December 1938.

82   "Airplane Factory Built in Eleven Weeks," in *Engineering News Record*, June 22, 1939. Also highlighting the speed of the construction: R. Barnes, "Aerial Plant Sets Record," *The Detroit News*, April 14, 1939 and "Martin Finishes Plant Addition in 11 Weeks," in *Construction*, June 5, 1939.

83   "Producer of Production Lines," in *The Architectural Forum*, June 1942, now also in K. Reid (ed.), *Industrial Buildings*, F.W. Dodge Corporation, New York 1951, p. 257.

84   A. Kahn. "Consequence of the Participation by Government…in the Preparation of Plans and the Carrying Out of Building Operations," in *Weekly Bulletin of the Michigan Society of Architects*, vol. 15, no. 38, September 23, 1941.

85   "Industrial Buildings. A Building Types Study," in *The Architectural Forum*, January 1942, now also in K. Reid (ed.) *Industrial Buildings*, p. 45.

86   A. Kahn, *Article on Windowless Factories*, typewritten, April 11, 1941 (AKA), p. 2.

87   A. Kahn. "Architecture in the National Defense Building Program," in *Weekly Bulletin of the Michigan Society of Architects*, December 30, 1941, p. 51.

88   A. Kahn, "Industrial Plants for Defense," Ibid., p. 61.

89   *Interview by Bernard Crandell United Press Staff Correspondent*, typewritten, March 17, 1941 (AKA), p. 2.

90   A. Kahn. "Architects of Defense," in *The Atlantic Monthly*, March 1942, pp. 359–360.

91   The Special Medal was presented on the occasion of the 74th Congress of the American Institute of Architects held in Detroit on June 24, 1942. See "Address of Mr. Albert Kahn, F.A.I.A.," in *Weekly Bulletin of the Michigan Society of Architects*, vol. 16, no. 28, July 14, 1942 (which contains the text of Albert Kahn's speech).

92   Among the most important obituaries, see P. Cret, "Albert Kahn," in *The Octagon. A Journal of the A.I.A.*, February 1943, p. 15–16; "A Great Architect Has Gone," in *Weekly Bulletin of the Michigan Society of Architects*, vol. 16, no. 50, December 15, 1942; "Albert Kahn 1869–1942," in *The Architectural Forum*, January 1943, p. 36; "Albert Kahn Architect 1869–1942," in *The Architectural Record*, January 1943, pp. 14–15. Among other testimonies there is also a letter from the Royal Institute of British Architects, dated February 2, 1943 (AKA) which communicated the intention of offering Kahn Honorary Corresponding Membership.

93   For works on the war period in general, see K. Reid (ed.), *Industrial Buildings*, and "Albert Kahn Memorial Issue." In particular, for individual projects, see *Curtiss-Wright Corporation. Columbus Plant*, typewritten, April 1, 1942 (AKA); "Building for Defense…A Propeller Plant in 68 Days," in *The Architectural Forum*, May 1941; "Naval Ordinance. The Amertorp Corporation," in *Factory Management and Maintenance*, vol. 102, no. 4, April 1944; "Mass Production Airplane Plant," in *The Architectural Forum*, June 1942.

94   See C.K. Hyde, *Detroit: An Industrial History Guide*, Detroit Historical Society, Detroit, undated [1980], pp. 26–27, site 1 (Tank Arsenal) and site 46 (Willow Run). In particular, on the Ford

plant at Ypsilanti, see "Ford Bomber Plant," in "Albert Kahn Memorial Issue," pp. 75–103.

95   L. Kahn, "Don't Let War Plants Scare You," in *Nation's Business*, April 1944, p. 27.

96   See S. Giedion, "Monumentality," and L.I. Kahn, "The Need For a New Monumentality," both in P. Zucker (ed.), *New Architecture and City Planning*, Philosophical Library, New York 1944.

97   L. Kahn, "The Future of Industrial Architecture," Ibid., pp. 13–14.

98   Ibid., p. 20.

99   Le Corbusier, *Vers une Architecture*, p. 28.

100   L. Kahn, "The Future of Industrial Architecture," p. 18.

101   Ibid., p. 28.

102   For an in-depth look at the works of Albert Kahn, Inc. beginning with the postwar period, see *Architecture by Albert Kahn Associated Architects and Engineers, Inc.*, Architectural Catalog Company, New York, 1948; "Industrial Buildings by Albert Kahn Associates," in *The Architectural Forum*, vol. 96, no. 2, February 1952, pp. 85–98 (part I) and vol. 96, no. 3, March 1952, pp. 149–160 (part II); W.B. Sanders, "Albert Kahn Associates 1942–1970," in *The Legacy of Albert Kahn*, Detroit Institute of Arts, Detroit 1970, pp. 137–149.

TEMPOS AND METHODS OF THE CREATIVE PROCESS
Scientific Management of Design Work

The design process of Albert Kahn, Inc. in the field of manufacturing plants was founded on a series of suppositions based on a constant relationship with large industries, in which the privileged contact with the Fordist experience was decisive. These exchanges, from which Kahn gained ideas for specific and autonomous elaborations and design management, offered a basis for a "Fordization" of the firm itself and for its projects as well.

As Henry-Russell Hitchcock wrote: "Albert Kahn took the lead around 1905, in developing a type of subdivision and flow of work in his office in Detroit comparable to the new methods of mass-production that his motor-car factories were specifically designed to facilitate."[1]

There are numerous articles in which, sometimes only obliquely, Albert Kahn spoke of the need to organize design work according to the principles of scientific management. These articles provide an outline of the essential elements of Kahn's ideas on organizational problems: most helpful is the text of the conference, entitled "Putting Architecture on a Business Basis," held at the Cleveland Engineering Society on December 15, 1930.[2] Through a series of observations, which, as was his custom, he pulled from his own experience, Kahn defined the tasks of the different professional figures involved in the construction of an industrial building. His objective was to demonstrate that mass industrial building problems could be resolved adequately only by resorting to team work and scientific management.

Referring neither to Taylorism nor to the assembly line, but not forgetting the habitual homage to Henry Ford, Albert Kahn talked of professional profiles and the specific functions of the technicians involved in designing an industrial building, often implying the possibility of translating his considerations into more general terms.

First, he spoke of the work of the architect: "The architect qualified to handle the problems of today must be a combination of many parts, and, as I recently read, must, like the conductor of a well organized orchestra, assume leadership in directing groups of men to produce concerted and harmonious results. Even thirty years ago, there were comparatively few firms employing more than fifty assistants. Today, we have numerous firms with hundreds of employees. Their practice must necessarily be managed with proper system and on a business basis.... There is no place here for the temperamental artist, the clear-headed business man must have charge. Don't misunderstand me—this clear-headed businessman-architect must not be devoid of artistic training or ability, for this must ever be the corner stone of the profession."[3]

Kahn proposed, then, an architect capable of directing a group of collaborators. The most significant collaboration was with the engineer, who concerned himself with the manufacturing processes, the structure and the mechanical plants. "The modern industrial building, as well, owes much of its success to the engineer, for to him is assigned the task of providing the network of mechanical veins and arteries of a modern structure nearly as complex as in the human body."[4]

Also essential to the construction sector is the contractor, who is responsible for ensuring that everything is implemented correctly in the actual construction of the building. Albert Kahn further specified the skills of the coordinator/designer. In order to establish a correct relationship with the various tasks, the architect—or better, a group of designers—had to be prepared to furnish detailed designs and instructions (to avoid delays and misunderstandings), pay attention to costs, insurance and payroll, oversee the phases of the construction, and provide inspection and assistance on the worksite.

Lastly, but most importantly, there was the client. For Albert Kahn, relationships with the client called for the observation of precise rules, as well as the mobilization of specific skills in areas of "building laws and restrictions, land values, the possible return on contemplated investments, the best methods of financing projects—in short, they like to confer with architects much as they would with their bankers."[5] In particular, designers of industrial buildings had to demonstrate "sincerity, honest frankness, openmindedness, common sense and aptitude to grasp requirements, directness and willingness to consider and accept the owner's point of view," in order to establish "a proper relationship."[6]

All this, according to Kahn, could be obtained only in a structure that included a designer, urban planners, and civil and mechanical engineers; an organization in which the teamwork of diverse collaborators, motivated by adequate salaries, was essential. In reality, such a conception meant a radical transformation of the internal relationships in a large professional firm.

Early on, Kahn realized the need to bring to his technicians not only the methods of mass industry, but also a very advanced system of direct participation in the profits of the company. Well beyond the traditional methods of incentives, he had made the decision to make his colleagues co-participants in the economic vicissitudes of the company, guaranteeing them both a certain percentage of the profits proportional to their responsibilities, and a life insurance policy redeemable every five years, as well as personalized bonuses according to the merits acquired in each specific job.

The results were favorable and Albert Kahn, in the article "Architectural Trend," published in 1931, declared the end of the era "of the individualist, the temperamental artist," replacing this figure with "the collective efforts of groups of men cooperating under proper direction."[7] This outlined a new role in the design field: a corporate structure exactly like the firm of Albert Kahn, Inc.

At this point, Kahn had synthesized the stages of growth of the company between 1918, the year in which Albert Kahn, Inc. was founded, and 1940, the year in which twenty-five of its oldest employees became associates of the company, thus creating Albert Kahn Associated Architects and Engineers Incorporated.

A brochure entitled "Albert Kahn Organization," published in 1942, presented the participants in this new proprietary organization.[8] In addition to the president, Albert Kahn, and the administrator, his brother Louis, there were the architects: Henry F. Altminks, William C. Bunce, Frederic A. Fairbrother, David Fettes, Joseph N. French, John Schurman, George K. Scrymgeour, Le Roy Lewis, Jr., Robert W. Hubel and Norman A. Robinson; the mechanical engineers: Frederick K. Boomhower, Saul Saulson, Paul Preuthun, Chester T. Roe, Sheldon Marston, Hubert E. Sloman, G.S. Whittaker and Herbert E. Ziel; and the structural engineers: O.L. Canfield, Edwin H. Eardley, John T.N. Hoyt, Joseph Matte, Jr., Robert E. Linton, George H. Miehls and Offer Preuthun.

The list of names and hiring dates[9] gave a good idea both of the managerial dimension of the firm from its first years of activity, as well as the contribution of the future associates. The size of the space in which the designing took place, the organizational scheme, and the image promoted by the company itself, all furnish additional information.

This last aspect had particular interest both for the foresight and the surprising timeliness of the initiative. It was Albert Kahn who concerned himself with the firm's public image, using systems that were applied in the public relations offices of large industrial companies. There were "communication bulletins," which, once a design was finished or a building was constructed, were sent to the daily newspapers of the city or to architecture magazines.[10] In the case of designs, Albert Kahn also sent a sketch done in his own hand to better publicize the work. One of the first testimonies of this attention to relations outside of the firm had to do with "the first office building of reinforced concrete in Detroit," constructed by the Trussed Concrete Steel Company (Julius Kahn's company) and published, still during the construction phase, by *The Detroit News Tribune* on January 27, 1907.[11]

Albert Kahn transferred his firm's offices to this building, where they remained until 1918, when the newly formed Albert Kahn, Inc. occupied the top floor of the Marquette Building. For these new headquarters of the company, there was an illustrated description appearing in the columns of *The Architectural Forum*. The text, by G.C. Baldwin, described the different work spaces. "In addition to execu-

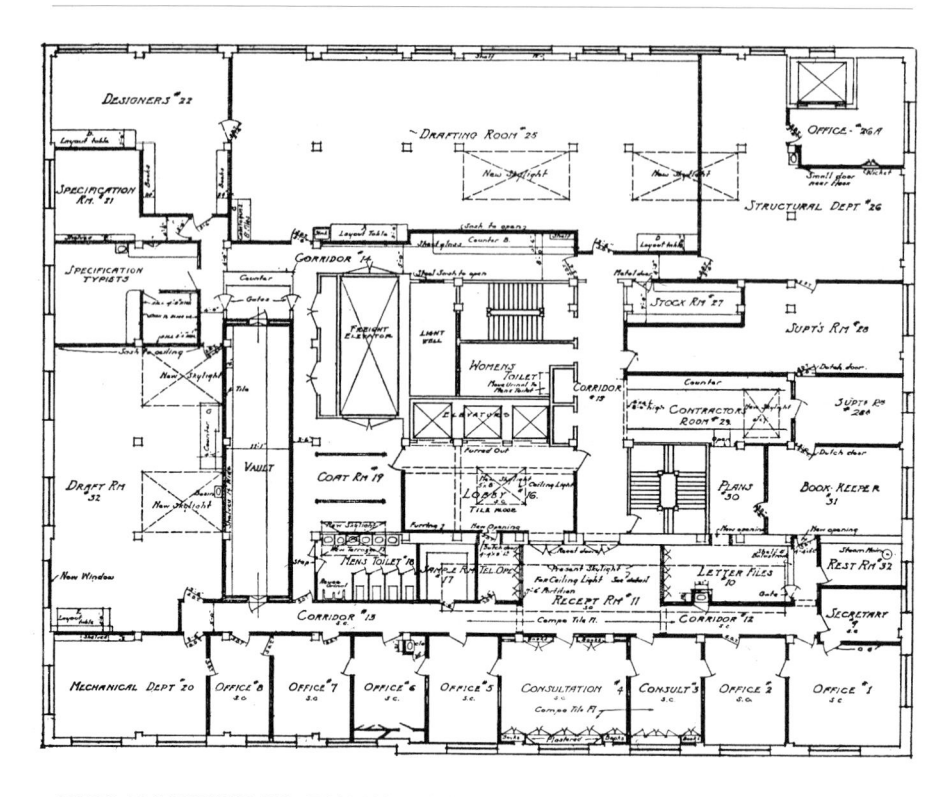

OFFICES OF ALBERT KAHN, INC., FLOOR PLAN: MARQUETTE BUILDING, DETROIT, MICHIGAN; 1918

tive and administrative offices, an atrium, corridors, underground passageways, facilities, sample rooms, dressing rooms, meeting rooms and a library, there are two large design rooms. There are also separate rooms for the mechanical and structural engineers, one area for design, two areas for specific technicians, one for the compilers of these specifics, a separate room for the typists, offices for the head superintendent and for the field superintendent, a room for the estimators, and two places for filing the contracts and correspondence. The offices for the executives and the meeting room are arranged along one side of the building, the design rooms along the other. The mechanical engineering and the structural engineering departments are situated in opposite corners.... The superintendents' offices are arranged in two groups on both sides of the meeting room. The hallways that serve them are floored with artificial, sound-proof tiles.... The designers' rooms are separated by clear glass divisions. The offices are enclosed by walls, and every office is equipped with a telephone for the city, an internal telephone, and an intercom."[12]

No differently than the factories, the space used for intellectual work was designed for maximum productivity. These principles, on which the arrangement of the firm depended, were believed to create the optimal environmental conditions for the maximization of energies and labor skills of the employees.

Every phase of the design was done in a specific place, conveniently laid out and equipped according to the principles inherent in many of Kahn's productions: functionalist essentials for the production departments, and echoes of classicism for the administration and the theorists.

The highest level of rationalization of labor manifested itself in the internal communications. Requests for materials, payments, daily relations between the department heads, and timetables for the designers were done by means of cards, notes, flyers and lists. All used the same form, but in different colors according to the procedure.

The daily control of productivity was quite rigorous. "Every department of the firm," wrote Baldwin, "had a graph of their work. At the beginning, the projected progress is indicated in a system of coordinates with a black curve; the actual progress of the moment is instead marked, day by day, in red. Every divergence between these two curves indicates a serious delay and a daily inspection makes possible an immediate provision to remedy it."[13]

After the First World War, in a special rating compiled annually by *The Architectural Forum*, relative to the total value of constructions designed, Albert Kahn, Inc. was in first place in America. The firm boasted a relative design activity that, in 1919, reached a value of twenty-three million dollars. This was quite an impressive statistic, considering that a medium-sized factory could cost from five thousand to one million dollars, and that the entire value of construction activity in the city of Chicago in the preceding year was about thirty-five million dollars.[14]

Such a volume of activity was possible due to the great number of persons assigned to managerial and executive positions. In 1927, commenting on an interview with Albert Kahn on the subject of an architect's work in industrial constructions, a journalist with the magazine *Management* observed that "The Albert Kahn organization now comprises around 250 people, including architects, structural engineers, mechanical engineers, and about 40 outside superintendents."[15]

In 1931, the company changed headquarters, and relocated to the New Center Building (now the Albert Kahn Building), in the new business center of Detroit, next to two other office buildings constructed by Albert Kahn: the General Motors Building and the Fisher Building, of 1922 and 1928–1929, respectively.[16]

The size of the firm increased with the volume of business. "In normal times the firm of Albert Kahn, Inc.," wrote George Nelson in 1939, "employs about 400 men and women; among them some 40 secretaries, stenographers, typists and file clerks;

about 15 accountants; 80–90 mechanical and electrical engineers; 40–50 field superintendents; some 30 specification writers, estimators, expeditors, etc.; 175 architectural designers and draftsmen."[17]

Both the increased concentration of employees and Kahn's method of controlling the entire process of conceptualization, construction and implementation of the industrial buildings, are clear indications of his affinity with the tenets of Fordism. The management of labor was decidedly Fordist. All the stages of conception and production of the project were ordered by a precise diagram that organized the work in a complex interdisciplinary procedure,[18] articulated in the specific skills of the two sectors that constituted the axis of the company: the Technical Division and the Executive Division.

The Technical Division, further divided into four departments, was responsible for the design of the buildings. The design department prepared the executive designs, the architectural department provided the stylistic definition of the buildings according to whether the structure was industrial or commercial, the structural department performed calculations on all of the structures, depending also on the relative specialization in steel or reinforced concrete structures, and finally, the mechanical department, divided into five sections, had jurisdiction over the design of mechanical aspects—sanitation facilities, heating, air conditioning, electrical systems, and the diagrams of operations.

Each of these departments was organized according to an identical hierarchical plan, composed of a job captain, technicians specialized in drafting designs, and staff assigned to control duties. The work was controlled by two groups: one that collected the work of the first three departments, and a second group devoted solely to the different sections of the mechanical department.

The ample supply of facilities for each section of the firm was explained, as Nelson noted, by the fact that: "All departments start work simultaneously instead of working in successive stages, and this, in addition to speeding up the work of making the drawings, means that plans and specifications for all trades can be submitted for bids at one time, thus enabling the client to determine the cost of the building in its entirety before starting to build."[19] This model of production was quite similar to the one adopted at River Rouge.

A similar search for the "greatest return" justified and encouraged rethinking every project and every concession, not only to improvisation but also to inspiration.

The Executive Division also held an important position within Albert Kahn, Inc. It was divided in two parts. The office management dealt with accounting and administration. Construction coordination, with a superintendent, announced the competitive bidding and chose (with the client) the best offers, coordinated the phases of construction, verified the schedules, assisted the work in progress, periodically informed the client of the progress of the jobs, and acted as liaison between the various enterprises. Finally, the superintendent ensured timely payment.

The creator of this precise organizational model was Louis Kahn, who began as an administrator and then, after Albert's death in 1942, became president.

It was Albert who recognized the merits of Louis, the youngest of his brothers: "Matters of policy, of supervision, the selection and handling of contractors, preparation of contracts, the receiving of reports of men in the field, the business management, collections and disbursements are entirely in the hands of my very able brother, Louis."[20]

Louis was born in 1885, when the family had already been in America for four years. He graduated from the University of Michigan with a degree in architecture and began to work in his brother's firm in 1908. From the first years of his career, he specialized in dealing with administrative problems and the organization of project tasks, and ended up preparing an enormous manual for use exclusively within the firm. All of the instructions for the operational management of every possible activity were documented in this manual.[21]

In a speech at the 75th annual meeting of the American Institute of Architects, held in Cincinnati in May, 1943, Louis underlined the need for each sector of industrial construction to be governed by a "complete architectural and engineering organization." Louis also presented some amplifications of the organizational model of the firm of which he was president.[22] The great bulk of work for the "Arsenal of Democracy" and the consequent need to speed up production time required, in his point of view, required specific sectors for each of the two operations. In that period of frenetic activity (and spending), these sectors assumed great importance. The estimating department prepared the estimates, and the contract division controlled and managed the contracts.

At the end of his speech, Louis Kahn manifested great optimism for the future: "In my opinion, industrial work is likely to be the principle field for architects, not only for the duration [of the war] but for a number of years following the cessation of hostilities."[23] Albert Kahn Associated Architects and Engineers Inc. was therefore prepared for the post-war industrial challenge, but Louis Kahn died in 1945 and was not able to see his predictions come true in the long expansive phase that preceded the fall of Motor City.

Fordism and Architecture Firms

The organizational example of Albert Kahn, Inc. prompted reflection on the possibilities of scientific management in architecture firms. The large Detroit firm certainly was not a novelty for North America, since Daniel Burnham's firm, after years of working with Root, became D.H. Burnham and Company, with more than 180 employees and headquarters in Chicago, New York and San Francisco.[24] But with respect to organizational layout, Burnham—the "colossal merchandiser" as Louis Sullivan described him with contempt[25]—was emblematic of an early managerial phase, founded on quantity. But Albert Kahn, from contact with the Ford industry, knew how to effect a decisive turning point in design work, applying the most advanced theories of scientific management and enterprise operation.

However, Albert Kahn was not a solitary figure even in this regard. Other leaders in the American architectural and engineering fields had begun to consider the importance of the organization of design projects since the beginning of the twentieth century.[26]

These theoretical elaborations, like those of Albert Kahn, Inc., demonstrated that the real transformation of work and the renewal of the construction industry could be realized only when the project operations were based on the rhythms of mass production. This would necessitate a complete overthrow of traditional methods of the profession.

During the first decades of the twentieth century, transformations in this direction first took place in the technical offices of major American industries that dealt with the conceptualization of products and the programmatization and management of the labor cycle.

The parallel examination of the great undertakings of architectural design firms like Albert Kahn, Inc., and those of the technical offices constituting the structure of control according to the Taylorist hierarchy, can be of help in understanding the common process of reorganization that involved these two spheres of intellectual labor. The two areas are, in fact, related by analogous processes of rationalization that impose the prefiguring of the manufactured products to be produced in series, the specification of the components and, finally, the defining of the ideal procedures for their production.[27] The analogy can be pushed further in the comparisons of the methods of workmanship at Albert Kahn, Inc., and in publications regarding the rational and economical use of production capacities in the technical offices of large industrial plants.

The growing need to create a continuous flux of information between company management, the technical office, and the workshop required efficient management of personnel, and the application of precise rules to make technical language simultaneously uniform and more easily understood.[28]

In particular, the methodology of representation was made uniform, thus ordering the growing number of elaborations (technical drawings and instructions of workmanship, schedules and write-ups) produced by the technical offices, that guided the course of the production cycle. Towards this same end was the tendency to reuse proven technical solutions, thereby reducing the time spent planning. Maximum clarity in the drafting and filing of designs thus became a necessity.[29]

This rationalization was carried out within the technical offices with the application of general norms for the construction of the work environment.[30] The necessity to obtain an ordered flow of labor by means of a rational conformation of space implicated problems similar to those inherent to workshop organization. In this case, too, skills and experimentation in different areas were established—circulation, sanitation, and study of heating, ventilation and lighting systems. Additionally, the influence of Fordism is clear in the distinction between departments, the regulation of production, and the close attention paid to materials and their circulation.

The theoretical reflection on the management of design work interested and involved much of the American architectural field. Beginning in 1923,[31] *The Architectural Forum* ran a series of articles by Howell Taylor, a partner in Schmidt, Garden & Martin of Chicago. Taylor wrote on technical and administrative production in architecture firms, and suggested that the maximum return of labor and the ready response to the augmentation of employees and to the turn of events could be achieved by adopting the same criteria that ruled scientifically organized industries.

Hierarchical ordering was considered capable of satisfying the wishes of management, but Taylor also pointed out the need for specialized professional skills in every member of the staff. The result was the creation of a pivotal figure, the Liaison Assistant, who was responsible for controlling the progress of work in the firm, and for establishing an effective bridge between design and construction.

The Liaison Assistant's role was of the utmost importance in that it established a bond between the sketches and their actual execution, once they had been enriched with technical knowledge.

The interest in this kind of study led to the publication of several manuals specifically directed at establishing norms for a "good business practice" as a determining component of professional practice. An important work on this subject is the volume by Royal Barry Wills, *This Business of Architecture*, edited in 1941. It is a manual of instructions for the formulization of contracts, relationships with clients, the promotion of the firm's public image, the analysis of costs, and general information ranging from filing to waste disposal.[32]

In the first half of the twentieth century, Europe presented decidedly less dynamic activity. There were, nevertheless, some reflections on the creative process and on the articulation of skills.

At the XI International Congress of Architects, held in Amsterdam in 1927, specific attention was paid to the distinction between the consulting architect and the managerial architect.[33] Balance sheets were laid out, illustrating the changes within the world of construction and making reference to the widening overlap and confusion of tasks between architects, engineers, building managers and qualified masters. There emerged a consciousness of the distance that separated the entire construction sector from the radical transformations in large industry.

Confirming the intention to maintain a separate destiny for architecture than that of the technical innovations and cultural conditions placed by mass industry, the congress outlined a type of intellectual technician. This position was to be distant and immune from those relations on which other architects were basing a refoundation of the discipline. A clear distinction was made—between the architect's purely technical and artistic activity, and his direct involvement in construction enterprises. The latter was considered harmful to both the quality of architectural design and to the integrity of the professional field.

This insistence on the separation between architects and construction was likewise enforced in European architecture schools,[34] where intellectuals and theorists maintained a cultural hegemony. The activity of the architect, according to the academics, could have been prejudiced by interference with commercial activities and with the entrepreneurial spirit to which new technical construction gave impetus.[35] A very similar attitude, though manifested through more detailed positions, was present in the influential informational manuals of the professional world. Some of these works, in fact, far from being schematic expositions of distributive, technical and constructive solutions, ranged from technical questions to problems of conducting professional studies.

The Italian *Manuale dell'Architetto* by Daniele Donghi (reprinted several times, with few modifications, from 1905 to 1929)[36] fit this definition. In particular, the pages dedicated to the profession of architecture emphasized the need to reunify artistic skills and technical knowledge, which the modern age had separated, with negative consequences.

The differences between the type of firm of which Donghi spoke, and the complex articulation of the American firms was evident.

In the chapter entitled "The Profession of the Architect and of the Engineer-Architect," (a chapter which remained unchanged from the first to the last edition) Donghi examined the "systematization of the office or firm," the "work of the architect," the "capacity and its very accountability," the "responsibility" and finally the "social function of the architect."[37] Those whom he described as assistants to or partners of the architect were sketchy figures: an assistant knowledgeable about construction materials charged with verifying the execution of projects, a measurer or verifier expert in surveying the execution of sketches and accounting, a number of designers varying in relation to the order of size of the jobs, and finally, a typist, a clerk, and an errand boy.

Thus emerged the centrality of the "shop" of the architect as a place of professional formation and direct assimilation of knowledge.[38] Direct contact with building contractors was given the same amount of importance, and a relationship with construction practices was desirable as long as no professional hierarchy was overturned.

A similar imposition was overcome, at least on a theoretical level, by a part of the European architectural community more inclined to accept and actually practice the standardization and the tempos of mass production. References were made to this at the XIII International Congress of Architects, held in Rome in 1935.

The speech given by Gaetano Minnucci on the subject "New Material From the Point of View of the Conception of the Design and its Production, and the Results Offered by its Use," presented arguments that he had been developing since the 1920s.

The greatly innovative aspect inherent in modern construction techniques was, in his judgement, bound to the possibility of scientifically predetermining the applications. This availability of exact data was destined to change not only the design process, but also the characteristics of construction and the utilized forms of buildings. "The perfecting of every area of construction," wrote Minnucci, "has made it possible that the house, in its construction, can reach the precision and the refinement of a machine, and can fulfill those characteristics of functionality by now universally recognized and desired."[39]

The preponderance of industrial products and their subsequent technical innovations began to influence an ever-growing number of architects and builders, no longer confined to the activities of avant-garde groups that had long ago chosen to champion the industrial aesthetic.

Despite the international dimensions of this tendency, there are few examples of faithful adaptation of scientific management principles by design firms. The only distinguishable references remain in the purely theoretical realm.

Architects sought to renew the foundations of their discipline, as it seemed to be losing contact with modern society, and they felt as though they had become relegated to being merely organizers and engineers. Le Corbusier's experiments in determining a dwelling as a "organisme rationnel, impeccable, économique,"[40] became somewhat of a guide in that he specified the use of mass-produced materials and Fordist distribution criteria.[41]

Le Corbusier's interpretation of Fordism was conscious of the differences between the potential of the production line and the limitations of the construction sector in Europe,[42] but did not focus as much on the principles of Fordist logic. Le Corbusier's research concerned solely the former, and was certainly not organized in a particularly rational or scientific way.[43]

The inclusion of rationalized design work as an integral part of construction reoccurred during the post-war period in the problems posed by the introduction of new construction techniques. Faith in the renewal of society through new technological means was shared by European intellectuals in the 1920s and 1930s, who chose (or were politically forced) to wholeheartedly support the new North American ethic. Among the cultural exchanges that this international enthusiasm effected, those of Walter Gropius and Richard Neutra[44] are of noteworthy significance.

The analysis done by Gropius in the 1950s—in light of his experience as a professor at Harvard University—manifested the perseverance of some unbridgeable gaps between the processes of design and construction.

Since, in his judgement, the traditional figure of the professional architect ended up noticeably marginalized, especially in determining the timetable and materials of construction, Gropius maintained that the centrality of the architect could be reconquered by participation in the design of the industrial components of buildings.

Central to Gropius's aspirations, therefore, was the creation of a labor method founded on the participation of individuals in a collective creative process, by means of which it might be possible to attain results of higher quality than by the traditional isolation of the designer. "I predict," affirmed Gropius, "that AIA will lose many architects who will refuse to be restrained any longer from a natural urge to take actual part in a team effort with the industry to produce buildings and their parts. The emphasis, I believe, will be more and more on the *team*."[45]

This position widely reflected North American cultural influences, but was interpreted as a utopian vision, inspired by the tradition of the great pre-modern builder's yard. However, this stance was ridiculed by several masters of the Modern Movement, including Jacobus Johannes Pieter Oud, who in 1952 wrote: "Look around you; you will see immediately that the truly significant monuments of world architecture have always been produced by one spirit only, and are attributed to only one man....My colleague Walter Gropius can detest the work of an architectural prima donna, but I doubt that a world entirely conforming to his architectural canons (whose products I would call choral architecture) would end up so attractive. A building that has the power to move us within can not result from a collective work. The individual is necessary, with his creative force, with his energy, with his passion."[46]

While Oud expressed a sentiment born of the European idea of an architect, "work in collaboration" had already become the motto of the American architectural community. Gropius's model is recognizable in the organizational arrangement of Richard Neutra's firm—Neutra had become quite assimilated in the architectural attitudes of North America.

Thanks to a rigorous filing system, the organization of Neutra's firm provides a glimpse of the compensations and time frames necessary for the different stages of design and construction. An issue of *L'Architecture d'aujourd'hui* dedicated to Neutra's work read: "Neutra's employees receive extremely precise directions for developing designs. They have in hand, first of all, the general procedural instructions for the perfection of the first sketch of the idea to be used. All designs are executed on pages of standard size, with a heading that includes all the necessary directions. After a first implementation of the design, one proceeds to a preliminary application of all the details, leaving only one part of the design unfinished. All of these details must be, as much as possible, typical solutions.... The designer is consistently reminded that he must make himself understood by the laborer who is not necessarily familiar with the particular type of work required."[47]

These examples constituted a first step in the itinerary that crossed disciplines interested in industrial building design. The firm of Albert Kahn, Inc. acquired particular significance because it joined art and science in a managerial organization comparable to the most advanced models adopted in mass production.

This brief comparison of the points of view of some of the more influential figures in modern architecture demonstrates how the organization of design work, structured in the firm of Albert Kahn according to the Fordist model, elsewhere followed a more complex evolution, centered on the role and the cultural identity of a designer faced with the fragmentation of professional knowledge.

NOTES

1 H-R Hitchcock, *Architecture: Nineteenth and Twentieth Centuries*, Penguin Books, Harmondsworth (1958), 1987, p. 547.

2 Kahn, *Putting Architecture On a Business Basis*, text of the conference held at the Cleveland Engineering Society on December 15, 1930, typewritten (AKA). Slightly modified text under the same title was published in two parts in *Weekly Bulletin of the Michigan Society of Architects*, January 6 and 13, 1931; an abridged version appeared in *Wolverine Builder*, February 1931.

3 A. Kahn, *Putting Architecture on a Business Basis*, typewritten, p. 3.

4 Ibid., p. 7.

5 Ibid., p. 11.

6 Ibid., p. 12.

7 A. Kahn, "Architectural Trend," in *The Journal of the Maryland Academy of Sciences*, vol. II, no. 2, April 1931, p. 133. "Problems of the architect include knowledge of old and new materials, familiarity with drawing up million-dollar contracts, concepts of finance and knowledge of land value, the ability to counsel proprietors about what they want to construct and what will result in an optimal investment with minimum risk of devaluation over time, and finally an architect must have the ability to finance a project" (p. 143).

8 *Albert Kahn Organization*, published in-house, 1942 (AKA).

9 Information on some of Albert Kahn's employees can be found in the following obituaries: "Saul Saulson," in *Jewish News*, July 25, 1975; "John Schurman," in *Monthly Bulletin of the Michigan Society of Architects*, January 1962; "George H. Miehls," in *The Monday Morning Sun*, December 1, 1975; "Clair W. Ditchy," in *Monthly Bulletin of the Michigan Society of Architects*, September 1967; "Joseph N. French," in *The Detroit Free Press*, September 28, 1985; "Robert W. Hubel," in *Weekly Bulletin of the Michigan Society of Architects*, December 19, 1944; "William C. Bunce," in *Weekly Bulletin of the Michigan Society of Architects*, December 12, 1944; "LeRoy Lewis," in *Weekly Bulletin of the Michigan Society of Architects*, February 8, 1944; *David Fettes*, typewritten, October 9, 1953 (AKA); *O.L. Canfield*, typewritten, September 22, 1955 (AKA); *Joseph Matte*, typewritten, undated (AKA).

10 See the numerous typewritten texts on single projects (AKA) often used in the course of this work. To better understand the spirit of Albert Kahn's initiative it is useful to determine how much was done by Henry Ford, the central argument of the excellent work by D.L. Lewis, *The Public Image of Henry Ford*, Wayne State University Press, Detroit, 1987.

11 "Eight-story office building for Trussed Concrete Steel Co.," in *The Detroit News Tribune*, January 27, 1907.

12 G.C. Baldwin, "The Offices of Albert Kahn, Architect, Detroit, Michigan," in *The Architectural Forum*, vol. 29, no. 5, November 1918, pp. 125–126.

13 Ibid., p. 126.

14 "Review of building activity in 1919," in *The Architectural Forum*, vol. XXXII, no. 1, January 1920, pp. 3–8.

15 "Combining Utility with Beauty. An Interview by D.G. Baird with Albert Kahn, President Albert Kahn Incorporated, Detroit," in *Management*, April 1927, p. 38.

16 On the New Center Building, see "New Center Project Seen A Timely Business Stimulant," in *Michigan Manufacturer and Financial Record*, October 4, 1930.

17 G. Nelson, *Industrial Architecture of Albert Kahn, Inc.*, Architectural Book Publishing Company, New York 1939, p. 19.

18 G. Nelson provides the organizational scheme, *Industrial Architecture of Albert Kahn, Inc.*, p. 21 and *Architecture by Albert Kahn Associated Architects and Engineers, Inc.*, Architectural Catalog Company, New York 1948, pp. 10–11, gives evidence of the amplified organizational scheme after World War II.

19 G. Nelson, *Industrial Architecture of Albert Kahn, Inc.*, p. 19.

20 Quoted in *Louis Kahn. 1885–1945*, typewritten, April 30, 1946 (AKA) and in G.S. Koyl, "Louis Kahn," in *Journal of the A.I.A.*, March 1950.

21 A very brief biographical profile is also found in *Biographical Encyclopedia of America*, vol. I, New York 1940, which erroneously reports the date of birth as 1886.

22 Speech by L.K. at A.I.A. 75th Annual Meeting at Cincinnati on May 26/43, typewritten, undated (AKA).

23 Ibid., p. 6.

24 See T.H. Hines, *Burnham of Chicago. Architect and Planner*, The University of Chicago Press, Chicago–London 1974. In addition to Burnham, on pioneers in scientific management of design work, we can not forget George B. Post; see D. Balmori, "George B. Post: The Process of Design and the New American Architectural Office (1868–1913)," in *Journal of the Society of Architectural Historians*, vol. XVVI, no. 4, December 1987, pp. 342–355. Concerning this subject, see B.M. Boyle, "Architectural Practice in America, 1865–1965. Ideal and Reality," in S. Kostof (ed.), *The Architect. Chapters in the History of the Profession*, Oxford University Press, New York 1977, pp. 309–344.

25 L.H. Sullivan, *The Autobiography of an Idea*, 1924, Dover, New York 1956, p. 292.

26 On the origins of the introduction of scientific management in architectural design, an interesting case to compare with Albert Kahn, Inc. is that of the Austin Company of Cleveland, which was cited in the account of Ford's work in Russia. See M. Greif, *The New Industrial Landscape. The Story of the Austin Company*, The Main Street Press, Clinton, N.J. 1978.

27 On the development of American technological culture between the nineteenth and twentieth centuries, see D. Noble, *America by Design. Science, Technology and the Rise of Corporate*

Capitalism, Knopf, New York 1977; D. Houndshell, *From the American System to Mass Production: The Development of Manufacturing Technology in the United States, 1850–1920*, Doctoral dissertation, University of Delaware, 1978; O. Mayr, R. Post (ed.), *Yankee Enterprise: The Rise of the American System of Manufactures*, Smithsonian Institution Press, Washington D.C. 1982.

28 See H.G. Tyrrell, *A Treatise on the Design and Construction of Mill Buildings and Other Industrial Plants*, The Myron C. Clark Publishing Co., Chicago–New York–London 1911, pp. 401–483—the part entitled "Engineering and Drafting Departments of Structural Works." The first edition of this volume was printed in 1900, but did not include this chapter.

29 Among the most interesting American contributions on standardized materials, see J. Gaillard, *Industrial Standardization: Its Principles and Applications*, Wilson, New York 1943, and A. Edwards, *Product Standards and Labeling Consumers*, Ronald Press, New York 1940.

30 On the rational conformation of intellectual work space, one can find interesting materials both in publications dedicated to general management of labor as well as those referring with greater specificity to technological innovations. See O.E. Perrigo, *Modern Machine Shop Construction. Equipment and Management*, New York 1906, Fr. trans. *L'atelier moderne de construction mécanique. Construction, outillage et direction*, Dunod, Paris 1920, pp. 152–168; and for Europe, M. Ponthière, *Le bureau moteur. Fonction et organisation des bureaux*, Dalmas, Paris 1935, pp. 224–262 and A.M. Morgantini, "La disposizione degli uffici come elemento di razionalizzazione," in *L'Organizzazione Scientifica del Lavoro*, III, no. 1, January 1929, pp. 33–34.

31 See H. Taylor, "Organization in the Architect's Office," in *The Architectural Forum*, vol. 34, no. 2, August 1923, pp. 55–58, the first of a series of articles on this subject.

32 R.B. Willis (with the collaboration of L. Keach), *This Business of Architecture*, Reinhold Publishing Corporation, New York 1941, a text that furnishes directions on the formation of contracts, client relations, cost analyses and more general information on the organization of the firm (from filing of materials to the organization of space).

33 *XI Congrès International des Architects*, official acts, Amsterdam 1927, in particular pp. 148–161. There were four questions posed to the members of the commission charged with this argument: "A) In your country, is the architect responsible for designing the plans and controlling the execution of the construction of the majority of urban housing? B) If not, what are the reasons for which the architect is excluded from this kind of work? And what would be some ways to obtain this kind of work? C) Can you indicate to the Congress some works by contract architects which had satisfactory results? Express your evaluation of these works on artistic, technical and economic grounds. D) Is it necessary to continue to maintain an essential separation between the position of the consulting architect and the contract architect and what measures should be taken in this regard within the Societies and Unions of Architects?" (p. 148).

34 For an interesting reconstruction of the events that, in a more or less direct way, led to the formation of the Schools of Architecture in Italy and France, see R. Gabetti, P. Marconi, *L'insegnamento dell'architettura nel sistema didattico franco-italiano (1789–1922)*, Facoltà di architettura del Politecnico di Torino, Edizione Quaderni di Studio, Turin 1968.

35 This kind of position was maintained in 1929 by Gustavo Giovannoni. See G.G. (G. Giovannoni), entry "Architettura," in *Enciclopedia italiana di scienze, lettere e arti*, vol. IV, Bestetti e Tuminelli, Milan–Rome 1929, p. 61.

36 D. Donghi, *Manuale dell'Architetto*, Utet, Turin (1905), 1929. For a critical evaluation of the concepts expressed in this manual, see C. Guenzi (ed.), *L'arte di edificare. Manuali in Italia 1750–1950*, Be-Ma, Milan 1981, pp. 155–164.

37 D. Donghi, *Manuale dell'Architetto*, pp. 449–486.

38 "If his employees are young, at the beginning of their careers, and beginning their careers in his office, he has the moral obligation to compensate them for the help that they give him commensurate with their knowledge and ability, instructing them in everything that experience has taught him, bringing them his works, having them attend discussions with contractors, with suppliers and, when he thinks it possible and convenient, also with clients and inspection operations. The student, so to speak, will be appreciative and will work with passion to the full benefit of his master" Ibid., p. 454.

39 G. Minnucci, "Paper on Subject no. 1," in *XIII Congresso Internazionale degli Architetti*, atti ufficiali, Rome 1935, p. 95.

40 Le Corbusier, "Architecture d'Epoque Machiniste," in *Journal de Psycologie normale et patologique*, XXIII, 1926, p. 328.

41 In their paper to the II International Congress of Modern Architecture, held in Frankfurt in 1929, Le Corbusier and Pierre Jeanneret wrote: "Domestic life consists of a regular sequence of precise functions. The regular sequence of these functions constitutes a phenomenon of circulation. The exact, economic circulation is the fulcrum of contemporary architecture. The precise functions of domestic life require different spaces whose minimum extension can be fixed with a certain exactness; for every function there is needed a minimum, necessary and sufficient standard ability (human scale). The sequence of these functions is established according to a logic that is of a biological rather than geometric order. One could elaborate this model of these functions according to a continuous line." Le Corbusier, P. Jeanneret, "Analyse des éléments fondamentaux du problème de la Maison Minimum," in AA.VV., *Die Wohnung für das Existenzminimum*, Julius Hoffmann, Stuttgart 1933, p. 25.

42 On the Taylorist and Fordist influence on Le Corbusier's work, see Le Corbusier, *Précisions sur un état présent de l'architecture et de l'urbanisme*, Vincent, Fréal & C., Paris 1960 [1930], where in the text from the second conference in Buenos Aires, in addition to "standardization, industrialization, Taylorism," referring to Pierre Jeanneret, one finds, "Il a lu Ford, il est fordiste!" (p. 56).

43 The essay of M. Bédarida, "Rue de Sèvres 35. Dietro la scena," in AA.VV., *Le Corbusier. Enciclopedia*, Electa, Milan 1988, pp. 416–423, testifies to the total absence of organizational criteria in the master's studio.

44 Naturally this deals with the experiences cited for their adherence to the analysis of changes in the course of design work. On another level there is the discussion regarding other successful immigrants like Mies van der Rohe and Hilberseimer.

45 "Gropius Appraises Today's Architects," in *The Architectural Forum*, May 1952, p. 174. See

also W. Gropius, *Scope of Total Architecture*, Harper and Brothers, New York 1955.

46 J.J.P. Oud, "Bowen en teamwork," in *De Groene Amsterdammer*, February 9, 1952. The English translation of this text was not accepted by *The Architectural Record* in the same year.

47 "Méthodes de travail," in *L'Architecture d'aujourd'hui*, no. 6, 1946, p. 16.

ECLECTICISM FOR MOTOR CITY
Detroit: Architecture and a City Between Modernity and Tradition

Few American cities, especially Eastern ones, rich with an urban tradition at least 200 years old, have an architectural history as overlooked as Detroit's. New York, Chicago, Boston, Philadelphia, Washington, Pittsburgh and, on the West Coast, San Francisco and Los Angeles are the significant landmarks in American architecture. Buffalo, Baltimore, New Haven and Newport may also come to mind, but very rarely is Detroit mentioned.[1]

Yet Detroit played a large role in the economic and social history of the United States, with its rapid industrialization in the automobile sector and its strong union movement.[2] The image of Detroit is so indissolubly linked to enormous industrial complexes, that American travel guides rarely mention the city without noting its strong link to factories and industry.[3]

And yet in the architectural and urban design history of Detroit, there are still projects outside the industrial framework worthy of mention. Two projects, of two different eras, which, had they been realized would have surely modified Detroit's image, were the Woodward Plan of 1806–1807, and the Gratiot Project of 1956–1963.

After the fire of June 11, 1805 that destroyed the old center of the city—the area around Fort Pontchartrain du Detroit founded by Antoine de la Mothe Cadillac in 1701—Judge Augustus B. Woodward convinced the governing authorities of the need to reconstruct the city using a precise, regulating plan. This resulted in what historian John W. Reps called "one of the most unusual city plans ever devised."[4] Taking his lead from Pierre Charles L'Enfant's plan for Washington, Woodward came up with extremely different results.

The design that he proposed was founded on a large-scale expansion of an equilateral triangle, with a side of about 1249 meters (4,000 feet), divided in six triangles, each of which became a section. Long tree-lined avenues cut between the sections, and each section then contained gardens and large open spaces which took their circular form from the blunted angles of the blocks.

The aesthetics of Woodward did not coincide, however, with the interests of the investors who took advantage of his absence and resorted to what was basically a bureaucratic conspiracy to malign the project. By 1817 all traces of the complex system of triangles were erased, and the only evidence of the original plan remained visible in the forms of the Campus Martius and the Grand Circus. The rest of the city was designed and laid out according to a more traditional "checkerboard" system.

"What would Detroit be like if Woodward's vision had been followed?"[5] Though difficult to answer, the question is an interesting one, as Woodward's plan was certainly an advanced urban model for its time.[6]

One hundred and fifty years later, with the Gratiot Project, Detroit missed yet another opportunity for comprehensive redesign inspired by the most advanced theories in urban planning. However, this project did succeed in leaving some visible changes in the city.

After World War II, the area between Gratiot Avenue and Lafayette Street, a run-down neighborhood established during the first wave of immigration, became the focus of a rehabilitation effort founded on a vast public housing program.

After a failed first attempt by the Housing Commission (the enthusiasm for the New Deal had given way to public apathy), a group of industrialists formed the Citizen Residential Corporation and commissioned the redevelopment of the plan to two design firms, who then assigned the task to Oscar Storonov and Minoru Yamasaki. The plan met with considerable resistance and, in 1956, two Chicago builders intervened and entrusted the new development plans to Ludwig Mies van der Rohe and Ludwig Hilberseimer, who at the time were both professors at the Illinois Institute of Technology.

The Gratiot Project offered Hilberseimer the opportunity to try out the city planning concepts he had developed in the 1940s, and it allowed Mies van der Rohe to build the Lafayette Park Pavilion Apartments complex, completed in 1959. The death of one of the buyers, Herbert Greenwald, interrupted the work of the two German masters, and the buildings were parceled out to local firms and were finished with no regard for the initial plans. Thus, modernism's attempt to breathe new life into the "American dream" was a failure.[7]

Detroit became a ghost town, and was deserted in the industrial crisis. Though, some well-defended strongholds (efficiently served by highways that cut through the city) did emerge from the social and urban degradation. The Renaissance Center, the Medical Center, the Cultural Center, and the New Center, were attempts to revitalize the downtown, but the absence of a comprehensive plan to organize the city left them mere citadels, separate and incapable of re-establishing or linking themselves to the pre-existing urban structure.[8] It was an inglorious end to a city once called "the Paris of the West," a name that rendered homage to an architecture that united the tendencies of New York eclecticism and the new language of the Chicago school.

The architects who did build in Detroit were Henry Hobson Richardson (Bagley Memorial Armory, 1886, Bagley Memorial Fountain, 1887, still standing in the Campus Martius); Daniel H. Burnham (Majestic Building, 1896, Ford Building, 1909, Dime Building, 1910, David Withney Building, 1915); McKim, Mead & White

(Peoples State Bank, 1900); George B. Post (Hilton Hotel, 1914); Cass Gilbert (Detroit Public Library, 1921, J. Scott Fountain, 1925); and Paul Philippe Cret (Detroit Institute of Arts, 1927).[9]

An unfortunate circumstance prevented Detroit from being home to a work by Frank Lloyd Wright. In 1909, Wright was commissioned by Henry Ford to build a private residence in Dearborn, on the banks of the Rouge River (where, ten years later, he would build his gigantic industrial plant). But in that year, Wright had a stormy affair that ended in his running off to Europe with the wife of a client, and he left Hermann Von Holst responsible for completing his projects. Graduated from the Massachusetts Institute of Technology in 1896 and with a newly formed firm in Chicago, Van Holst took over the work for Ford, in collaboration with George Mann Niedecken, an interior designer to whom Wright frequently turned for furniture design. After the work had already begun, however, Ford decided to assign the project to an obscure Pittsburgh architect, William Van Tyne, who disregarded the original plans and built Ford an anonymous, English-style home in 1915.[10]

Also important to Detroit's architectural history were Eliel and Eero Saarinen. Eliel, after achieving success in his native country with the design of the Helsinki station, and in the United States with the 1922 Chicago Tribune competition, was asked to teach at the University of Michigan in Ann Arbor. There he met George G. Booth, editor of *The Detroit News* and founder of the Detroit Society of Arts and Crafts. Booth commissioned him to design a school inspired by the ideals of the Arts and Crafts movement, in Bloomfield Hills, not far from the city of Detroit: Cranbrook Academy of Arts. Cranbrook was directed by Saarinen himself, and became one of the most prestigious cultural centers of the Mid-West. Eliel's son, Eero, also became a leader in the American architectural scene of the fifties and sixties, and made a significant mark in Detroit with his General Motors Technical Center, completed in 1951.[11]

So despite Detroit's relative anonymity among architects, there is actually no shortage of examples of architectural and urban import. These works can also be evaluated in terms of Albert Kahn's specificity of method,[12] as his firm and its practices were quite influential in Detroit.

An understanding of the work and work ethic of Albert Kahn, Inc. necessitates an examination of the personal motivations of Albert Kahn. Without doing so, an evaluation of the projects would be incomplete. Albert Kahn felt that the architect was a technician at the complete disposal of the client. This affected, in turn, the architectural product, especially in Detroit and actually, in much of the United States, where the clientele had a natural inclination towards eclecticism.[13] This clientele desired function and economy for factories and offices, the bucolic elegance of the English country home for residential areas, and monumental styles of the past for institutions.

Much to the dismay of the European avant-garde, Kahn was happy to find "stylistically" specific solutions for each of these needs, demonstrating his ability to swing easily from the functionalism of structures for mass production to the employment of an encyclopedic historical lexicon for public architecture.[14]

This whole-hearted acceptance of eclecticism brought a sort of schizophrenia to Albert Kahn's work. He designed public buildings and residences conforming to highly esteemed academic traditions, but he also created industrial buildings that, designed to accommodate scientifically organized labor, were unquestionable contributions to modern architecture. To ignore one of the two parts of Kahn's work, or to take the "inconsistency" of his work as pretext for excluding him from architectural history would be an unfortunate error.

Even as early as Kahn's first independent commissions, he demonstrated sensitive compositional differences according to the function that the buildings were to serve. In the Scripps Library and Art Gallery, built in 1898 with George Nettleton, he used English Gothic for the library, and Dutch style for the art gallery, because it was to house Scripps's collection of Flemish art.[15]

Temple Beth El, built in 1893, was based on the Roman pantheon, but its decorations were in the Louis XIV style, all of which hid an avant-garde structural system. Twenty years later, in the new building for the congregation of Beth El, Albert Kahn reproposed "free use of classic forms" with an interior "in the character of the Italian Renaissance of the period of Raphael and Giulio Romano."[16]

Albert Kahn did not always conform to the styles of the eclectic European tradition. The Palms Apartment Building, designed from 1901 to 1902 with George Mason, was a six-story building in reinforced concrete (a complete novelty for Detroit), with walls of limestone blocks. There were no decorative concessions and the facade had bay windows at the sides, and a projection in the center that recalled Burnham & Root's Argyle Apartment Building in Chicago (1886).[17] While Kahn generally did draw from historical lexicons, in designing office buildings he tended to incorporate ornamental elements into the simplicity of the grid structure of reinforced concrete. The Trussed Steel Company (the Owen Building) of 1907 was designed to have only clean and essential lines: its eight stories in reinforced concrete were used as the headquarters of the offices of Albert and Julius Kahn. The Owen Building held resemblances to skyscrapers of the Chicago School: the Kresge Building and the Vinton Building, of 1914 and 1917, specifically.[18]

Beginning with these first projects, Albert experimented with a work method that he perfected over the years until it solidified to form the backbone of Albert Kahn, Inc. He gained the reputation as an architect and a manager who could coordinate different specialized skills to meet the client's needs, and who, at the same time, was involved

ECLECTICISM FOR MOTOR CITY 147

TEMPLE BETH EL: DETROIT, MICHIGAN; ALBERT KAHN, GEORGE MASON, 1903

OWEN BUILDING: DETROIT, MICHIGAN; ALBERT KAHN, ERNEST WILBY, 1907
PALMS APARTMENT HOUSE: DETROIT, MICHIGAN; ALBERT KAHN, GEORGE MASON, 1902

following pages:
UNIVERSITY OF MICHIGAN, HILL AUDITORIUM: ANN ARBOR, MICHIGAN; ALBERT KAHN, ERNEST WILBY, 1913

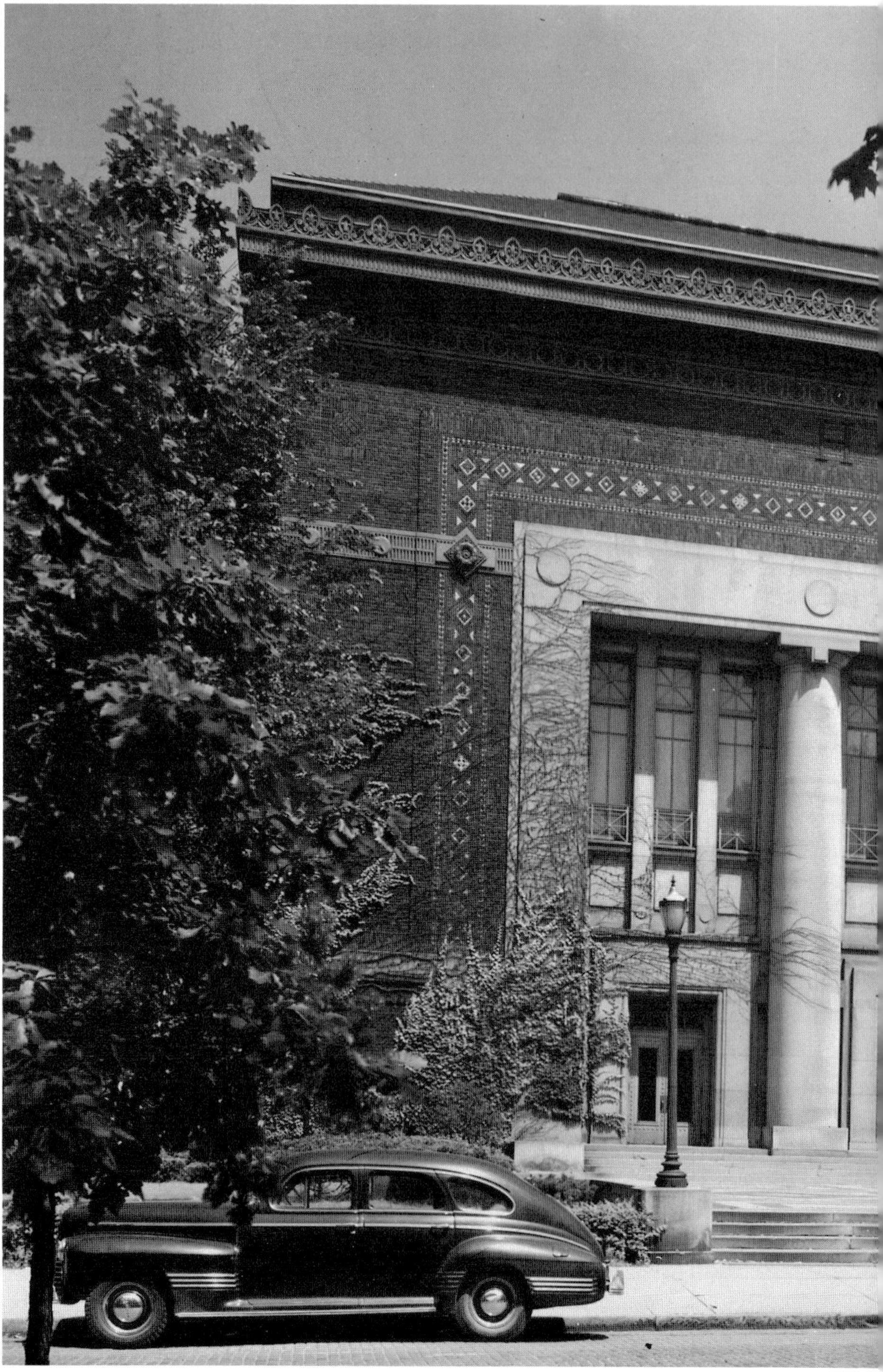

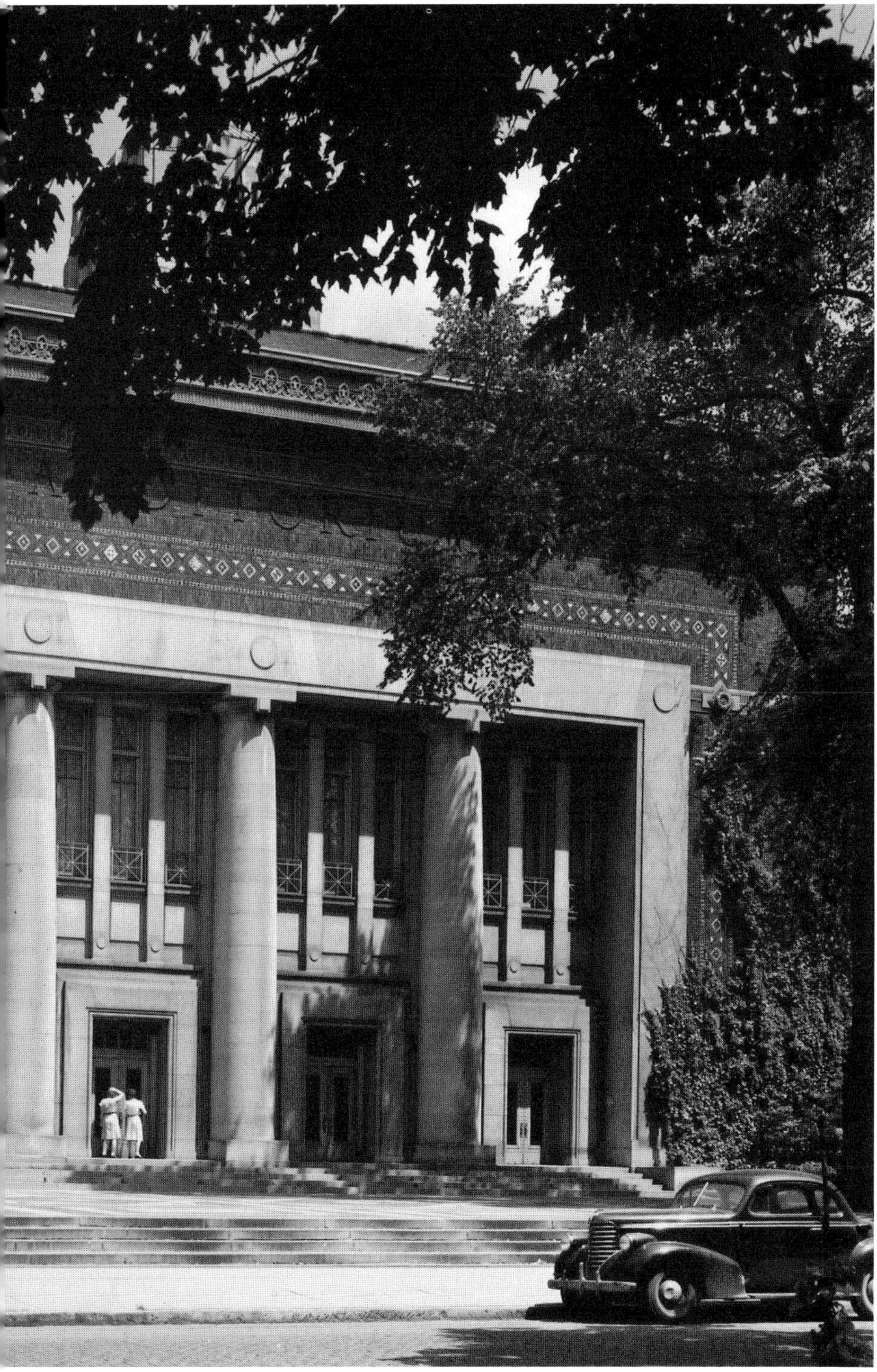

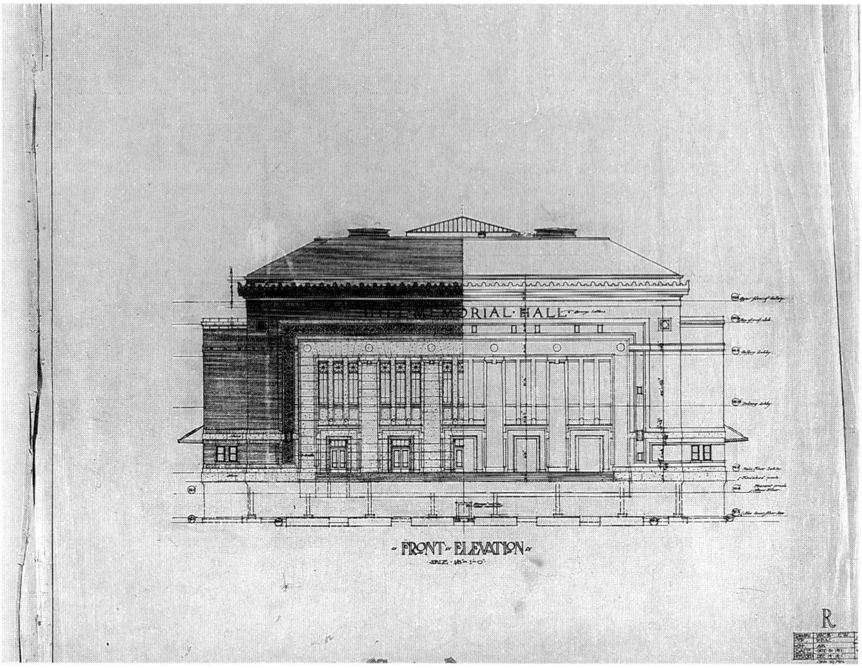
MEMORIAL HALL
FRONT ELEVATION

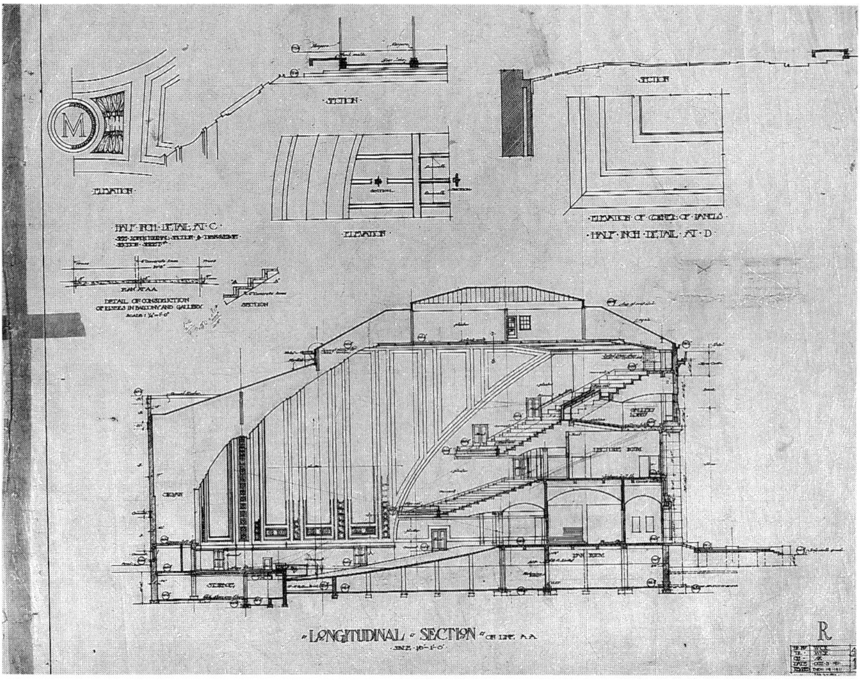
LONGITUDINAL SECTION

in monitoring and maintaining the quality of his firm's work in order to earn more commissions. That the work was eclectic did not seem to be an obstacle in gaining recognition and appreciation from clients, who instead were pleased to be able to choose from such a rich variety of styles.

Important to this aspect of Kahn's work was his collaboration, from 1903 until 1918, with Ernest Wilby. Born in England in 1868 but raised in Canada, Wilby was the designer of the decorative details that characterized the firm's first works. Remembering his old colleague in 1941, Kahn wrote that "one of the best investments I made early in my professional career was the engagement of Ernest Wilby."[19] The first project of "Albert Kahn Architect, Ernest Wilby Associate" was the Engineering Building (1903) at the University of Michigan at Ann Arbor (which was a structure of reinforced concrete and as such, required the collaboration of Julius Kahn as well). In this university town, about fifty kilometers (31 miles) from Detroit, the firm of Albert Kahn built twenty-six buildings between 1898 and 1937. They form a series of very different structures, whose differences can be explained for various reasons: the era in which they were designed, the typological differentiations, and above all, the wishes of the client. The latter was a factor to which Albert Kahn, as previously discussed, paid a great deal of attention.

Ten years after completing the Engineering Building, Kahn and Wilby finished the Hill Auditorium, a theater which, because of its acoustic and compositional particularities, has been compared to Chicago's Auditorium Building, done by Adler and Sullivan.[20] It was built in reinforced concrete with a veneer of classical brick (characteristic of Michigan architecture) from which the designers patterned a decorative texture. The entrance was imposing and rather heavy, with four stone columns. The overall result was a somewhat poorly resolved combination of the classical tradition to which Albert Kahn was inclined, and the local vernacular; a dualism that in an article analyzing the project—published in *Michigan Alumnus* in February 1912—was pointed out as a distinctive trait of the new architecture of the Mid-West. "Architecture in America is often divided into two schools—the Eastern and the Western. The Eastern school is known by its adherence to classic tradition; the Western school by its freedom from traditional form. Considering this fact, some may discern in this building a character which is appropriate to the ideals of a middle-Western University, because it fuses the spirit of the classic and conservativism of the East with the freedom of ideas which becomes the new West."[21]

opposite page:
UNIVERSITY OF MICHIGAN, HILL AUDITORIUM: ANN ARBOR, MICHIGAN; ALBERT KAHN, ERNEST WILBY, 1913
Elevation, section, and details

UNIVERSITY OF MICHIGAN, MEDICAL BUILDING: ANN ARBOR, MICHIGAN; ALBERT KAHN, INC., 1925

opposite page:
UNIVERSITY OF MICHIGAN, HOSPITAL: ANN ARBOR, MICHIGAN; ALBERT KAHN, INC., 1920
UNIVERSITY OF MICHIGAN, CARILLON TOWER: ANN ARBOR, MICHIGAN; ALBERT KAHN, INC., 1936

ECLECTICISM FOR MOTOR CITY 153

THE ALBERT KAHN SUMMER HOUSE:
WALNUT LAKE, MICHIGAN; ALBERT KAHN, 1917

THE H.E. DODGE HOUSE: GROSSE POINTE, MICHIGAN;
ALBERT KAHN, ERNEST WILBY, 1910

THE EDSEL B. FORD HOUSE:
GROSSE POINTE SHORES, MICHIGAN;
ALBERT KAHN, INC., 1926

THE KUHN HOUSE: GROSSE POINTE, MICHIGAN;
ALBERT KAHN, ERNEST WILBY, 1914

In this project, as in the Natural Science Building (1917) and the General Library (1919), terra cotta was widely used for decorative expression. The University Hospital (1920) signaled the end of a decade of the severity and sobriety of brick, and the beginning of a period of neoclassicism. Its adherence to functional needs was evident in both the organization of the plant and in the design of the exterior. This was because Kahn saw a similarity in the organization of labor in hospital buildings and industrial plants.[22]

In the 1920s, Kahn broke with Wilby and was left to design the stylistic flourishes himself. Kahn adapted himself to the academic tendencies, utilizing a Doric colonnade for Angell Hall, an Ionic colonnade for the Medical Building, and settled on Vignola's design for the casino at the Villa Farnese (he had visited the villa on his third trip to Italy), for the Clements Library (1922).[23]

Finally, there was the Carillon Tower, behind the Hill Auditorium, built in 1936 with commemorative intentions but also to serve the University's future school of music. Of the tower, Albert Kahn himself said that "in its exterior treatment no particular precedent has been followed."[24]

Wilby's influence manifested itself primarily in the firm's single-family homes. The residences built by the firm were, for the most part, situated in the Grosse Pointe area. Grosse Pointe was the preferred residential area of Detroit's upper-middle class, and became a showcase of provincial eclecticism, where architects and their clients competed to outdo each other with reinventions of European styles.[25]

Built in the first half of 1918 (during the collaboration with Wilby), the Grosse Pointe houses revealed Wilby's ability to interpret English domestic tradition in an original manner. Designed in this style were the homes of C.M. Swift in 1903, H.E. Dodge in 1910, J.S. Newberry in 1911, P.H. McMillan in 1912, Kuhn in 1914, and H.B. Joy in 1918. The sole exception was the Edgar house of 1915. The Edgar house was not considered a success as it was in the classical style, which Detroit had abandoned to embrace the Italian villas of Charles Platt. The three later residences demonstrated Kahn's unconditional adherence to the architectural caprices of his prestigious clients. In 1926, Kahn designed the home of Edsel Ford, Henry's son, to reflect his passion for the architecture of the Cotswold area of Worcestershire. Henry Ford and his son saw much of England during their numerous trips taken on the occasion of the construction of the plant in Dagenham, near London. So Albert Kahn satisfied the wishes of his biggest client (the Rouge River construction was in full swing) and created a Cotswold cottage. The brochure designed for the sale of the house read, "The Fords made many visits to the Cotswold district; they engaged in considerable research on the history and construction of Cotswold houses; and then they secured the services of the late Albert Kahn, architect, to design and build [their] home."[26]

Soon after, Kahn received commissions to build the Macauley house in Grosse Pointe, and the James Couzens house in Bloomfield Hills.

Finally, there was the summer residence for the Kahn family at Walnut Lake. Free from the constraints of clients, the Detroit architect paid homage to Frank Lloyd Wright's Prairie houses.[27] Whether it was a casual choice or the expression of a personal orientation is unclear, but does comment on just how influential a role Kahn's clients tended to hold.

In 1915, Wilby and Kahn designed the Detroit News Building, headquarters of the most important daily newspaper in Detroit. It was yet another example of how, for Kahn, the efficacious response to functional demands did not necessitate the exclusion of decorative aspects. An article published in *The Architectural Forum* in 1918 described in detail both the plan and the facade of the building. The reinforced concrete exterior was characterized by "richly sculpted" arches on the first floor, and on the higher floors, according to the author of the article, by "strong vertical movement further intensified by the stone window mullions running through the second and third stories."[28] The building was crowned by a heavy cornice with decorative panels and sculptures of publishing pioneers. The definition of the interior space was consistent, again according to the description in *The Architectural Forum*, with the characteristics of the facade. The ease with which Kahn passed from one style to another was remarkable. "The decoration of the public portions of the building is in a modified Renaissance manner characterized everywhere by a sense of dignified restraint. The vaulted ceiling of the lobby is painted in various colors and gold following simplified Florentine precedent. An accesory of special interest is the central lighting fixture, an iridescent glass globe leaded and in color to reproduce the medieval maps. The editing and business offices are wainscoted in oak and have flat coffered ceilings, which, with the neutral tints of the plastered walls, contribute to a restful simplicity of effect. The private suite of offices on the second floor and the president's suite on the mezzanine floor have been decorated in a modified Elizabethan style, with characteristic oak paneling and modeled plaster ceilings."[29]

The building's monumentality and return to authoritative styles of the past, in order to underline the presence of the newspaper headquarters in the heart of the city, did not at all compromise its functional needs. The Press Room on the first floor and the sky-lit Composing Room on the top floor were planned out in accordance with criteria for industrial buildings. However, the decorative exterior gave no indication that the spaces within were governed by a specific and rational layout that responded to the rhythms and organizational needs of editorial production.

The Detroit News Building served as a model for similar projects that Albert Kahn designed in the 1920s and 1930s—the headquarters of both *The New York Times* in Brooklyn (1929) and *The Detroit Times* in Detroit (1928).[30]

ECLECTICISM FOR MOTOR CITY   157

DETROIT NEWS BUILDING: DETROIT, MICHIGAN; ALBERT KAHN, ERNEST WILBY, 1915

NEW YORK TIMES BUILDING: BROOKLYN, NEW YORK; ALBERT KAHN, INC., 1929

following pages:
THE DETROIT TRUST COMPANY: DETROIT, MICHIGAN; ALBERT KAHN, ERNEST WILBY, 1915

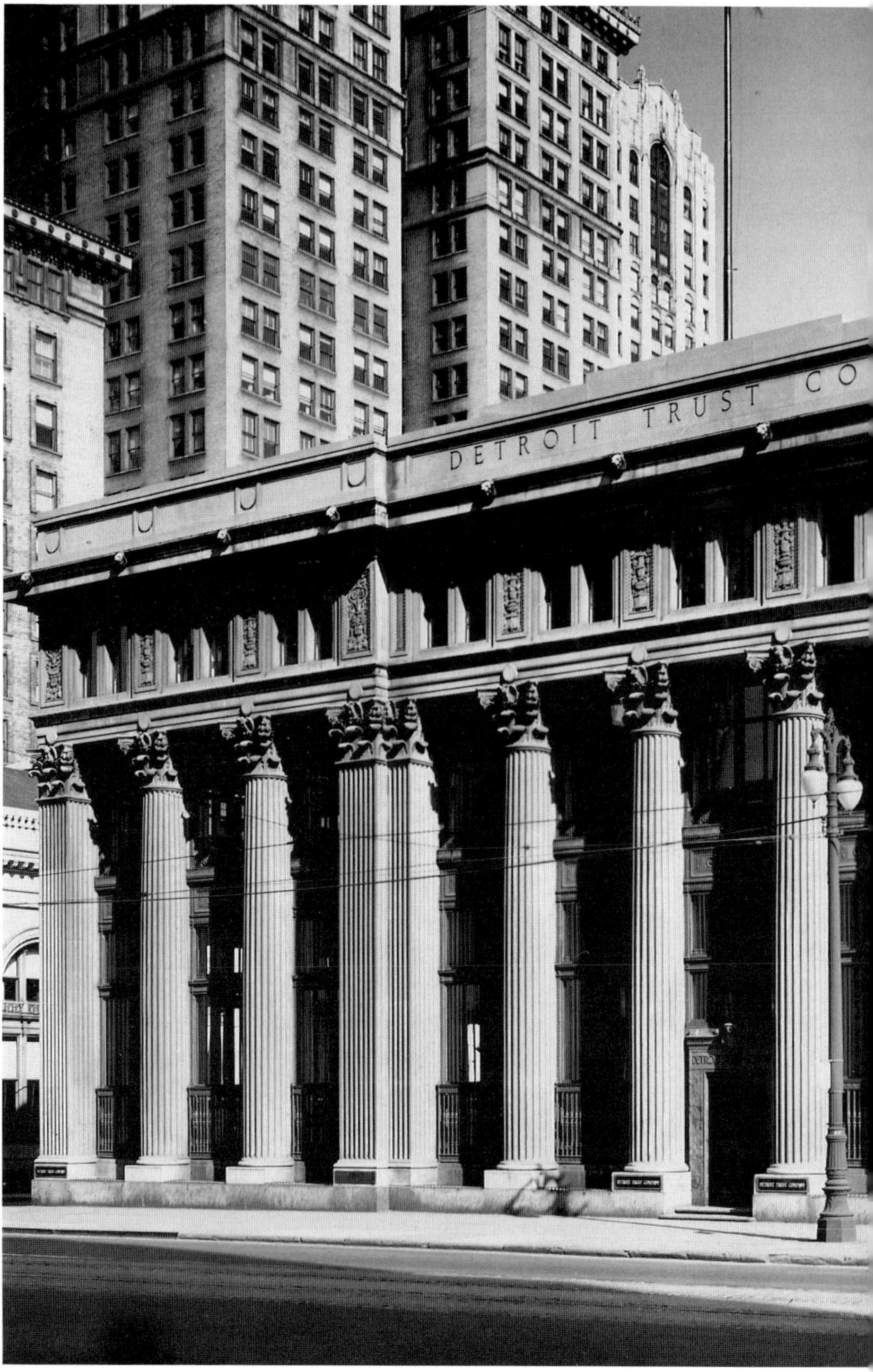
DETROIT TRUST CO

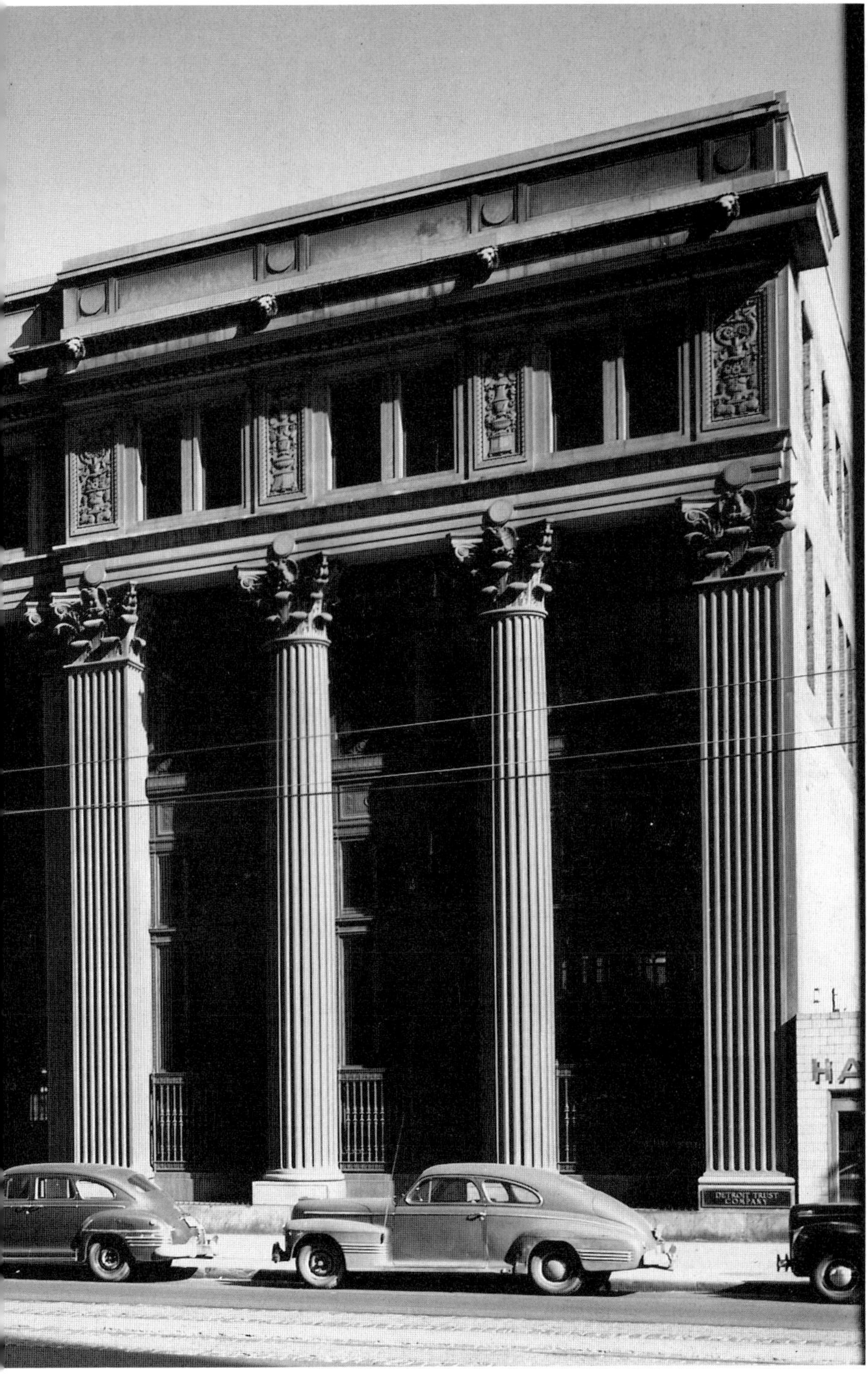

clockwise, from top left:
DETROIT ATHLETIC CLUB: DETROIT, MICHIGAN; ALBERT KAHN, ERNEST WILBY, 1915
WAYNE COUNTY & HOME SAVINGS BANK: DETROIT, MICHIGAN; ALBERT KAHN, ERNEST WILBY, 1910
NATIONAL BANK OF DETROIT: DETROIT, MICHIGAN; ALBERT KAHN INC., 1922
POLICE HEADQUARTERS: DETROIT, MICHIGAN; ALBERT KAHN INC., 1921

The adherence to monumentality freed the architect to manipulate the internal layout. Kahn took advantage of this in his scheme for the Detroit Athletic Club (1915), an exclusive club with a gymnasium, a pool, a dining room, and a game room. As Kahn himself remarked, the exterior and the interior were both Italian Renaissance but masked a reinforced concrete structure built by the Trussed Steel Company. The same style was employed for the headquarters of the Detroit Police Department[31] and for the various financial headquarters that Kahn designed. Given the representative quality of these buildings, Albert Kahn conceded to the use of "Classical lines."[32] Stylistic variations were dictated by advertising purposes, to define the image of a particular financial society. Therefore, Kahn used the Doric style for the Detroit Savings Branch Bank, Ionic for the Highland Park State Bank, and Corinthian for the National Bank of Commerce. He used Corinthian columns again for the Detroit Trust Company (1915), which resembled McKim, Mead & White's Knickerbocker Trust Company in New York, and for the National Bank of Detroit (1922), a twenty-four story building in the late Burnham style.[33]

Between eclecticism and the clean lines of Kahn's industrial buildings, were the Automobile Sales and Service Buildings, the showrooms and repair shops that the automobile industries built nationwide. The idea to create a network of affiliates was Henry Ford's, who in this way enlarged the market for his Model T (whose success was indeed attributed in part to this extensive network of maintenance facilities).[34] The first designs for these buildings were done by two young architects in Albert Kahn's firm, Frederic A. Fairbrother and Wirt C. Rowland. Two articles published in *The Architectural Forum* in 1920 and 1921 discussed the buildings' plans and structure, respectively.[35] These two works clearly show a highly refined functional articulation and definition of workshops, showrooms, and different offices for each service. The structure as a whole, was simple and somber, with subtle echoes of traditional architecture.

With the foundation of Albert Kahn, Inc. in 1918, the firm shifted its focus from public architecture to projects for the professional sector. Albert Kahn, Inc. contributed, particularly during the 1920s, to the development of Detroit's new business center at the intersection of Woodward Avenue and Grand Boulevard, well served by the transportation network and just a few kilometers from the Detroit River.

The pivotal event in the great speculation and building boom of the 1920s was the opening of the General Motors Building in 1922. Occupied by both General Motors and other businesses, the building took up an entire block. It housed offices (standard size of 4.5 x 6 meters, 15 x 20 feet), a 1200-seat auditorium, a bank, refreshment lounges, stores, and display areas. The complex united business, maximum use of land space, and scientific management of labor. Its plan was based on the designs for the

PACKARD SALES AND SERVICE BUILDING: DETROIT, MICHIGAN; ALBERT KAHN, ERNEST WILBY, 1915

CHRYSLER CORPORATION, SALES AND SERVICE BUILDING: DETROIT, MICHIGAN; ALBERT KAHN, INC., 1933

GENERAL MOTORS BUILDING: DETROIT, MICHIGAN; ALBERT KAHN, INC., 1922

automobiles sales and service buildings. A rectangular body (152.4 x 76.2 meters, 500 x 250 feet)—containing the new car showrooms, the auditorium, and stores—was marked by a great arched Ionic colonnade. Above this were four fourteen-story rectangular volumes of offices (140 per floor) joined by a volume that housed, among other things, a bank of twenty-four elevators. The exterior of these four office towers was a simple grid of windows and structural support. To the top floor, however, Kahn applied a Corinthian colonnade. As the top floor housed the directors' offices, the restaurant, and the boardroom, Kahn explained that decorative details had been used "only at important points."[36]

Along the entire length of the back of the complex ran a five-story factory occupied by the General Motors laboratories, and another large showroom area. In addition to building a successful industrial edifice with historical references, Albert Kahn had also developed a new typological precedent: the office building as self-sufficient "fortress," complete with all the services necessary for work.

Albert Kahn completed another project diagonally across the Grand Boulevard from the General Motors Building: the Fisher Building, financed by the Fisher Body

FISHER BUILDING: DETROIT, MICHIGAN; ALBERT KAHN, INC., 1928–1929
View of the building, 1979

Corporation, built in 1928–1929. Its functions were the same as the those of the General Motors Buildings: offices for rent, various services, plus a garage and a 3000-seat theater. However, the organization of the complex on its site was quite different from that of the General Motors Buildings: a twenty-eight story tower and two eleven-story buildings ran at right angles along Second Boulevard and West Grand Boulevard, and the rest of the block was taken up by the garage and the theater.

The Fisher Building was highlighted in the February 20, 1929 issue of *The American Architect*. In the introductory article, in addition to underlining the far-sightedness of the clients (the Fisher brothers, who spared no expense "to erect a thoroughly high class building"[37]), Albert Kahn outlined the building's stylistic characteristics and the labor method. The construction was clearly inspired by the new language of tall buildings like Eliel Saarinen's entry for the Chicago Tribune competition. Since 1924 (the time of the Detroit River Front proposal), Kahn had been fascinated by the work of the Finnish architect,[38] and he employed some of Saarinen's compositional strategies in the Fisher Building. The accentuation of the verticals recalled the "telescopic" form that Saarinen used to express and emphasize verticality in his projects.

Other influences were visible in the Fisher Building as well. "The Fisher Building," wrote one newspaper of the time, "with its rectilinear lines, and vertical style of architecture, is an American adaptation of the Gothic."[39] The interior spaces (the theater in particular), however, made reference to Native American ornamentation, with decorations inspired by Mayan civilization. Albert Kahn's homage to pre-Columbian America contradicted the formal choices of a number of American skyscraper designers, but was influenced by Hugh Ferris's primitive romanticism. However, of more interest is the method by which the Fisher Building was designed.

As in the construction of industrial buildings, Albert Kahn, Inc. divided the work into specific skill areas. The point of departure was the L-shaped scheme, which had been modified at least fourteen times. After pinpointing the client's preferences, Albert Kahn entrusted his engineers with the design of the structure, the mechanical systems, and the construction of the impressively modern garage. He assigned his architects the task of designing the exterior and interior, and for the ornamentation, he engaged professional artists. Finally, the theater project was subcontracted to a specialized architecture firm.

Fordist Architecture: A Model for Europe

"And I saw great massive buildings with windows so big and clear that flies crashed into them. Through the windows I could see men moving, but barely moving, as if they were struggling weakly against I don't know what impossibility. Was that Ford? And then all around and above as high as the sky, a heavy, deafening, and hard noise of torrents of machinery, stubborn machinery, turning, rotating, groaning, always close to breaking but never breaking." Louis Ferdinand Celine in *Voyage au bout de la nuit* (1932) recorded his impressions of the Ford Motor Company plants at River Rouge.[40] While literature and other media expressed the sense of anxiety caused by the Ford revolution, it also brought about a renewal of interest in modern architecture.

"The grain silos of Canada and [North] America, the coal bins of the great railroad lines, and the most modern industrial hangars of the North American trusts withstand the comparison, in their monumental force, to the constructions of ancient Egypt. Their architecture is so precisely defined that everything appears clear to the observer, with extraordinary energy, the meaning of the structure." In 1913, with references to ancient Egypt and with photographs of American silos and factories (including one of Highland Park), Walter Gropius launched a campaign that glorified American industrial buildings, and that figured in the theoretical elaborations of the European architectural avant-garde.[41]

Ten years later, Le Corbusier echoed Gropius, in articles in *L'Esprit Nouveau* which he re-examined in *Vers une Architecture*. He even used the same photograph of Highland Park. After becoming familiar with Taylorist concepts, gathering concrete design experience, and arranging his theories, Le Corbusier, in the pages of *Quand les cathédrales étaient blanches*, approached empassioned praise of Fordism: "I'm going out of the Ford workshops in Detroit. As an architect, I am in a kind of stupor.... With Ford, everything is collaboration, unity of vision, unity of intentions, perfect convergence of the totality of thought and action."[42] In addition to Gropius and Le Corbusier, Erich Mendelsohn romanticized and exalted American industrial buildings in his widely published photographs.[43]

Adolf Behne, Bruno Taut and Richard Neutra were more interested in the technical innovations of American industrial buildings. In *Der Moderne Zweckbau*, published in 1926 (but written three years earlier), Adolf Behne quoted "the declarations of Henry Ford concerning industrial architecture" and published two photographs of Albert Kahn's factories.[44] Bruno Taut in the chapter "Industrie-Bauten" of *Die Neue Baukunst in Europa und Amerika* (1929) included—next to the works of Hans Mehrtens in Cologne, Adolf Myer in Frankfurt and the tobacco factories in Rotterdam

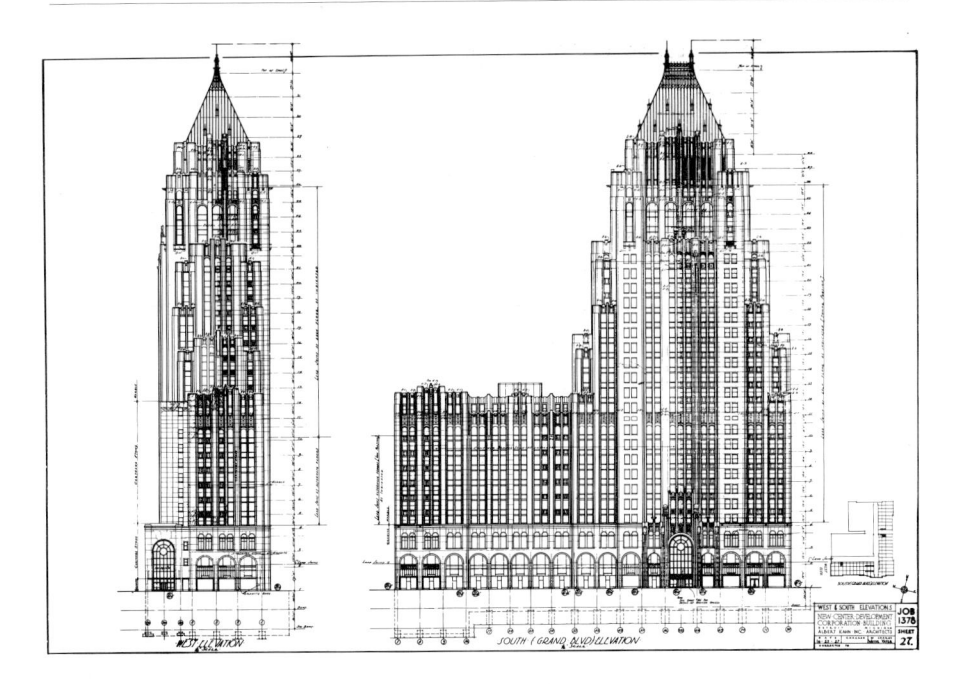

FISHER BUILDING: DETROIT, MICHIGAN; ALBERT KAHN, INC., 1928–1929
Elevations

done by Brinkman and Van der Vlugt—four pictures of Ford factories with the following caption: "Architeckten Albert Kahn, Inc., Detroit."[45] Richard Neutra, in *Amerika*, described the new type of closing devices for industrial buildings introduced by Albert Kahn, Inc.[46]

European interest in the work of Albert Kahn was most noticeable in Italy, where the American style came in contact with the ideological open-mindedness of a polytechnical culture. In Italy as well, there was no lack of literary interpretation. Emilio Cecchi, in *America Amara*, wrote: "I passed some hours at Edgewater, in the most modern and perfected assembly workshop of the Ford Motor Company.... One has the sense of an invisible presence, like in front of an embrasure of a castle. And this sense of a working and hidden awareness, it intervenes and accompanies you with every footstep, from when, having climbed to the first floor of an endless hangar, you find yourself in front of the assembly belt on which the car first begins to take shape and

following pages:
FISHER BUILDING: DETROIT, MICHIGAN; ALBERT KAHN, INC., 1928–1929
Detail of the entrance

SECTION B

DETAIL OF BOULEVARD ENTRANCE AND SOUTH EAS[T]

DENTILS
CARVED ORNAMENT
GRANITE
MARBLE
SECTION C
BLVD. ENTRANCE
NEW-CENTER-DE
CORPORATION
OF BLDG.
1/4" SCALE

then leave, after about six hours, perfect and tested, on the ground floor, at the other end of the assembly line."[47]

Aside from this testimony, Italy's first information on the technical innovations of the Ford Motor Company industrial plants concerned Albert Kahn's buildings at Highland Park. In 1915, the magazine *L'Industria* carried articles on the construction particulars, and in 1916, on the new methods of scientific management adopted in the American complex.[48]

The Highland Park complex was an inspiration to Giacomo Mattè Trucco, the engineer who, between 1914 and 1916, designed the Lingotto workshops of Fiat in Turin, the first factory in Europe to use an assembly line. The workshops improved the system used at Highland Park, in that the entire cycle of production, down to final inspection (performed on the track on the top of the building), was carried out in one building. Otherwise, the same principles were adopted: mass production concentrated under a single roof, production flow from one floor to another, careful use of space, and consideration of the psychological and physical well-being of the workers.

Similarities between the two buildings existed on a formal level as well. Like the architecture of Albert Kahn, the Lingotto workshop became both a symbol of industrial potential and a model for rules and discipline for production. "One of the most impressive sights of the industry" for architects, but also "the most rational…prison" for workers.[49]

While the Turin plant was a significant example of the influence of American-style scientific management in Italy,[50] the two countries were still separated by profound differences, due to the untimeliness and limited scope of the implementation of Fordist methods. The delay was also due to the inability to value the revisions of the pre-World War I ideology. In 1924, the year in which Lingotto became fully functional, Albert Kahn, Inc. was finishing the River Rouge plant for the Ford Motor Company, with a radically new conception of mass production.

However, the River Rouge complex did intrigue Italian technicians. In 1925, the magazine *Ingegneria* published a two-part account of engineer Carlo Ferrari's visits to the Ford industries: a detailed description of the "River Rouge plants" that the Italian engineer defined as "architectonically a gigantic complex of monolithic steel structures."[51] Ferrari's favorable impressions were echoed by Enrico Bonicelli, professor of the Regia Scuola d'Ingegneria of Turin, who, in his manual on industrial architecture, judged "the Ford workshops…very interesting in their architectural aspect."[52]

Of all the River Rouge buildings, the Engineering Laboratory received the most recognition from the architectural avant-garde.

Gaetano Minnucci, in a famous article published in *Architettura e Arti Decorative*, highlighted the "beautiful solution for low, extended buildings," and concluded that it was "a splendid example of mixed construction: pillars and lintels in reinforced concrete, covered in steel."[53]

Also during the postwar period, Alberto Sartoris, who since the 1920s, had followed the effects of scientific management on architectural design, in discussing American architecture of the period, cited the work of Albert Kahn as a departure from the academic mold: "Among the exceptions is Albert Kahn's (1869–1942) Ford Engineering Building in Dearborn, Michigan. The originality, elegance, sobriety, lightness, and greatness flow exclusively from an artistic ideal supported by good sense."[54]

Italy's and Europe's familiarity with the work of Albert Kahn, Inc. depended mainly on American texts like the 1938 issue of *The Architectural Forum* and the 1939 Nelson monograph, that circulated among organizers of production engineers and in architectural circles most attentive to transformations introduced by the industrial world.

Francesco Mauro, an expert in scientific management and the localization of industrial plants, and a man well familiar with Fordism (and who became an unheeded spokesman of Italian industrialists), was among the first Italian engineers to study the work of Albert Kahn. Speaking of Nelson's monograph as a "well-known work," Mauro stated: "the magnificent volume illustrates the works of the famous industrial engineering firm (famous for design and consulting) of Albert Kahn, connected to the names of Ford, General Motors, Chrysler, Glenn L. Martin, Pratt & Whitney, and Republic Steel."[55]

Another Italian interested in the work of Albert Kahn was Ugo Gobbato, an engineer with Alfa Romeo. After his visit to the Ford Motor Company plants in Highland Park and River Rouge, Gobbato made observations that assigned industrial architecture a central role in the business economy. In the second volume of an influential manual published in 1930, Gobbato wrote: "Always try, when giving shape to a design of an immobile object, to imagine and ideally fix your production cycle in the space, and to surround it only with what is indispensable, not what is indispensable at the moment but also what is durable and economic in time. And so you will have, from envisioning your cycle, the ideal industrial environment. Decorative facades, architectural monuments, all things beautiful for other types of architecture, are superfluous in an industrial setting, and, as such, are expenditures that one day may be sorely and irremediably regretted."[56] Nine years later, when Alfa Romeo was preparing designs for the Pomigliano d'Arco plant, Gobbato came to know of the new American industrial architecture through correspondence with a United States consultant, Michele Caserta. Caserta sent news on technical details with a copy of the monograph issue of *The Architectural Forum* dedicated to Albert Kahn, commenting, "it doesn't get any better!"[57]

The Fordist practice of the organization of space and land also had a great influence on the Olivetti experience, as shown in the magazine *Tecnica e Organizzazione*, published in Ivrea from 1937 to 1942.[58]

The work of Pasquale Carbonara was specifically important for the popularization of Italian architecture. In an exchange program for recent graduates of the University of Rome and Columbia University, Carbonara was able to visit the United States and report his impressions in a volume in which Albert Kahn, Inc. was defined as "the largest architectural firm specialized in industrial construction."[59] The rationalists, too, although slightly disloyal to Le Corbusier, became directly interested in the work of American engineers. In September, 1942, the magazine *Costruzioni Casabella*, in the second monograph issue dedicated to industrial architecture, edited by Ireneo Diotallevi and Franco Marescotti, included three examples of the work of "the famous firm A.K. Inc., specialized in works of industrial nature."[60]

American Style versus International Style

While many major European engineers and architects between the two World Wars looked to the work of Albert Kahn as a model for industrial constructions, the Detroit architect turned his interests to the history of European architecture, from the classical age to nineteenth-century eclecticism; Italy occupied a privileged position.

Albert Kahn spent most of his European travels in Italy (1891, 1911, 1919 and 1924). He visited Rome, Naples, Venice, Florence, Palermo, Bologna, Siena, and Milan, to which his sketches and photographs attest. In addition to this material, his interest in Italy was also documented in his personal library, for which he collected the books of Camillo Boito, Luca Beltrami, Adolfo Venturi, Pietro Toesca, studies of the Renaissance, and monographs on individual buildings. Together with the collection of illustrations of furnishings, decorations and architectural details of historic monuments, these books composed a rich iconographic archive from which he could draw to please any client's wishes.[61]

The attention to historical precedent was paired with the spirit of the business architect to better win the admiration of the client. Albert Kahn was thus able to propose factories admired by European rationalists and residences that adhered to the principles of the Beaux-Arts movement.

As a product of the machine age, Kahn simultaneously represented both the figures of the "American engineer" and the "American architect" from which Le Corbusier distanced himself.[62] But for Kahn, there was no contradiction: he strove to consistently satisfy his clientele. To read his work only within the framework of the slogan "architecture is 90% business and 10% art"—which was often said—does not do complete justice to the analysis of Albert Kahn or the work of Albert Kahn, Inc.

"Albert Kahn was not a theorist," wrote Paul Cret in Kahn's obituary.[63] Cret's assertion was well-founded only up to a certain point. Even though it was true that the Detroit architect did not produce a body of systematic theory, he still lectured and spoke of his theories at public functions and conferences, particularly after 1930.

Additionally, Kahn's writings showed a well-defined critical point of view, which, in a certain sense, changed opinion to interpretative perspective. This made Kahn the most versatile of the eclectic architects, capable of using even the compositional language of the Modern Movement.

Surprisingly enough, Kahn's criticisms of the European avant-garde are quite similar to those of the American architectural community today. His criticisms of the Modern Movement were rooted in reflection on specific characteristics of American architecture.

In an undated typewritten text (probably from 1931) entitled "Architecture in the United States," Kahn gave an historical account of the emerging leaders in the American architectural community, together with personal preferences and interesting critical points.[64]

Particular consideration was given to the eclectic work of the New York firm of McKim, Mead & White, as well as to architects like Cass Gilbert, Paul Cret and Charles Platt. While Kahn greatly praised the work of Louis Sullivan, he did not hesitate to criticize the romantic individualism of Henry Hobson Richardson, and he even directed some biting remarks toward Frank Lloyd Wright.[65] Finally, pausing to note the importance of Daniel Burnham's White City, which had triumphed at the 1893 Chicago Expo, Kahn underlined "The debt which this country owes to the French government for the liberal treatment accorded Americans in the École des Beaux Arts."[66]

Aside from being an ode to eclecticism and the academic tradition, the piece focused on a subject that occupied a central place in Kahn's theoretical reflection: the search for a national architecture. Indeed, the twenty-three type-written pages of the text began with a declaration that defined an architectural language solidly anchored to the national context: "Architecture, more than any other art, images the character of a people. It is the mirror of the national consciousness and reveals the social tone of the Nation."[67]

This theme was developed in what may have been the definitive work on Kahn's views of non-industrial architecture: the article entitled "Architectural Trend," in the April 1931 issue of the *Journal of Maryland Academy of Sciences*.[68] "But what is a purely American style? The wigwam of the Indian or the adobe hut of the Pueblo? Are these to serve as our inspiration?" The answer leaves no room for doubt. "Just as the American people is a composite of many nations, just so its architecture must be a composite; but just as American characteristics influence American life, so they influence American architecture. If, in re-employing older forms and applying them to our newer problems, we have done wrong, then all architecture of the past is wrong, for all of it is but a development of what was done before....Those who so deplore the non-existence of an American architecture need merely look about. It has been here for years only they do not know it."[69] Thus, eclecticism became the architectural melting pot of the American city.

Similarly, Kahn voiced a criticism of two well-renowned American architects: Sullivan (whom he had previously praised) and Wright. In his point of view, "Theirs was not an architecture that sprang from the soil, even though hailed as such. It was an individual effort which did not acquire even sufficient momentum to interest a reasonably large group, and collective effort is always necessary to form a new school."[70]

Some years later, at a conference held at the Adcraft Club in Detroit on January 22, 1937, Albert Kahn confirmed his adherence to the Beaux-Arts tradition, but modified his stance towards the Chicago School and enlarged his horizon of thought to include other architects.[71] His preferences tended towards the architecture of Eliel Saarinen, "a foreigner from Finland who had never built a skyscraper [who showed] us in his remarkable competitive design for the Chicago Tribune Building, the real solution of the problem."[72]

The most important reflections from this occasion regarded the relationship between industrial and public architecture. In underlining how the use of reinforced concrete, which made possible the substitution of glassed surfaces for walls, revolutionized the architecture of the factory and created a new type of building, Albert Kahn was quick to emphasize: "I can see a very close analogy between the modern industrial building and the modern box-like, flat roofed house, so many of which are erected today. At that, while I admire many of the modern factories, I can't say as much for many of these houses. Indeed, much already done and being done under so-called modernism, is to me extremely ugly and monotonous."[73]

This was the duality inherent in Albert Kahn's work: the designer of perfect labor machines theorized the refusal of these machines for dwellings. In the 1930s, when the preoccupation was exclusively with industrial architecture with noteworthy, quality experimentation, the Detroit architect launched an intense campaign primarily against Le Corbusier.

In his entry for the *National Encyclopedia* on industrial architecture, Albert Kahn criticized the excessive use of glass in industrial buildings designed by the European avant-garde.[74] This was a technical charge relative to means of construction of industrial buildings—a terrain in which the Detroit architect was the indisputable leader and was irrefutably superior to any European architect—but beyond that, the criticisms that he directed towards the Modern Movement were more general.

There were some noteworthy occasions on which the American architectural community confronted the Modern Movement.

From February 10 to March 23, 1932, the Museum of Modern Art in New York held the exhibit *Modern Architecture* curated by two young Harvard graduates: thirty-one-year-old Henry-Russell Hitchcock and twenty-six-year-old Philip Johnson. The exhibit presented photographs and models of the works of Wright, Gropius, Le Corbusier, Oud, Mies van der Rohe, Hood, Howe & Lescaze, Neutra, and the Bowman Brothers, and a section dedicated to Housing, curated by Lewis Mumford.

In the introduction to the exhibition catalog, Alfred Barr, Jr., director of the museum, explained the choices made by Hitchcock and Johnson.[75] According to Barr, the Colombia Expo of 1893 and the competition for the Chicago Tribune Building in 1922 represented the milestones of a period of American architectural history marked by contradictory and confusing language. The new architecture, called "International Style," indicated a new road to travel. Referring to its exhaustive treatment in *The International Style: Architecture Since 1922*[76] by the two exhibit curators, Barr synthesized the thesis, pointing out the essential principles of the new style: volume, regularity, flexibility, technical perfection, and the absence of decoration. The precedents and references were clear: Wright was the spiritual father and Gropius, Oud, Le Corbusier and Mies were "the four founders of the International Style."

The homage to the European avant-garde was deceptive, as the theses expressed were based on American production, with the intention of conferring cultural dignity, and inclusion in the international architectural debate in which it had been marginalized.

Examples of the International Style included the McGraw Hill Building by Raymond Hood (a decisive turning point in the career of this architect, famous for the Neo-Gothic Chicago Tribune skyscraper), the Health House of Los Angeles by Richard Neutra, the Philadelphia Savings Fund Society Building by George Howe and William E. Lescaze, and the Lux Apartments by the Bowman Brothers. Oddly enough, all of these architects soon abandoned the International Style.

Neutra arrived in the United States in 1923 from Vienna, where he had worked with Adolf Loos. After two years with Wright in Chicago, he moved to Los Angeles to begin his own architectural firm. For Doctor Lovell's Health House, Neutra studied and ultimately shared the passionately health-conscious life philosophy of the client, and created an appropriate setting for him. The morphological and technological aspects of the work, from its horizontality to its asymmetry, from its steel skeleton to its concrete frames, became a symbol of the new style, and fit right in on the West Coast. Despite the success of this building, Neutra soon distanced himself from the formal models of the International Style, and tried an approach called "biorealism," which aimed to create a physical environment which would not interfere with "natural human gifts."[7]

Howe and Lescaze, too, dissolving their firm in 1934, deserted the International Style after building the Philadelphia skyscraper. Howe had begun his teaching career after graduating from Harvard University and from the École des Beaux-Arts in Paris. In 1928, he joined William E. Lescaze, a Swiss architect and student of Werner Moser at the Polytechnic in Zurich, who had come to the United States some years earlier. The design of the Philadelphia Savings Fund Society, completed in 1932, brought their studio great renown.[78] The base of the building had a beveled angle designed to house offices, and its unornamented tower (whose structural elements were visible) signaled a new generation of American skyscrapers, rightfully entering—along with Raymond Hood's McGraw Hill Building—the series of successes of the International Style in America in the field of tall buildings.

However, for Hitchcock and Johnson, the works that demonstrated the success of the International Style were not limited to these few examples. In the essay "The Extent of Modern Architecture," included in the exhibit catalog, the two curators cited for every nation those architects whose designs were closest to their proposals. In Germany there were Schneider, Scharoun and Haesler; in Holland: Rietveld, Van Eesteren, Duiker, Brinkman and Van der Vlugt; in France: Lurçat, Chareau and Roux Spitz; and finally in the United States "the magnificent factories of Albert Kahn in Detroit."[79]

Many illustrations and photographs of these works of architecture (Albert Kahn's were excluded) filled the book *The International Style: Architecture Since 1922*. The manualistic intentions of the book were evidenced by its enumeration of principles: from judgements on European functionalism and the formulation of the historical path. Twenty years later, in a famous article that reconsidered the original pronouncements but confirmed the fundamental conception, Hitchcock warned against what he had once wanted to make "an academic rulebook."[80]

Even in their flexibility, the rules clearly defined an "idea of style" as a common thread of design experience. Catchphrases like "mere planes surrounding a volume," "flat roofs," "continuous space," "continuity of surfaces," "regularity," "asymmetry," "horizontality," "avoidance of applied decoration," "natural colors," and "free planning," became the ten commandments of modern architecture.[81]

In establishing the boundaries of a new style, the International Style completely upset the research of the Modern Movement to satisfy American architecture's need to refer to European models. The eclectic repertory could now be further enriched. Along with French gothic and Italian renaissance buildings, there were now also the "white houses:" the Tugendhat House, the Weissenhof, and the Bauhaus.

Of course, the apparent clarity of Hitchcock and Johnson's thesis did not convince everyone, especially American architects.

"But most new 'modernistic' houses manage to look as though cut from cardboard with scissors, the sheets of cardboard folded or bent in rectangles with an occasional curved cardboard surface added to get relief. The cardboard forms thus made are glued together in box-like forms—in a childish attempt to make buildings resemble steamships, flying machines or locomotives." With this pronouncement, Wright ridiculed European modern architecture, in one of his lectures at Princeton University in 1930.[82]

Referring to the New York exhibit, in an article published in the May 1932 issue of *Pencil Points*, Albert Kahn also aligned himself with Wright. "I have before me the catalog of an exhibition of 'modern architecture' being held at the moment in this country...would it be possible by the wildest stretch of the imagination to believe either the Lovell House at Los Angeles by Neutra or the Lux Apartment House by Bowman Brothers things of beauty or a joy forever? May Providence and our common sense save us from such aberrations!"[83]

Speaking then of the European architects cited as founders of the new movement, Kahn turned his attention to the condemnation of the same compositional formulas adapted for every situation and for every building type, disapproving "of making all buildings look like factories."[84]

Kahn advised the study of styles of the past, but at the same time urged architects not to forget "the local color" through the use of forms and materials characteristic of the geographic context where the building was located. Kahn's critique of architecture was tempered by regionalism, and was attentive to producing a continuity with the past.

These different facets of Albert Kahn's position regarding American and European architecture found a definitive formulation in the text "Architecture. Whence and Whither," read at the Cleveland Architectural Society on December 6, 1936.[85]

On this occasion Kahn deepened his condemnation of the leaders of the Modern Movement, Le Corbusier most of all, but at the same time declared that he valued much of twentieth-century European architecture.

Among the Germans, he showed a preference for the works of Kreis, Fahrenkamp, Behrens, Messel, and Hoffman to those of Mendelsohn, Gropius, and Poelzig; among the French the Perrets were preferable to Le Corbusier, Lurçat, and Mallet-Stevens; in Holland, Kahn cited the work of Dudok; and finally, Kahn also showed admiration for Nordic classicism.

In the end, Kahn reproached these modern architects because he realized that "It would be sad indeed if an International Style based upon their theories became a reality. Imagine not only a city but many lands building in accordance with one formula, and that applied to residences as well as to hospitals, and schools and hotels, railroad stations, factories, prisons and State Capitols, as well. What monotony would result? A building to be good, even today, must express its purpose and look like what it is. To make all appear alike may be modern according to Corbusier but certainly not good architecture or common sense."[86]

Albert Kahn was a designer capable of providing a decisive contribution to the aesthetics of the machine, an ambassador of eclecticism, a businessman-architect that privileged the demands of the client, a manager of a large firm organized according to the principles of scientific management, and a self-taught critic capable of singling out reference models, of advancing operative principles, and of voicing unusual opinions.

NOTES

1 The bibliography on the American city is quite vast; for an introduction, see C.N. Glaab, *The American City. A Documentary History*, Dorsey Press, Homewood, IL 1963.

2 An in-depth study on the social history of Detroit: O. Zunz, *The Changing Face of Inequality: Urbanization, Industrial Development and Immigrants in Detroit, 1880–1920*, University of Chicago Press, Chicago 1982, also available in an abridged edition in French: *Naissance de l'Amérique industrielle. Detroit, 1880–1920*, Aubier, Paris 1983.

3 See the difference between the travel impressions of an Englishman: A. Archer, *America Today. Observation & Reflections*, Heinemann, London 1900, with those of thirty years later by an Italian: F. Ciarlantini, *Incontro col Nord America*, Edizioni Alpes, Milan 1929.

4 J.W. Reps, *Town Planning in Frontier America*, Princeton University Press, Princeton, NJ 1969, p. 368; this text is the abridged edition of Reps's study, *The Making of Urban America. A History of City Planning in the United States*, Princeton University Press, Princeton NJ, 1965 (for the history of Detroit, see pp. 267–269). On the general urban history of Detroit, see the fundamental work of R. Conot, *American Odyssey*, Wayne State University Press, Detroit 1986 (on the Woodward Plan, pp. 8–17).

5 J.W. Reps, *Town Planning in Frontier America*, p. 376.

6 For a history of American urban planning in the nineteenth century, see D. Schuyler, *The New Urban Landscape. The Redefinition of City Form in Nineteenth-Century America*, The Johns Hopkins University Press, Baltimore–London 1986. On L'Enfant's Plan for Washington as a connection to Woodward's urban solutions, see J. Reps, *Monumental Washington*, Princeton University Press, Princeton, NJ 1967. For its novel aspects, the Woodward Plan can be likened to Cerdà's for Barcelona. See I. Cerdà, *Teoria general de la Urbanizacion*, 1867, A. Lopez de Aberasturi (ed.), Seuil, Paris 1979.

7 For an analysis of the Gratiot Project, see W.H. Ferry, *The Buildings of Detroit. A History*, Wayne State University Press, Detroit 1968, pp. 371–373; L. Hilberseimer, *Entfaltung einer Planungsidee*, Ullstein, Berlin 1963, chapter XXV. D. Spaeth, "Ludwig Hilberseimer's Settlement Unit. Origins And Applications," in R. Pommer, D. Spaeth, K. Harrington, *In the Shadow of Mies. Ludwig Hilberseimer Architect, Educator and Urban Planner*, The Art Institute of Chicago and Rizzoli International Publications, New York 1988, pp. 63–64; F. Schulze, *Mies van der Rohe. A Critical Biography*, The University of Chicago Press, Chicago 1985. For a direct testimony, also see L. Hilberseimer, *Mies van der Rohe*, Theobald, Chicago 1956.

8 See R. Conot, *American Odyssey*; S. Conti, *Dopo la città industriale. Detroit tra crisi urbana e crisi dell'automobile*, Angeli, Milan 1983; P. Ceccarelli, "Due città fragili: Detroit e Torino. Ovvero, come non si dovrebbe costruire la città moderna," in *Il Mulino*, XXXII, no. 1, January–February 1983.

9 On the construction history of Detroit, see W.H. Ferry, *The Buildings of Detroit. A History*, and for a useful guide, K.M. Meyer (ed.), *Detroit Architecture. A.I.A. Guide*, Wayne State University Press, Detroit 1971 (see also the 1980 revised edition, M.C.P. McElroy (ed.)). Some images of the city prior to 1900 can be found in *Neely's Photographs. Views of Prominent American Cities. Buffalo–Detroit–Cleveland–Milwaukee–Cincinnati*, Tennyson Neely Publisher, London–New York–Chicago 1899.

10 On the contact between Ford and Wright, see G.C. Manson, *Frank Lloyd Wright to 1910: The First Golden Age*, Reinhold Publishing Corporation, New York 1958, p. 213. On Van Holst, see E. Harrington, "International Influences on Henry Hobson Richardson's Glessner House," in J. Zukowsky (ed.), *Chicago Architecture. 1872–1922. Birth of a Metropolis*, The Art Institute of Chicago and Prestel Verlag, Munich 1987, p. 205. On Niedecken and his work for Ford, see R.G. Wilson, "Chicago and the International Arts and Crafts Movements: Progressive and

Conservative Tendencies," Ibid., pp. 212 and 218. Finally, for the Van Tyne construction, see C.K. Hyde, *Detroit: An Industrial History Guide*, Detroit Historical Society, Detroit 1980, site 48.

11 On the works of the Saarinens, see the monographs, (still valid although somewhat dated) by A. Christ-Janer, *Eliel Saarinen*, The University of Chicago Press, Chicago 1948, and A. Temko, *Eero Saarinen*, Braziller, New York 1962.

12 The other large firm which, with Albert Kahn, Inc., divided a great part of the construction commissions in Detroit, is that of Smith, Hinchman & Grylls. See T.J. Holleman, J.P. Gallagher, Smith, Hinchman & Grylls: *125 Years of Architecture and Engineering, 1853–1978*, Detroit 1978.

13 On eclecticism and its revival in American architecture, see W.C. Kidney, *The Architecture of Choice: Eclecticism in America. 1880–1930*, Braziller, New York 1974 and M. Whiffen, *American Architecture Since 1780. A Guide to the Styles*, MIT Press, Cambridge (MA)–London 1969. For an examination of the problematic aspects of eclecticism in international architecture, see L. Patetta, *L'architettura dell'Eclettismo. Fonti, teorie e modelli, 1750–1900*, Mazzotta, Milan 1975 and Ibid., "Alcune considerazioni sull'architettura dell'eclettismo," in *QD. Quaderni del Dipartimento di progettazione dell'architettura del Politecnico di Milano*, no. 6, December 1987, pp. 7–21.

14 Albert Kahn's penchant for getting himself published is evidenced in *Albert Kahn architect. Detroit, Michigan*, Architectural Catalog Co., New York, undated (the copy consulted by the author carries the following dedication helpful in determining the date: "with the best wishes Albert Kahn, Nov. 18th 1921"), which contains photographs and designs, but no text, of thirty-three constructions including offices, banks, and residences.

15 See W.H. Ferry, *The Buildings of Detroit. A History*, p. 264.

16 A. Kahn, *Temple Beth-El*, typewritten, 1923 (AKA), p. 3. On Temple Beth-El of 1922 (still standing at 8801 Woodward Avenue thanks to the 1982 nomination by the National Register of Historic Places), see "Breaths Spirit of God's House," in *The Detroit News*, November 4, 1922; "Temple Beth-El," in *The Architectural Forum*, vol. XL, no. 5, May 1924, tables 73–74.

17 See W.H. Ferry, *The Buildings of Detroit. A History*, pp. 180–181.

18 Ibid., p. 187.

19 A. Kahn, *Ernest Wilby*, typewritten and sent to "Talmage Hughes," March 19, 1941 (AKA), p. 1. See also "Ernest Wilby Dies At Home in Windsor," in *The Detroit Free Press*, December 12, 1957.

20 "The interior of Hill Auditorium in Ann Arbor (by Albert Kahn with Ernest Wilby as designer) is located near the Auditorium Building by Adler and Sullivan as one of the most intelligent solutions to the problem" L. Mumford, "A Backward Glance," in L. Mumford, (ed.), *Roots of Contemporary American Architecture*, 1952, Dover Publications Inc., New York 1972, p. 23. Mumford praised Albert Kahn as well in *The Brown Decades, A Study of the Arts in America 1865–1895*, 1931, Dover, New York 1959, p. 179.

21 "The Arthur Hill Memorial Hall," in *The Michigan Alumnus*, February 1912, p. 191 (plans of the building; the October 1911 issue featured perspectives of the building just before its construction). See also J.L. Beckstrom, "Hill Auditorium Still Going Strong at 75," in *Ann Arbor Scene Magazine*, September 1987, pp. 18–20.

22 On hospital architecture, see S.S. Goldwater, "Current Hospital Trends," in *The Architectural Forum*, vol. LVII, no. 5, November 1932, pp. 387–390 (which carried the illustration of Herman Kiefer Hospital in Detroit designed by Albert Kahn, Inc.) and H.E. Hannaford, "Planning the General Hospital," *The Architectural Forum*, pp. 391–398.

23 A. Kahn, *Library at Ann Arbor*, typewritten and sent to "Mr. Wm. W. Bishop, Librarian,

University of Michigan, Ann Arbor, Michigan," January 14, 1920 (AKA).

24 A. Kahn, *Carillon Tower*, typewritten, "sent to Dr. Robbins for his brochure," undated (AKA); and *The Charles Baird Carillon. The University of Michigan*. December 4, 1936, Ann Arbor 1936 (AKA). This brochure, published on the occasion of the building's inauguration, in the parts described carried—without citing the author—the text drafted by Albert Kahn.

25 See W.H. Ferry, "The Mansions of Grosse Pointe. A Suburb in Good Taste," in *Monthly Bulletin of the Michigan Society of Architects*, March 1956.

26 W.H. Ferry, *The Buildings of Detroit. A History*, p. 272.

27 On Prairie Houses, see H.A. Brooks, *The Prairie School: Frank Lloyd Wright and His Midwest Contemporaries*, University of Toronto Press, Toronto 1972 (p. 342 indicates Albert Kahn who, the author writes, "in his first works was occasionally influenced by the Prairie architects").

28 "The Detroit News Building. An Imposing Example of Commercial Architecture and an Efficient Newspaper Plant. Albert Kahn, Architect; Ernest Wilby, Associate," in *The Architectural Forum*, vol. XXVIII, no. 1, January 1918, p. 27.

29 Ibid., p. 28.

30 See, respectively, the brochure *A Newspaper Jewel Box. The Brooklyn Plant of The New York Times, New York*, undated (AKA) and M. Kahn, "Planned To Make Newspaper Work Easy," in *The American Architect*, March 1930.

31 On the Detroit Athletic Club, see A. Kahn, "An Architectural Triumph," in *Detroit Saturday*, April 17, 1915 and "The Detroit Athletic Club. Mr. Albert Kahn, Architect. Mr. Ernest Wilby, Associate," in *The American Architect*, vol. CVIII, no. 2064, July 14, 1915 (which published numerous illustrations, primarily detailing the interior). On the project for the police headquarters, see "Police Station Plans Drawn," in *The Detroit News*, March 7, 1920.

32 A. Kahn, *The First State*, typewritten, undated (AKA), p. 1.

33 See Albert Kahn, Inc., *Architectural Treatment of Bank Buildings*, Detroit 1929 (AKA); J.M. Donaldson, "Branch Offices of State Banks in Detroit," in *The Architectural Forum*, vol. XXXII, no. 4, April 1920, pp. 135–140 that carried illustrations of Kahn's designs. On the headquarters of the Detroit Trust Company, see the brochure *Detroit Trust Company. Fifteen Years of Service*, Detroit 1916 (AKA).

34 On the spread of these services in the Ford Motor Company, see P. Lehideux, *Ford. Entreprise internationale*, Presses Universitaires de France, Paris 1953, particularly the chapter "L'aspect geographie commerciale."

35 See F.A. Fairbrother, "The Planning of Automobile Sales and Service Buildings," in *The Architectural Forum*, vol. XXXIII, no. 2, August 1920, pp. 39–44 and W.C. Rowland, "Architecture and Automobile Industry," in *The Architectural Forum*, vol. XXXIV, no. 6, June 1921, pp. 199–206.

36 A. Kahn, *General Motors Building*, typewritten, December 31, 1921 (AKA), p. 1. The complete description of the building (location, services offered and architectural parts) is found in the two advertising brochures (conserved in AKA): *Durant Building*, Durant Building Corporation, Detroit, undated (which documents the building plan with numerous designs. The name Durant Building, in honor of the General Motors president, was later changed) and *A Great Business Community. General Motors Building, Detroit, Michigan, U.S.A.*, Detroit, undated (with numerous photographs that document the construction).

37 A. Kahn, "Fisher Building," in *The American Architect*, vol. CXXXV, no. 2563, February 20, 1929, p. 211. In addition to the introduction by Albert Kahn (pp. 211–220), the index of this issue of the magazine dedicated to the Fisher Building follows with: "A Group of Plates Illustrating the Fisher Building," (pp. 221–244; with thirty designs and photographs);

"Engineering Contributions To the Design of the Fisher Building" (pp. 245–250); an article signed by the engineers of Albert Kahn, Inc. on the complex installation system); "Editorial Comment" (pp. 251–264; illustrated with numerous designs of construction details); "Fisher Building Garage" (pp. 265–268) and "The Fisher Theater" (pp. 269–274; signed by the firm of Graven & Meyer Architects and Leiberman & Hein Engineers, to whom Albert Kahn had entrusted the theater project). The various commercial services that the building offers are more thoroughly illustrated in the advertising brochure *Concerning the Fisher Building, Detroit*, Detroit 1929 (AKA). The Fisher Building won the Architectural League of New York prize for "the best building constructed in America" in 1928 (see "Albert Kahn Is Awarded Medal," in *Weekly Bulletin of the Michigan Society of Architects*, April 23, 1929).

38 A. Kahn, *Memorandum Regarding the Saarinen Plan*, typewritten, undated (AKA). On Saarinen's plan for Detroit's Riverfront, see M. Tafuri, "La montagna disincantata," in G. Ciucci, F. Dal Co, M. Manieri Elia, M. Tafuri, *La città americana dalla guerra civile al New Deal*, Laterza, Bari 1973, pp. 464–465.

39 "Fisher Building Office to Open About September First," in *Trio*, vol., no. 35, May 15, 1928, p. 1. The Fisher Building was pointed out as well in a European publication dedicated to American architecture; see F. Washburn, *Riesenbauten Nordamerikas*, Fussli, Zurich–Leipzig 1930, p. 20.

40 L.F. Celine, *Voyage au bout de la nuit*, 1932, Gallimard, Paris 1952.

41 W. Gropius, "Die Entwicklung Moderner Industriebaukunst," in *Jahrbuch des Deutschen Werkbundes*, 1913, pp. 17–22, Eng. trans. "The Rise of Modern Industrial Architecture," in D. Gifford (ed.), *The Literature of Architecture*, Dutton, New York 1966. On the Taylorist and Fordist influence on Gropius's work, see W. Nerdinger, *Walter Gropius*, Mann, Berlin 1985.

42 Le Corbusier, *Quand les cathédrales étaient blanches. Voyage au pays des timides*, Plon, Paris 1937, p. 247. On Le Corbusier's position with respect to the subject of industrial production, see M. McLeod, "Taylorismo," in AA.VV., *Le Corbusier Enciclopedia*, Electa, Milan 1988, pp. 471–476 and S. von Moos, "Industria," *Le Corbusier Enciclopedia*, pp. 227–239.

43 E. Mendelsohn, *Amerika. Bilderbuch eines Architekten*, Rudolf Mosse, Berlin 1926, and E. Mendelsohn, *Russland Europa Amerika. Ein Architektonischer Querschnitt*, Rudolf Mosse, Berlin 1929.

44 A. Behne, *Der Moderne Zweckbau*, Masken, München-Wien 1926, pp. 25–26 (for Ford quotes) and plates 3–4 (for photographs of Albert Kahn's factories).

45 B. Taut, *Die Neue Baukunst in Europa und Amerika*, Julius Hoffmann, Stuttgart 1929, pp. 94, 96, 99.

46 R. Neutra, *Wie Baut Amerika?*, Julius Hoffmann, Stuttgart 1927.

47 See E. Cecchi, *America amara*, Sansoni, Florence 1941, p. 32. In particular, on the subject of images of the United States in Italy, see M. Nacci, *L'antiamericanismo in Italia negli anni Trenta*, Bollati Boringhieri, Turin 1989.

48 See "Le officine della Ford Motor Co. a Detroit negli Stati Uniti," in *L'industria*, XXIX, no. 26, June 27, 1915, pp. 414–415 and "L'organizzazione del lavoro in una fabbrica di automobili degli Stati Uniti," in *L'industria*, CCC, no. 50, December 10, 1916, pp. 799–800.

49 Respectively: XXX (Le Corbusier), "Les usines Fiat du Lingotto a Turin," in *L'Esprit Nouveau*, no. 19, undated (December 1923, according to the date suggested by the Foundation Le Corbusier), pages unnumbered; and by a flyer entitled "La cellula comunista di Portolongone," in D. Bigazzi, "Gli operai della catena di montaggio. La Fiat Lingotto, (1922–1935)," in *Società e Storia*, II, no. 5, 1979, p. 483. For the history of the building, see M. Pozzetto, *La Fiat Lingotto. Un'architettura torinese d'avanguardia*, Centro studi piemontesi, Turin 1975 and M.G. Daprà Conti, "Produzione meccanica e progetto: lo stabilimento del Lingotto," in *Casabella*, XLVI, no. 486, December 1982, pp. 40–47.

50 For a critical evaluation of the particularities of the Italian situation, see G. Sapelli, *Organizzazione, lavoro, e innovazione industriale nell'Italia tra le due guerre*, Rosenberg & Sellier, Turin 1978; Ibid., "Gli organizzatori della produzione tra struttura d'impresa e modelli culturali," in *Storia d'Italia. Annali 4. Intellettuali e potere*, Einaudi, Turin 1981, pp. 591–696.

51 C. Ferrari, "Produzione in massa. Le industrie Ford," in *Ingegneria*, IV, no. 7, July 1925, p. 252 (the second part of the article was published in the no. 10, October 1925 issue). Another visit by an Italian engineer to the Ford plants, with interesting descriptions of labor methods, is that of V. Magliocco, *Detroit, U.S.A.*, Edizioni dell'Associazione Nazionale Fascista dei Dirigenti di Aziende Industriali, Rome 1931.

52 E. Bonicelli, *L'architettura industriale nei suoi elementi costruttivi e nella sua composizione*, Unione Tipografico–Editrice Torinese, Turin, p. 469.

53 G. Minucci, "L'architettura e l'estetica degli edifici industriali," in *Architettura e arti decorative*, V, vol. 2, 1925–1926 (the article is dated May 1926), p. 564.

54 A. Sartoris, *Encyclopédie de l'architecture nouvelle. Ordre et climat américains*, Hoepli, Milan 1954, p. 93. For the Italian rationalist architects' interest in the principles of scientific management of labor which particularly involved Sartoris and Piero Bottoni, see G. Tonon, "Dagli stili alla ricerca come stile, 1922–1929," in G. Consonni, L. Meneghetti, G. Tonon (ed.), *Piero Bottoni. Opera completa*, Fabbri, Milan 1990, pp. 44–46.

55 F. Mauro, *Impianti industriali*, Hoepli, Milan 1948, p. 656, note 43.

56 U. Gobbato, *Organizzazione dei fattori della produzione*, vol. II, Torino 1930, p. 107.

57 In the Alfa Romeo general archives, document 95/I; thanks to Duccio Bigazzi for having furnished me with this precise information. On Gobbato's activity as director of Alfa Romeo, see D. Bigazzi, "Organizzazione del lavoro e razionalizzazione nella crisi del fascismo, 1942–1943," in *Studi Storici*, no. 2, 1978, pp. 367–396.

58 On this topic see G. Consonni, "Il Piano A.R.: un progetto nella tradizione dell'Illuminismo lombardo," now in G. Consonni, *L'internità dell'esterno. Scritti sull'abitare e il costruire*, Clup, Milan 1989, p. 52. The magazine deals with "new cars, industrial architecture, social assistance;" the industrial architecture articles were signed by Riccardo Rothschild.

59 P. Carbonara, *L'architettura in America. La civiltà nord-americana riflessa nei caratteri dei suoi edifici*, Laterza, Bari 1939, p. 130.

60 "Fabbrica di bilance automatiche Toledo nell'Ohio;" "Edifici di montaggio e spedizione automobili Chrysler a Detroit;" "Officina di montaggio aeroplani a Baltimore" in *Costruzioni Casabella*, XV, no. 177, September 1942, pp. 24–27, 33. See also *Casabella*, X, no. 113, May 1937, p. 33 which shows an illustration of a "Ford plant in Michigan (A. Kahn)." Afterwards, during the Reconstruction period, the American experience in the field of industrial construction became a valuable reference model, and in this case as well, the work of Albert Kahn, Inc. appeared. See R.G. Angeli (ed.) *Documenti di architettura. Composizione e tecnica. Edifici industriali*, Ballardi, Milan 1949 and V. Zignoli, *La produttività e la nuova tecnica di produzione*, Hoepli, Milan 1945. For an historical account, see B. Zevi, *Storia dell'architettura moderna*, Einaudi, Turin 1955, which points out the work of Albert Kahn, Inc. as "for an honest and very pure industrial construction" (p. 478).

61 Albert Kahn's personal library has been donated to the Lawrence Technological Institute of Southfield, Detroit. In addition to the Italian volumes dedicated to architecture history and art history, there are other volumes on architecture by Le Corbusier, Mendelsohn, Wagner, Lurcat, Aalto, Gropius, Taut, Sartoris, Garnier, Hilberseimer, Oud, Mallet-Stevens, and of course, writings by and about Wright. AKA conserves the collection of photographs of historical European edifices (several images courtesy of Studio Alinari, Florence).

62 "Let's listen to American engineers, but beware of American architects." Le Corbusier, *Vers une Architecture*, 1923, Vincent, Fréal & C., Paris 1958, p. 29.

63 P. Cret, "Albert Kahn," in *The Octagon. A Journal of the A.I.A.*, February 1943, p. 16.

64 A. Kahn, *Architecture in the United States*, typewritten, undated [circa 1931] (AKA).

65 Ibid., p. 3 (for Richardson); pp. 4–6 (Sullivan); pp. 7–10 (McKim, Mead & White); pp. 11–12 (Gilbert); pp. 16–17 (Cret); p. 18 (Platt); p. 23 (Wright).

66 Ibid., p. 13.

67 Ibid., p. 1.

68 A. Kahn, "Architectural Trend," in *The Journal of the Maryland Academy of Sciences*, vol. II, no. 2, April 1931, pp. 106–136.

69 Ibid., p. 107.

70 Ibid., p. 117. In the successive pieces dedicated to American architecture, Albert Kahn modified this heavy judgement, but, even while recognizing its importance, he did not pass up the opportunity to criticize Wright's work. On this subject there is the interesting exchange of shots during a conference held by Wright in Detroit in October 1938 (see H.C. Bower, "Architecture Talk Given by Expert," in *The Detroit Free Press*, October 19, 1938). Expressing admiration for the Ford factories, "even if they're 90 per cent business and 10 per cent art," Wright added that Albert Kahn could be considered only a "builder" and invited the Detroit architect, present in the audience, to defend this accusation. Kahn refused, but later, during the dinner, Albert Kahn publicly praised Wright's work and asked him to give an example of modern architecture. Wright answered, "not a factory and not done by yourself."

71 A. Kahn, *Thirty Minutes With American Architecture and Architects*, text of a conference given at the Adcraft Club in Detroit on January 22, 1937, typewritten (AKA).

72 Ibid., p. 10.

73 Ibid., p. 11.

74 See A. Kahn, *Article on Industrial Architecture for Collier Encyclopedia*, typewritten, August 1931, (AKA), in part published in the entry "Factory Building," in *National Encyclopedia*, Collier and Sons, New York 1932.

75 A.H. Barr, Jr., "Foreword," in *Modern Architecture. International Exhibition*, Museum of Modern Art 1932 (exhibit catalog), pp. 12–17.

76 H.R. Hitchcock, P. Johnson, *The International Style: Architecture since 1922*, Norton & Company, New York 1932. On the influence of the International Style on American architecture during the 1930s and 1940s, see A. Gowans, *Images of American Living. Four Centuries of Architecture and Furniture as Cultural Expression*, 1964, Harper & Row Publishers, New York 1976, pp. 435–444; M. Whiffen, *American Architecture Since 1780. A Guide to the Styles*, pp. 241–246; D.P. Handlin, *American Architecture*, Thames and Hudson, London 1985, pp. 197–231.

77 See R. Neutra, *Survival Through Design*, New York 1954. On Neutra's work, see also E. McCoy, *Richard Neutra*, Braziller, New York 1960.

78 See W. Jordy, "PSFS: Its Development and Its Significance in Modern Architecture," in *Journal of the Society of Architectural Historians*, XXI, no. 2, May 1962, pp. 47–83; A.H. Brooks, "PSFS: A Source for Its Design," *Journal of the Society of Architectural Historians*, XXVII, no. 4, December 1968, pp. 292–303.

79 H.R. Hitchcock, P. Johnson, "Extent of Modern Architecture," in *Modern Architecture. International Exhibition*, p. 22. The inclusion of Albert Kahn's work among the representatives

of the new style surpassed national confines. At the V Triennale of Milan in 1933, where the Museum of Modern Art was commissioned to prepare the panels dedicated to American architecture, the photo montages presented the work of Neutra, Howe and Lescaze, together with Kahn's industrial buildings. See *V Triennale di Milano. Catalogo ufficiale*, Ceschina, Milan 1933, pp. 82–83. It must be added that critic Henry-Russell Hitchcock often cited the work of Albert Kahn: he did so more in-depth at the conference "Architecture of The Mid-Twentieth Century" held at the Detroit Institute of Arts on October 16, 1945, now in *Weekly Bulletin of the Michigan Society of Architects*, no. 45, November 6, 1945, pp. 1–3.

80 H.R. Hitchcock, "The International Style Twenty Years After," in *The Architectural Record*, August 1951, now also in H-R Hitchcock, P. Johnson, *The International Style*, Norton & Company, New York-London 1966 (originally published under the title *The International Style: Architecture Since 1922*), p. 242.

81 The quotations are taken from H.R. Hitchcock, P. Johnson, *The International Style*, pp. 40–88.

82 F.L. Wright, *Modern Architecture*, Princeton University Press, Princeton, NJ 1931. Now also in F.L. Wright, *The Future of Architecture*, Horizon Press, New York 1953, p. 130.

83 A. Kahn, "The Approach to Design," in *Pencil Points*, vol. XIII, no. 5, May 1932, p. 300.

84 Ibid.

85 A. Kahn, *Architecture. Whence and Whither*, text of a conference given at the Cleveland Architectural Society on December 6, 1937, typewritten (AKA).

86 Ibid., p. 12.

SOURCES OF ILLUSTRATIONS

Albert Kahn Associates Inc. Architects and Engineers, Detroit
pp. 28, 32, 34–36, 40, 41, 44–48, 51–53, 55–57, 59, 60, 64, 82–83, 87 (below), 88 (top two), 93, 94 (above), 98–99, 100, 110, 147, 150, 154, 162, 163, 167, 168–169.

Hedrich-Blessing Studio, Chicago
pp. 80, 85 (above), 86, 87 (above), 88 (last), 89, 104, 106–107, 109 (first, third, last), 112–113, 114, 152, 158–159, 160 (above right, below).

Forster Studio, Detroit
pp. 62–63, 85 (below), 103, 148–149, 153.

Manning Brothers, Madison Heights (Michigan)
pp. 156 (above), 160 (above left).

R.M. Damora, New York
p. 88 (third).

F.S. Lincoln, New York
p. 156 (below).

B. Korab, Troy, Michigan
p. 164.

G.A. Ostertag, Buffalo
p. 109 (second).

Soyuzphoto, Moscow
p. 94 (below)

The Architectural Forum, November 1918
p. 128.